The *Optimal* Life

Empowering Health, Healing & Longevity

"Dr. Bizal presents these magnificent steps to creating and maintaining wellness. They are truly gifts given by a higher power through this humble servant, who is truly a proclaimer of the good news that can make an incredible difference in the quality of our health and life. This is a 'must' reading for every human being."

—Donald Jolly-Gabriel, Ph.D.
Director, Hyperbaric Medicine
Whitaker Wellness Institute

"Dr. Bizal's book reveals how different expressions of energy are interconnected to shape our being. In today's life - dominated by reductionism and lack of mind-body-spirit-emotion education - Steve's book offers a great chance to pro-actively improve our own greatest asset: health. "The Optimal Life" is an invaluable tool to make us aware of our potential and ease the amazing journey of living."

—Luca G. Guidotti, M.D., Ph.D.
Associate Professor, Dept. Molecular and Experimental Medicine,
The Scripps Research Institute, La Jolla, CA
Head, Division of Liver Diseases, San Raffaele Scientific Institute, Milano, Italy

"I wanted to take a moment and express my gratitude to you . . .for making the event extremely informative and for sharing your knowledge with us. In ten years of attending re-licensing seminars both through Innercalm Associates as well as other companies, I must say that your seminar was by far the most informative and helpful."

—Dr. Keyvan Eghbali, D.C.

"I have attended Dr. Bizal's seminars and his session "The Wholistic Health Model" is easy to understand, revolutionary, and fundamental to creating a totally vibrant healthy life."

—Kardena Pauza, Ms America Fitness 2007

"Just wanted to let you know that I took one of your seminars about a year ago and I think you are fabulous. You exude such loving energy and vitality and are very inspiring. I have no other reason to email you except to express my gratitude for the experience I had in your class. Keep up the good work and keep loving life. You touch people more than you know."

—Dr. Michele Lesser, D.C.

"I wanted to thank you for a GREAT seminar this past weekend . . . I truly enjoyed it. While I have always been interested in wellness, juicing and living/raw food are relatively recent passions of mine. I'm in the process of transitioning from omnivore to a mixture of vegan and living foods.

—Dr. Steven Schlais, D.C.

"I have taken a few motivational, inspiring seminars like with Mark Victor Hansen, Zig Ziglar, read a few books like Deepak Chopra's *Seven Spiritual Laws of Success* and other books like *See You At The Top*, but, like I said, it seems to all wear off too soon. I felt that you were the real deal, talked the talk and walked the walk."

—Dr. Sayel Fakhoury, D.C.

"Doctor Bizal lives by his Wellness words. He has set out a model which we can easily follow, in fact, embrace with much energy and joy."

—**Lou Ringler, Ph.D.**, President, Innercalm Associates

"Your seminar was intelligent, informative, well researched and uplifting. I know how interesting, at times challenging, it can be to teach to other doctors and your material was thought provoking as well as accessible. Following your departure, I overheard several attendees commenting on how they would use the information presented. You are doing good work and I wanted to thank you. Yours, in enlightening wellness."

—**Dr. Pamella Joy Foster, D.C.**

"WOW!! Thank you so very much for all this wonderful information. My father & I look forward to implementing much of this in our practice. We very much enjoyed your seminar this past weekend; much to our surprise. We came with the perception that we would be extremely bored sitting through yet, another C.E. seminar. However, your wealth of information caught us off guard . . . much to our surprise! Thank you for your dedication to our profession and humanity, that is so very transparent in your teaching approach!"

—**Dr. Carisa S.E. Boshoff-Novak, D.C., Cad.**

"Many thanks for the informative, concise and real-life facts lecture. You are a very inspiring speaker and were prepared to give the audience just what 'the doctor ordered' instead of being another tedious lecturer that we have all experienced at least once. I sincerely appreciate your nutritional input as well as your knowledge of the energy system of the universe. Thank you again for your enthusiasm and sagemanship."

—**Dr. Greg Ball, D.C.**

"I wanted to thank you again for your wonderful seminar. I have not been so inspired . . . since I was first introduced to NLP, several years ago . . . . My husband Jon and I were both moved by your words as well as your delivery from beginning to end. I just wanted you to know that. Thank you for inspiring us to be better human beings, better doctors and even better to each other. You are a valuable asset to our world."

—Dr. Ann Clevinger, D.C.

"Just wanted to send you a little note on how much I enjoyed your presentation . . . . Your energy, passion, and vibrant health were very motivating. It was very motivating to me as I have fallen from the "healthy lifestyle" I once lived and feel the results. I look forward to implementing some of the changes inspired by your talk both with myself and family and with my patients. Anyways, good luck to you and keep on spreading the truth. Best wishes."

—Dr. Curt Collins, D.C.

The *Optimal* Life

Empowering Health, Healing & Longevity

Dr. Stephen Bizal, D.C.

WC

A Wellness Communications Publication

Wellness Communications
4533 MacArthur Blvd. Ste. A #166
Newport Beach, CA 92660
Tel: (949) 222-6681 Fax: (949) 222-6681
www.WellnessCommunications.org

Ordering Information:
On-line Sales. *The Optimal Life* is available for purchase @ www.TheOptimalLife.net.

Quantity Sales. Special discounts are available on quantity purchases by corporations, associations, educational institutions, and others. For details contact Wellness Communications at the address or phone number above.

Individual Sales. Wellness Communication publications are available on-line @ www.TheOptimalLife.net. They can also be ordered directly from Wellness Communications @ (949) 222-6681.

Disclaimer: This book is for reference and informational purposes only and is in no way intended as medical counseling or medical advice. The information contained herein should not be used to treat, diagnose, or prevent any disease or medical condition without the advice of a competent medical professional. The author and Wellness Communications shall have neither liability nor responsibility to any person or entity with respect to any loss, damage, or injury caused or alleged to be caused directly or indirectly by the information contained in this book.

Interior Design by Kira Fulks • www.kirafulks.com

Printed in the United States of America

Library of Congress Cataloging-in-Publication Data available upon request from the publisher.

ISBN 978-0-9800116-0-9

To My Mother
In Memory of My Father
In Memory of Dr. Steve Zara

Dedicated to the EmPOWERment of the human spirit

ACKNOWLEDGEMENTS

As with every endeavor to create something of enduring value there are always the "others" who played critical and significant roles in bringing what was initially merely an idea to fruition for the benefit of humankind.

Thank you to the team that evolved over time to support this project with their energy, talents, gifts, and contributions to bring this work to completion:

Pete Johnson, Johnson Communications, for early and final book title concepts, early book cover design concepts and internal illustrations, as well as the wisdom and insights offered during our numerous conversations over several years.

Bruce McAllister, book consultant, who helped frame the direction that this work evolved.

Linda Coss, Plumtree Marketing, Inc., whose copyediting prowess helped clean up my raw material.

MaryEllen O'Brien, The Writer's Place, whose editing skills and proofreading eagle eyes put the finishing grammatical usage touches to this work.

Allura Dunn, Image Website Design, whose talents, gifts, and artistic eye for colors and element of design grace the final book cover and web sites.

John Dunn, Marketing Resultants, Inc., whose creative marketing genius is probably responsible at some level for getting this book into your hands, and who has been a dear friend (more like a brother), mentor and confidant as well as a marketing guru for the past 28 years.

Jim Riordan, Seven Locks Publishing, Inc., for his publishing wisdom, insights and guidance on the practical matter of managing the internal book design, layout and printing of this book.

Book designer, Kira Fulks, whose artistic talents turned a plain vanilla word document into a work of art.

A special thank you to Anita Edson, MFT, who proved to be my greatest advocate and provided moral support during the early stages of developing this work. Her love and support through challenging times was a gift and a blessing.

FOREWORD

November, 1982

Mr. Stephen Bizal
PERSONALIZED HEALTH AND FITNESS
4500 Campus Drive,   Suite 628E
Newport Beach, California 92660

Dear Steve:

The most exciting aspect of my successful weight
loss was that after 36 years on the face of this earth
you convinced me that I was Important above all other
things. It is unbelievable how the system turns your
mind around. My jobs, investments, projects, daily
routine and fight for survival in everyday life became
more important than ME!

I realize now that all the money I spent on commercial
weight loss programs was actually a waste. These programs
do not address themselves to real life issues, but rather
the fads and gimmicks better known as the easy way---there
is no easy way, and once YOU are the priority in your life
it doesn't have to be easy, it just has to be done.

After 18 months of your personal coaching, and a 100
pound weight loss, I feel the need to say thank you for
caring. My personal and professional life will now mature
more fully and reach higher potential as a result of having
learned to control my physical destiny.

My hope is that you reach out to other people as you
have me, and provide them with the same personal interest
in helping them help themselves to "look good and feel
great".

On a positive ♪,

John J. Dunn

The *Optimal* Life

Empowering Health, Healing & Longevity

CONTENTS

Figures – Tables – Exercises

INTRODUCTION

Most of us want optimal health and a superior quality of life, but few claim it. After all, a healthy and vibrant physical life, free from illness and disease, is a prerequisite for achieving happiness and fulfillment and reaching your highest human potential. You can be pain-free, disease-free, medication-free and doctor-free . . . but only you can create it. It is possible! This book can show you how.

The Optimal Life was originally conceived to help the 76 million baby boomers—the 40 to 65 year olds—who are inching toward senior living. National statistics report that over 90% of these baby boomers will spend the remainder of their lives taking 12 to 15 prescription medications each day as they become participating members of the senior population. What's wrong with this picture? How did this happen? Why is this acceptable to us? Can we reverse this trend? And if we can reverse it . . . *how*?

Creating your optimal life is not a mystery. Living a pain-free, disease-free and medication-free life *is* possible. Most roadblocks to achieving optimal health and healing are due to:

- ❖ lack of motivation
- ❖ lack of understanding
- ❖ lack of motivation & lack of understanding

Although *motivation* is a uniquely personal issue, *understanding* is entirely possible in this Information Age. Today, thanks to the internet, there is no lack of information about health and wellness, nor lack of access to this information. The real challenge is to ferret out the accurate information—the *truthful*—and separate it from the inaccurate—the *untruthful*. Then and only then will we be able to implement what works—utilizing *truth*—to achieve the results we want.

Best of all, accurate information will stand the test of time and will never fail you. Although the concepts and principles presented here were originally intended for baby-boomers, they are valid for every age group, and can help you optimize your life, as well as the lives of your loved ones, for generations to come.

WELCOME TO *THE OPTIMAL LIFE*

The Optimal Life is a reader-friendly reference guide to health and healing—short, concise, practical information based upon a philosophy of living that is in alignment with nature's wisdom and the Universal Principles that govern the health and un-health we experience. This is your "Owner's Manual" for taking care of your body. *The Optimal Life* is the primer on wellness that you never received on your way out of the womb: a combination of a "how to" self-help guide to creating well-being and the "why" behind the "how to."

My intention is to provide you with an initial frame of reference, a starting point, for reclaiming your health, the cornerstone of human potential. The material presented avoids going too deeply into any one topic; my hope is to get you in the ballpark and onto first base, a safe place from which you can continue to build your health destiny. The downside to this approach is that the treatment of a topic may in some cases lack enough scientific accuracy to satisfy those of a more rigorous academic and scientific nature. Of course, there is still much that we do not fully understand about this complex, sophisticated, magnificent creature we call a human being, despite our best scientific and medical research efforts!

Whether you want this information or not, if you want to be in charge of your health destiny you need to know what is in these pages. Health—or maybe we should say *un*-health—will become an issue for you at some time in your life, and you need to have a working knowledge of the basic facts . . . though maybe not all the details.

My experience working with people over the past 25 years as a healthcare provider and wholistic health educator as well as a personal fitness trainer and nutrition counselor, has taught me that a great majority of folks don't need the *deep* stuff—they just need the *right* stuff. And, as national health and mortality statistics tell us, there is a great deal of misunderstanding and confusion about what it takes to create a healthy life. Unfortunately, this is a problem shared by both lay people and all too many health professionals.

So what does it take to create *The Optimal Life?* It starts with a belief that things can be better and that you have the innate power to make things better, no matter what it takes. It takes an open mind, a genuine desire to change, a personal commitment to improve the quality of your life, a willingness to accept total responsibility for your current state of health, the ability to take action, and the discipline to stick with it . . . even in the face of adversity.

All the information in the world will not heal you from your current illness, keep you healthy, or prevent you from developing some disease. It takes action. The road to optimal health and healing is an experiential and uniquely personal journey of self-discovery. You have to be willing, determined, disciplined, and

adventurous to succeed. Wimps need not apply! The road out of
illness into a state of consistent health and well-being is not an
easy journey. Your health is the cornerstone for achieving your
highest human potential.

The Optimal Life was written in response to a huge gap that
exists in the general understanding of how to create health. It is a
tool designed specifically for you. Use it in good health!

MY JOURNEY TO OPTIMAL HEALTH

My first major life lesson on my own personal journey for greater
understanding about the potential of the human body began when
I was a teenager. At the age of 15 I fractured my pelvis during a
high school gymnastics competition. I remember the "popping"
sound made as the hamstring tendon pulled a chunk of the bone
away from the bottom of my pelvis. I remember lying on the gym
floor in excruciating pain, unable to move after dropping into a
split. I remember the inside of the ambulance that rushed me to the
emergency room of our local hospital. I remember the emergency
room. But mostly I remember the pain.

Because of the pain, I was heavily sedated for the first several
days. During that time, the doctors debated over whether or not to
surgically repair the fracture. Fortunately for me, the medical team
ultimately decided not to operate. Instead, the doctors decided to
let the pelvis "heal on its own," since at age 15 the bone growth
centers located in the pelvis were still active, and would therefore
generate the new bone that would facilitate healing.

It was a decision that ultimately changed my life.

The road to recovery for this type of injury was a painful,
long, drawn-out process. Nothing about it was easy or pleasant.
The first week of my two-week hospital stay was spent lying flat
on my back, unable even to roll on my side without a nurse's

assistance. In the days immediately following the injury the pain was deep and unrelenting. Needless to say, there were other medical complications and "elimination" difficulties that I won't bother to go into as a result of the trauma to my groin area. Once I got out of the hospital, I was on crutches for 3 months. I was able to stand up or lie down but could not sit. During the next several months I carried a circular pillow, what they call an orthopedic "donut," with me everywhere I went, just to make the simple act of sitting more bearable.

I was a couple of months into the healing process when the orthopedic surgeon gave us the *real* bad news. During one of my weekly follow-up doctor visits, he quietly and with great certainty explained to my mother that my athletic career was over. He went on to explain that by the time I was 40 years old I would have "severe arthritis of the pelvis," and that I would need a cane, or crutches, or even a wheelchair, just to move around.

It was devastating information . . . but I refused to believe a word of it.

For whatever reason—most likely, nothing more than my youthful rebellion—I never bought into the doctor's story. I remember saying to myself, "Not me. No way! Whatever you are saying doesn't apply to me." I know now, in retrospect, that it was the power and energy of my initial thoughts —my unshakable *intention* and *determination*—that directed my personal path for healing. There is no doubt in my mind today that it was my unrelenting belief that I was going to heal from this injury and be back to 100% that "guaranteed" my recovery.

Over time my body did indeed heal itself, and I went off to college to experience an accomplished athletic career. Today, at age 54, as I complete the writing of this book in the fall of 2007, I experience no residual limitations due to that early injury.

The experience did teach me one life-altering lesson: the body *can* and *does* heal itself, and there *are* ways we can improve our ability to heal and improve the quality of our health.

Meanwhile, my own journey was far from over. At age 32, during midterm week halfway through Chiropractic College, I was working as a gymnastics coach for part-time income at a nearby gymnastics training center. It was a cold rainy Valentine's night. While doing some "extreme" gymnastic tumbling passes—what we called "power" tumbling—I ruptured both Achilles tendons at the same time. Ouch!.

The pain felt like someone took two blow torches up the back of my lower legs. I remember hitting the mat and crumbling to the ground. I remember being on the ground once again in excruciating pain. With everyone else in the gym at a loss for what to do, I was forced to orchestrate what to do next. I got two of the other gymnasts to pick me up, carry me out of the gym, put me into the back seat of my car, then drive me to the nearest hospital emergency room.

After taking x-rays of both ankles to rule out the possibilities of any bone fractures, the ER surgeon on duty informed me that I had ruptured both Achilles tendons and that I would need immediate surgery to repair the damage. Having some knowledge of my injury and with no broken bones detected from the x-rays, I declined his offer to "cut" on both legs and informed him that I would be seeing an orthopedic surgeon who had seen me for other athletic injuries, for a second opinion.

The second opinion revealed that surgery was not warranted. My orthopedic surgeon who had experience with this type of athletic injury explained that this was because it was a complete functional rupture (i.e., the tendons did not "snap" and roll up into the back of the leg). Instead, the injury produced more of an extreme stretch tear where the tendon tissue was still connected within the sheath, and there were therefore no blunt ends that could be pulled back together and sewn.

Once again, I was able to avoid surgery. Four sets of leg casts and eight weeks later—*without* surgery—the tendons repaired themselves. Granted, it took longer than that to walk normally, but over time there was no pain and no residual functional limitation or restriction due to the injury. Once again, I experienced first hand the body's potential and ability to heal itself.

The body's ability to heal itself applies to chronic degenerative health conditions as well as orthopedic injuries.

By age forty, I successfully *healed* myself from life-long asthma.

As an infant in the crib I was diagnosed as "asthmatic." Throughout my childhood, teenage, and early adult years, I suffered from severe allergies and breathing difficulties on an on-going basis. Now, as a health practitioner with greater awareness and understanding about the body and its innate healing ability, I discovered how illness and disease is created not just in response to physical and environmental factors but also in response to different mental and emotional states.

I was able to eliminate the symptoms of the allergies and asthma. By healing my *heart* as well as my *mind* I was able to resolve the physical ailments as well. My personal healing journey dealt with addressing two non-physical aspects of my health condition. First, dealing with my personal belief system and gaining a new understanding about what the asthma and allergy represented in my life. Second, identifying and dealing with the unfinished emotional business and the unresolved painful feelings from childhood, my *emotional incompletions,* that were the origin of the health problems. The short version . . . my body was able to heal itself once I dealt with the unfinished emotional business from my past.

At age 49, on my last ski trip, I "blew-out" my right knee. I had to be hauled off the mountain during a blizzard, strapped into a rescue gurney. Thank you ski patrol! Orthopedic tests and an MRI confirmed two partially torn ligaments in the right knee, and two out of three orthopedic surgeons recommended immediate reconstructive surgery.

"No, thank you," I said. "No surgery. Also, no pain medication." I wanted to be able to listen to everything, I mean *everything*, that my body was telling me so that I could be in complete charge of orchestrating my own healing process based upon unfiltered messages. Once again the knee healed after many months of conscientious self-managed physical therapy, including a strict nutritional regimen that supported and maximized the body's natural healing powers along again with visualizations and an unwavering positive attitude and belief in my body's innate ability to heal itself. That was more than five years ago. Today, as I share these stories, my knee is pain-free and I have no residual functional limitation and enjoy normal activity.

In case you are wondering, all-in-all I have been on crutches 14 times in my life between the ages of 15 and 50, due to athletic injuries and numerous accidents related to other extreme physical activity. I have also geared back quite a bit from the aggressive and "extreme" sports of my younger years. I no longer test the physical limits of my body because I know that everything physical wears out over time.

Where I do continue to "push the envelope" is in my pursuit of greater understanding of the spiritual, emotional, and psychological domains of the human condition and how they relate to the human potential equation. So, what have I learned through all this? What I do know for certain, through study, observation, and personal experience, is that the mind, body, spirit, and emotion all work together to *heal* everything that ails us, if only we are willing to allow and support what is essentially a natural process.

HELPING MYSELF, HELPING OTHERS

What I have learned on my own personal journey of healing has been useful in helping others as well. When I was 27 years old, a good friend and business associate approached me during a family Thanksgiving get-together and asked me if I would help him lose weight.

My friend was 35 years old and weighed 365 pounds. He shared in confidence that he had recently completed an extensive medical diagnostic workup, performed by a world-renowned cardiologist who specialized in treating the critically obese (people who are more than 100 pounds over their ideal body weight). He had a number of health-related problems, all stemming from his excess weight. Apparently, at the conclusion of this comprehensive diagnostic work-up, the cardiologist sat my friend down behind closed doors and had what my friend described as a "come-to-Jesus" meeting with him.

The doctor informed him that, primarily due to his obesity, the pericardium, the protective sac around his heart, was filling up with fluid. In fact, it was already about 70% full of fluid. "The doctor told me that at the rate I was going I would be a 'dead man' in the next three to six months," my friend shared, with a sense of heightened concern in his voice. "I'm literally drowning my heart, suffocating it."

Well, fear of death can be a tremendous motivator. My friend went on to share how he had tried numerous popular weight loss programs over the years with little success, and didn't know what to do next. I believe he asked me for help based upon his observation of my health and fitness lifestyle, which was in stark contrast to the lifestyle habits of most of the other people we worked with in corporate America. Over the next 12 months my friend and I worked together daily to create an eating, activity, and lifestyle regimen based upon nature's wisdom.

During that period, not only did we work together for 10 hours a day in corporate America, but we also became roommates so that I could closely monitor the process and his progress. We created an ideal situation—I was able to "shadow" his daily activity from the time he awoke in the morning until the time he retired at night. We tracked and documented his vital signs, eating regimens, physical activity programs, changes in body fat, changes in weight, changes in attitude, and changes in perceptions about what it takes to create optimal health.

Over the next 12 months he lost 120 pounds and reversed every health problem he was suffering from. He even weaned himself off of every medication. Over the following six months he dropped an additional 45 pounds by continuing with his new routines.

His amazing recovery taught me that the principles that I had applied to myself in creating my own wellness worked just as effectively for others. It was through this experience that I learned one of the greatest lessons for working with others: *People want to know how much you care, before they care how much you know.*

Consequently, I have spent the last 25 years empowering others in achieving optimal health for the greater purpose of reaching their highest human potential.

THE FOUR REALIZATIONS

My personal life experiences have brought me to four important realizations in my understanding about what it takes to create health, healing, and *The Optimal Life*:

REALIZATION #1

THE BODY HEALS ITSELF.

Every cell in the body has its own built-in "intelligence." At the moment of conception, every cell in the body is encoded with all the information and instruction—the DNA—it will ever need to perform its specialized function, replicate itself and repair itself, without the person's conscious intervention. Our only real responsibility is to support the natural healing power of the body and not interfere with this innate ability.

As a wellness practitioner and wholistic health educator I have never cured or healed anyone. I believe that I have contributed energetically, psychologically, emotionally, and mechanically to my patients, allowing them to experience a faster or more positive healing outcome, but I humbly submit to the wisdom of nature, innate intelligence, and the life force energy within all living things as the real agent of healing. As the Nobel laureate Dr. Albert Schweitzer proclaimed, "Patients carry their own doctor inside. They come to us not knowing that truth. We are at our best when we give the physician who resides within each of us a chance to work."

What is this *truth* that Albert was referring to? We shall cover this and other *truths* in Chapter 2, Rules of Health.

REALIZATION #2

THERE ARE NON-PHYSICAL AS WELL AS PHYSICAL FORCES THAT INFLUENCE OUR HEALTH AND GOVERN THE HEALING PROCESS.

Like every game, the game of health has its own specific set of rules. These are not rules created by human ideas or by the medical, pharmaceutical, scientific, or religious communities. These rules are the Universal Principles that govern the processes that determine the quality of health we experience. They apply at all times and in every situation without exception.

These Universal Principles include both Spiritual Laws and Laws of Nature. Spiritual Laws govern the realm of the non-physical aspect of life, like our thoughts and feelings. Laws of Nature, on the other hand, deal with physical realities such as our environment and the foods we eat. All Universal Principles work together, collectively, to influence body physiology: how the body works and how the body heals. From the "5,000 foot level," *health* appears to be the natural consequence of being in alignment with Spiritual Laws and Laws of Nature.

In contrast, illness and disease, *un-health*, are merely the natural consequences of violating either Spiritual Laws or the Laws of Nature, or both. If this is true then we could define *healing* as the process of getting back into alignment with both of these Laws. So the real challenge in the presence of illness and disease is to figure out how we are violating these laws and what we need to change to get back in alignment.

REALIZATION #3

HUMANS ARE WHOLISTIC.

A human being is more than the cells, tissues, and organ systems that make up the human body. Humans also have a spiritual, psychological, and emotional dimension to their existence. These factors work together, along with the physical, to create our experience of life and health. Because of this dynamic, any approach to health and healing that does not acknowledge and take into consideration this mind-body-spirit-emotion connection is inherently a self-limiting paradigm that is doomed to failure at the onset.

Our allopathic model of medicine and health care does not appear to recognize this wholistic, integrated dynamic in its approach to dealing with chronic degenerative diseases. Maybe this is what accounts for the high failure rate of conventional medicine (i.e. drugs and surgery) in treating and preventing cancer, heart disease, stroke, diabetes, and the rest of the lifestyle diseases.

Western medicine is a "reductionist" model. This approach recognizes and treats the human body as a mechanical model made up of separate parts. This "reductionistic" mentality does not recognize the significance of how our thoughts and feelings are expressed in the physiology of every cell throughout the human body. Some health professionals have figured it out, but most have missed the boat.

REALIZATION #4

WE ARE EACH 100% RESPONSIBLE
AND ACCOUNTABLE FOR OUR EXPERIENCE OF LIFE,
INCLUDING OUR EXPERIENCE OF HEALTH.

In his twilight years, the late actor, comedian, and centenarian George Burns is attributed with saying, "If I knew I was going to live this long, I would have taken better care of myself." Although George may have been going for the joke, his words speak to a greater wisdom, a wisdom expressed in his acknowledgement that his health was *his* responsibility, and his alone.

In the U.S., the food manufacturers create and market artificial foods designed to increase your craving for, and consumption of, these unhealthy products.

The pharmaceutical industry leads you to believe that your only solution for the health maladies that you are suffering from—while you're eating artificial foods and living an unhealthy lifestyle—is to introduce more foreign substances, synthetic chemicals, into your system.

The medical research and health care community tells you that it is not your fault that you are fat and depressed, but rather that the reason you are falling apart is because of your genes: you are the victim of being born human.

The music in the background being sung by the health insurance companies is that it is okay for you to not be responsible or accountable for how you lead your life, because when you start falling apart there is health insurance that, for a small up-front price, will pay to have you put back together again.

As for various government entitlement programs, wasn't it Abraham Lincoln who once suggested that you cannot improve the quality of a man's life by doing for him that which he needs to do for himself?

Who is responsible here? At a fundamental level, isn't the out-of-control spiraling cost of health care being driven primarily by increased utilization of health services and drugs for the treatment of chronic degenerative diseases? Isn't the increased utilization of health services simply due to more illness and disease and the continued deterioration in the general health of the population? If these are the facts, then the simplest, most direct, and most effective solution is to focus on educating people about basic healthy lifestyle issues and supporting them in that process.

The only obstacle I can see to implementing the above solution is that it does not appear to be in alignment with the profit motives and economic appetites of the food, pharmaceutical, insurance, and health care industries . . . collectively no small adversary. What this means is that ultimately your health is in your hands. Why? Because, when it comes down to it, nobody else really cares!

How This Book Can Work For You

Part One of the book, The Wholistic Health Model, begins with a discussion in Chapter 1, Mind-Body-Spirit-Emotion of the wholistic nature of human beings, and an explanation of how this relationship is represented graphically as "The Wholistic Health Model." Chapter 2, Rules of Health, discusses the Universal Principles—Spiritual Laws and Laws of Nature—that are the "rules of the game" that govern health outcomes. Chapter 3, Why People Get Sick, explores the fundamental nature of illness and disease.

Part Two, What the Body Needs, includes a chapter on each one of the "10 Principles of Wellness" for creating *The Optimal Life*. These 10 Principles offer a practical approach to creating a healthy life based upon the wholistic nature of human beings and the Universal Principles that govern health. The end of each chapter includes a "Must Know" summary and Chapters 3-13 also include a "Must Do" action list to help you on your journey. References to various research findings within the medical research literature are included to both entertain and enlighten, with the awareness that all research studies are inherently self-limiting; after all, they were designed by humans, so *all* "scientific" interpretation is open to scrutiny. In contrast, *truth* is self-evident by its very nature. It needs no scientific validation.

No claim of ownership is made by the author for the concepts, principles, laws, information, or knowledge shared in this publication. Although this manuscript represents my personal opinions and interpretation based upon my unique life experiences, the information contained in these pages has existed for all time and is in the domain of the living universe, available for the benefit of all humankind. All accurate and truthful health information is accessible at any time to anyone who is genuinely:

❖ open-minded
❖ seeking greater understanding
❖ willing to accept total responsibility for their health
❖ willing to do the work

This publication is offered as my best effort at this time, although I reserve the right to improve upon this work based upon an even greater understanding and awareness of the *truth* about health and healing as it is revealed to me.

Throughout this publication the term "(w)holistic" is used in lieu of the word "holistic" because I believe it reflects and portrays a more accurate visual message of the whole person concept. Throughout this publication the term "mind-body-spirit-emotion" is used to describe the wholsitic nature of human beings instead of the more common nomenclature of "mind-body-spirit." Even though, technically, the term "mind" refers to both our intellect and our emotions, I believe that the phrase "mind-body-spirit-emotion" imparts a more accurate and comprehensive visual message of the whole person concept.

I am grateful for all the time, energy and Herculean efforts of all the healers, authors, doctors, allied health practitioners, health educators, researchers, and scientists whose works I have benefited from on my own distinctive journey of wellness and self-discovery, and in preparing this manuscript. As a wellness practitioner and wholistic health educator, I hope that sharing this information will help empower you on your personal journey to create greater health, happiness, and fulfillment on this beautiful planet.

If you strive to achieve your greatest human potential you will need to be healthy—this book is for you. Why? Because, optimal health is the cornerstone of all human potential.

If you are living with any chronic pain or degenerative disease and believe that life can be better . . . read on.

If you are suffering from any health problem and are open-minded enough to consider natural approaches that could transform your life . . . read this book!

If you believe you can be pain-free, disease-free, and medication-free, you can. You are a candidate for *The Optimal Life*.

Thank you and best in health!

The Optimal Life

PART ONE

THE WHOLISTIC HEALTH MODEL

The doctor of the future will give no medication,
but interest his patients in the care of the human frame, in diet,
and in the cause and prevention of disease.

Thomas A. Edison
Inventor

CHAPTER ONE

Mind-Body-Spirit-Emotion

THE WHOLISTIC NATURE OF HUMANITY

THE PREMISE

If it is true that humanity has spiritual, psychological, and emotional dimensions as well as a physical aspect, then in our attempts to fully understand how the human body works —why people get sick, what it takes to heal, and what it takes to stay healthy and prevent illness and disease—any health or wellness strategy we formulate that does not take all these factors into consideration is, by its own design, a self-limiting paradigm and doomed to failure from the onset.

Enlightenment is merely the emergence of truth when the obstructions to the realization of that truth have been removed. By analogy, the shining of the sun is not conditional upon the removal of the clouds; it merely becomes apparent.

—David R. Hawkins, M.D., Ph.D., *I, Reality & Subjectivity*

THE BIG PICTURE

The real challenge is to look at the big picture and figure out how the dots are connected: how the mind (intellect and emotion), body, and spirit work together in creating either health or illness and disease. According to metaphysical principles there exists an answer to every question and a solution to every problem, even health problems. Why? Because, a problem cannot exist without there already being in existence a specific solution to that problem. The solution to every problem lies in having a greater and more comprehensive understanding of all aspects of the problem. So how do we arrive at this greater understanding?

Sometimes far greater insight into the understanding of a problem can be gleaned by backing away from the problem a bit and viewing it from a distance, so that we can see the bigger picture rather than only viewing it "under the microscope." Why? Because the circumstances in which an event occurs, its *context*, determines its meaning and significance—it's *content*. When speaking of health issues, *content* refers to the specific illness or disease which we seek to better understand while *context* refers to spiritual, mental, emotional, and physical circumstances surrounding the occurrence of the illness or disease. *Context* therefore determines *content*.

THE WHOLISTIC NATURE OF HUMANITY

Humans are comprised of several different expressions of energy:

- ❖ physical energy (our body)
- ❖ mental energy (our thoughts)
- ❖ emotional energy (our feelings)
- ❖ spiritual energy (our life force)

Wholistic refers to the "whole" person, mind-body-spirit-emotion, and is a variation of the more common term "holistic." The term "holistic" (from the Greek word *holos* meaning "whole") in healthcare is used: (1) to describe that which is considered outside the mainstream of scientific medicine, and (2) to emphasize the importance of the whole person in its approach. Holistic also incorporates the holism doctrine that "the whole is greater than the sum of its parts."

This mind-body-spirit-emotion relationship describes what we call the wholistic nature of humanity. Although technically, when referring to the "mind" we are speaking of both the mental ("thought") and emotional ("feeling") aspects of a person, for the sake of our discussion we will be using the term "mind" when referring to the intellectual or conscious mind and will be using the term "emotion" when referring to the subconscious or unconscious mind.

Optimal health assumes a balanced and integrated relationship encompassing all these areas of human existence. A brief overview and description of the different health models practiced in America today will help us in our discussion as we move forward.

Two Different Health Care Models in America

There are fundamentally two contrasting health care models, two schools of thought, that exist in the U.S. today: medical and non-medical. While both aim to cure what ails you, they are based upon very different philosophical approaches. The medical model includes terms like **Allopathic**, **Western**, **Conventional** and **Scientific** medicine to describe itself. All of these medical models treat illness and disease from the same orientation: all focus on identifying and treating the symptoms of illness and disease with drugs and surgery.

Allopathic medicine is the standard practiced by medical doctors such as family and general practitioners, cardiologists, neurologists, oncologists, endocrinologists, psychiatrists, etc. **Western** medicine is what is practiced in the modern and Western cultures in North America and Europe, predominantly using drugs and surgery. **Conventional** medicine is that which is taught in medical schools and practiced in hospitals—exclusively drugs and surgery. **Scientific** medicine claims to be founded on scientific principles and only recognizes that which can be proven scientifically. It does not recognize theories or practices of healing illness and disease which have not been proven scientifically and therefore, in their eyes, have no validity within the scientific medical research community.

The non-medical approach to health and healing uses terms like **Wholistic** or **Holistic**, **Alternative** and **Complimentary** medicine, and **Natural Healing** to refer to these contrasting schools of thought. All are practiced by non-medical health practitioners (Chiropractors, Acupuncturists, Naturopaths, Clinical Nutritionists, Herbalists, etc.) and some medical doctors. These non-allopathic approaches identify and treat the cause of illness and disease from a whole-person perspective, and treat the symptoms using only natural remedies—physical medicine, herbs, nutrition, etc.—as the first-line strategy.

THE MEDICAL HEALTH CARE MODEL

Allopathic medicine's approach to treating illness and disease claims to be founded on scientific principles and is considered a "reductionist" model. Its emphasis is on the physical aspects, reducing a human being to a collection of systems. This scientific view sees a person as a machine. The "parts" of this machine— heart, brain, lungs, kidneys, muscles, joints, etc.—are prone to "breakdown" and either need time to repair or need to be replaced with "spare parts." Here, the purpose of medicine is to intervene to correct dysfunction and restore "normality" using drugs and surgery.

Allopathic medicine views what happens in the physical body as separate and distinct from what may also be happening simultaneously with that person at a psychological, emotional, and spiritual level. The modern medical research approach to understanding health problems is to isolate the sick or unhealthy cells from diseased tissues and organ systems, and study them under a microscope. This approach formulates an understanding and treatment strategy based upon this microscopic interpretation. Although there is value to understanding something at a microscopic level, it doesn't explain how it got there in the context of its surrounding physical, mental, emotional, and spiritual energy influences.

A limitation of this approach is that in extracting cells out of their natural setting within the human body and analyzing their mechanical and chemical nature, we are not only removing them from their normal relationship with other cells but also removing them from the context of the other wholistic factors— mental, emotional, and spiritual energy forces—that influence cell physiology. The danger with this reductionistic approach is that it leaves us open to making interpretations about and creating treatment strategies for health problems without considering the big picture. This creates a self-limiting paradigm. Although considered the best option for acute illness that is due to bacterial infections and/or physical trauma, allopathic medicine has not been effective in treating the chronic degenerative diseases, such as cancer, heart disease, stroke, diabetes, obesity, fibromyalgia, Alzheimer's, or Parkinson's.

THE NON-MEDICAL HEALTH CARE MODEL

Wholistic or **Holistic** medicine is designed to look at and treat the **whole** person, not just the disease symptoms. This approach looks at the mind-body-spirit-emotion relationship and how a person's spiritual, psychological, emotional as well as physical energy states contribute to creating the imbalances in the biochemistry of the body that contribute to illness and disease. The objective in Wholistic medicine is to identify, treat, and eliminate the cause of the disease itself, while simultaneously treating the symptoms.

This whole-person approach to treating illness and disease includes the analysis of physical, nutritional, environmental, emotional, social, spiritual, and lifestyle issues. It also focuses on patient education and the patient's personal responsibility for achieving balance and well being. From the wholistic perspective, the allopathic model is self-limiting by definition.

Alternative medicine—that which is not taught in medical schools or practiced in hospitals—is the term often used by the general public and some healthcare practitioners to refer to healing techniques which are either not well known or not accepted by the majority of "conventional" or "allopathic" medical practitioners (M.D.'s). Such techniques would include non-invasive, non-pharmaceutical approaches such as Chiropractic, Acupuncture, Naturopathy, Herbalism, Homeopathy, Massage, and many others.

However, the term **Alternative** medicine has also been used to refer to any experimental technique, drug or non-drug, which is not currently accepted by "conventional" medical practitioners. As non-invasive, non-pharmaceutical techniques become popular and accepted by a larger number of conventional practitioners, these techniques will no longer be considered alternative.

Complementary medicine refers to non-invasive, non-pharmaceutical techniques used as a complement to the conventional medical treatments of drugs and surgery. The term implies that conventional medicine is used as a primary tool and the non-invasive, non-pharmaceutical techniques (such as chiropractic, acupuncture, naturopathy, herbalism, homeopathy, massage, etc.) are used as a supplement when needed.

Natural Healing is the term used to describe those natural methods that support the wisdom of the body and the body's innate natural ability to heal itself as the primary emphasis for treating illness and disease instead of using drugs and surgery. The primary treatment objective here is to strengthen the systems that make up the body's immune response, including the digestive, cardiovascular, and lymphatic systems, as well as to strengthen specific organs such as the heart, lungs, liver, and kidney. Natural Healing refers to the use of nature's nutrition as well as all the natural physical healing techniques available: healing touch, massage, hot and cold water therapies, manual manipulation, breath work, oxygen therapies, etc.

The goal of all non-medical approaches to healing is to support the body's own innate natural ability to heal itself by strengthening the immune response. The major focus in natural healing is to neutralize and remove toxins from the body while nourishing the body back to optimal health using quality nutrients.

There is one more category: **Integrated** medicine. This approach attempts to combine what it considers the best of both the medical and non-medical approaches, for the maximum benefit of the patient.

To be **Wholistic**, any wellness program designed to cure and prevent illness and disease, improve quality of life, and achieve optimal health must take into account the spiritual, psychological, and emotional as well as the physical aspects of the human condition. We must then consider what we mean when we speak of the spirit, the mind, the emotions, and the body, and how they work together to create optimal health.

SPIRIT & SPIRITUALITY

When we speak of the "spirit", I believe we are referring to the essence of the individual at an energy level. When referring to the nature of an individual, we use terms like "gentle-spirited" or "mean-spirited" to describe our experience of that essence. Although difficult to measure and quantify by current scientific standards, the experience is undeniable. According to the theory of quantum physics, everything in the universe is energy. All physical matter, when continually broken down to its smaller and smaller units, becomes energy—there is a level of interface where physical matter eventually becomes pure energy and pure energy becomes physical matter.

At a very essential level, the universe is comprised of energy. It is also postulated that everything in the universe is connected and it is through our spirit, or spiritual energy, that we are connected at an essential level with every other human being and every sentient being on the planet.

So what do we mean when we speak of "spirit," "spiritual," and "spirituality"?

Trying to define these terms is like trying to hold water in the palm of your open hand or trying to grasp smoke out of thin air. It is certainly real—it's right there in front of you—but it is difficult to embrace, even when closing your fingers around it.

Spirit, spiritual, and spirituality seem to mean different things to different people, depending on orientation and personal beliefs. A cursory review of the current literature on the subject reveals varying perspectives depending upon the field of study from which the writer emerges—the religious community, the scientific community, or the metaphysical community. Each community defines spirituality within the context of its own discipline. The religious community embraces the concept of spirituality that has a strong association to their specific religious beliefs and dogma, i.e. Christian, Jewish, Hindu, Buddhist, or Muslim. Both the scientific and metaphysical communities define spirituality outside the context of an association with any specific religion or religious dogma.

For the sake of our discussions we will be referring to the term spirit and its derivations in a metaphysical context that is not associated with any specific religious dogma, while at the same time embracing all religious beliefs that embrace love as their highest guiding principle.

In this metaphysical context, the terms spirit, spiritual, and spirituality refer to the non-physical, non-material aspect of our being. The words spiritual and spirituality refer to those higher virtues that are an expression of divinity—love and truth as manifested in our thoughts, feelings, words, and actions. We experience these virtues as compassion, patience, tolerance, joy, kindness, gentleness, sensitivity, gratitude, non-judgment, and non-materialism in our dealings with ourselves and others.

These virtues call on us to engage in life with an *attitude of lovingness* in everything we do. Because everything in the world is connected at an energy level, every thought, every feeling, every word, and every action that is an expression of this *attitude of lovingness* benefits the recipient, the giver, and the entire universe.

What we refer to as spiritual qualities are beyond the perceptual world of form, although they do affect what happens in the physical world. They are subjective, experiential realities. They are states of knowing that are beyond perception.

> *The proper utilization of our intelligence and knowledge is to effect*
> *changes from within to develop a good heart.*
>
> —Dalai Lama, *The Art of Happiness*

THE MIND

What do we mean when we speak of the "mind"? What is the relationship between the mind and the body? How does the activity of our mind influence our health?

The mind we are referring to here is not the physical brain and central nervous system. The mind in this context is that part of human existence that is comprised of thoughts, attitudes, opinions, perspectives, feelings, and emotions. Mind includes both intellectual and emotional phenomena, both thinking and feeling. Both are forms of energy that influence the physiology of the body.

> *Mind includes your thoughts and emotions as well as all unconscious*
> *mental-emotional reactive patterns. Emotion arises at a place where*
> *the mind and body meet. It is your body's reaction to your mind—a*
> *reflection of your mind in the body.*
>
> —Eckhart Tolle, *The Power of Now*

OUR EMOTIONS & FEELINGS

Our emotions and feelings have a profound impact on our health. There is an intimate and direct relationship between our emotions and feelings and the physiology of the cells in the body. For every feeling there are physiological, hormonal, and chemical changes that occur in the body. Painful feelings like fear, anger, guilt, shame, and sadness adversely affect our state of well being. These painful feelings are the natural consequence of unresolved emotional issues ("emotional incompletions") from childhood that we carry forward into our adult life.

So, what are our emotions and feelings? How do they affect health? The terms "emotions" and "feelings" are used interchangeably by most authoritative sources. Webster's Third New International Dictionary defines emotion as "a physiological departing from homeostasis (balance) that is subjectively experienced in strong feeling (as of love, hate, desire or fear) and manifests itself in neuromuscular, cardiovascular, hormonal and other body changes . . ." Webster also defines feelings as "an emotional state." By this definition we see that emotion is described within the context of its effect on the physiology of the body.

As previously stated, quantum physics suggests that everything in the universe, at an essential level, is information and energy, and that energy possesses a vibrational frequency that describes the quality of itself. If this is true, then every emotion and feeling, also expressions of human energy, possesses a specific vibrational frequency that reflects some quality of energy, and it is the quality of this emotional energy that determines its effect on the physiology of the cells that in turn influences the quality of our health.

Research has shown that strong emotions, both joyful and painful feelings, cause changes in the biochemistry of the body. While positive emotions of joy, gratitude, and peacefulness enhance energy flow in the body and cause beneficial change to the physiology that support health, painful or negative emotions such as fear, anger, guilt, and shame restrict energy flow in the body, causing physiological, hormonal, and chemical change that lead to illness and disease. We could say that positive energy affects cells in a positive and healthy way, while negative energy affects cells in a negative and unhealthy way.

UNFINISHED EMOTIONAL BUSINESS

What do we mean by "unfinished emotional business" and how does it affect our health? Unfinished emotional business—*unresolved emotions or emotional incompletions*—represents the painful feelings such as fear, anger, resentment, guilt, shame, hatred, inferiority, worthlessness, and sadness that we initially experienced in childhood and are still carrying with us today as adults.

Our unfinished emotional business is considered unresolved and therefore incomplete because it was never dealt with, resolved, and the painful energy released at the time they were experienced. We could say that we got stuck in those painful feelings as children. The reason we got stuck in the first place is because as children we lacked the necessary tools—personal power, knowledge, and life's experiences—to accurately interpret and then deal effectively and appropriately with what happened to us.

The unfinished emotional business from childhood that we carry with us into adulthood continues to cause emotional discomfort. Every unresolved emotion in our lives is still an integral part of each of us as adults and holds your body in a state of energetic and physiological imbalance or "heterostasis."

The phenomenon that describes the body's ability to hold onto painful feelings from past events is called "cellular memory." Every emotional, psychological, and physical trauma you experience in your life is recorded in the memory of your cells. It is this cellular memory that explains why emotional discomfort experienced in childhood can still be present in our adult life, even though the emotional trauma may have happened long ago and has even been forgotten at a conscious level. Unresolved emotional issues remain an active and prevalent part of our subconscious mind until raised to a conscious level to be identified, confronted and resolved (healed). It is for this reason that there exists an intimate and direct relationship between unresolved, painful emotions in a person's life and illness and disease.

Some psychologists believe that depression is nothing more than unresolved anger turned inward, and that cancer is nothing but the physical expression of the energy of anger creating major physiological imbalance in the body. With greater awareness and understanding we would probably find that every illness and disease process is rooted in some way to unresolved emotional pain in a person's life.

The **Law of Responsibility** is another Universal Principle which states that everything we experience in our life we create at some level. This can be a difficult pill for some to swallow. We previously stated that most of the disease processes that we have created in our life have a strong connection to unresolved emotional issues. Our lack of awareness of this dynamic, whether out of denial or ignorance, will not excuse us from experiencing the *truth* and consequences of this reality. But based upon our power to create and our freedom to choose, we possess the ability to *recreate* anything and everything in our lives that is not working for us. We need only be genuinely open to the possibilities.

OUR THOUGHTS & BELIEF SYSTEMS

There is an intimate and direct relationship between the thoughts we think, what happens at the cellular level in our bodies, and the health we experience. Our thoughts are an extension of our belief systems. Our belief systems are that which we hold to be true about ourselves and the world around us. That which we believe to be true provides the foundation for our decision making processes: not only *what* we think, but *why* we think that way. Our judgments and subsequent actions are based upon these beliefs.

Our beliefs are either accurate—in alignment with *truth* and the way things really are, or inaccurate—not in alignment with *truth*. If our beliefs are in alignment with the way things really are, then the decisions we make and the actions we take create a certain outcome. On the other hand, if what we believe to be true is, in fact, not true, then the decisions we make and the subsequent actions we take based upon those decisions will create a different outcome. *All outcomes we experience reflect the accuracy of our beliefs.*

All health, illness, and disease we experience are an expression of the accuracy of our belief systems regarding the *truth* about health—what health is and what health is not.

It's not what we don't know that gets us into trouble. Its what we think we know that just ain't so.

—**Mark Twain,** American humorist, satirist, lecturer & writer

In Chapter 2, Rules of Health, we will explore the quantum physics concept that everything in the universe is comprised of information and energy, and that all energy possesses a vibrational frequency. This vibrational frequency describes the characteristic or "quality" of the energy. Energy itself has no meaning, quality, or characteristic other than the one we give it.

Thought is one expression of human energy. A thought is a *real thing* that possesses a vibrational frequency. Every thought we think, whether verbalized or not, is energy of a specific vibrational frequency that is released into the universe. The universe, then, simply takes our thought and works toward manifesting outcomes and events in the physical world that are in alignment with the quality of the energy of our original thought. The material form of that expression is inconsequential, at least to the universe, even though it matters to us. What is significant is the quality of the energy—the vibrational frequency—that is being expressed.

This principle applies at an individual level as well as at a group level, the *collective consciousness*. When we think a thought and implement an action that represents a quality of energy that expresses an attitude of lovingness toward ourselves and others, universal dynamics will manifest an outcome in the physical reality which is consistent with the quality of the energy of the original thought. Here is how the principle works: think happy thoughts, you create happiness; think unhappy thoughts, you create unhappiness. Think healthy thoughts, you create health; think unhealthy thoughts, you create illness and disease.

This is an example of a Universal Principle known as the **Law of Attraction**. It states that *energy attracts back to itself energy of like kind*. At an energy level, we attract health, people, and events into our life—regardless of how it may appear—that are in alignment with the quality of the energy of our thoughts, feelings, words, and actions.

So what does this have to do with health? What is this universal dynamic and how does it work? What is the connection between our thoughts and our physical health?

Simply put, that which you give *attention* to grows stronger in your life, and that which you give *intention* to transforms the un-manifest into the manifest. *Intention* transforms energy and information, thereby organizing its own fulfillment. Your thoughts can influence cellular physiology and biochemistry and therefore have power over your physical body.

What you *believe* to be true about health—whether actually true or not—will be manifested in your physical body. If you truly believe that the body and every cell in the body has the potential to heal itself, then by this genuine belief you engage the power of the universal laws that support that outcome and the physiological activity of every cell in your body will move in that direction, working toward a healing outcome. Of course, this assumes that everything else you are doing in your life supports and honors that belief. If, on the other hand, you genuinely believe that healing is *not* possible, then you create a dynamic that sets into motion physiological and chemical changes in the body that move you in the direction of *unhealth*.

> *Intention is the active partner of attention; it is a way we convert automatic processes into conscious ones. The decline of vigor in old age is largely the result of people expecting to decline; they have unwittingly implanted a self-defeating intention in the form of a strong belief and the mind-body connection automatically carries out this intention.*
>
> —**Deepak Chopra, M.D.**, *Ageless Body Timeless Mind*

It is through this universal dynamic that we become the thoughts that occupy our mind. This is how, at one level, we create either health or illness and disease in our life.

False information about health, how our bodies function, and the body's healing ability all contribute to a person's limiting beliefs about the body's innate and natural healing potential. Inaccurate information and limiting belief systems obstruct a person's natural ability to create a vibrant, healthy, pain-free, disease-free, and medication-free life.

Limited perceptions and restricted thinking lead to restrictions in energy flow in the body; restricted energy flow in the body leads to energetic and chemical imbalances and restricted physiology; restricted physiology leads to sub-optimal cell function; sub-optimal cell function leads to compromised immune response and subsequent health problems.

Just as healthy thoughts and action can never produce illness and disease in the body, unhealthy thoughts and action can never produce a healthy body.

Good thoughts and actions can never produce bad results; likewise, bad thought and action can never produce good results.
—David R. Hawkins, M.D., Ph.D., *Power vs. Force*

OUR BODY

Our physical presence on this earth, our body, is the vehicle through which we experience the world around us. It is the gift we were given, so we would be able to engage in and experience the universe and all things of creation at the physical level, on the material plane of existence, here on planet earth. It includes all the physical senses: our ability to see, hear, taste, smell, and touch.

All of life has intrinsic value. Our physical presence on this planet must have meaning and purpose, simply because *we exist*. Because of this existence we have potential that was meant to be expressed. Although our existence suggests an implied responsibility to this physical existence, the choice is still ours to make. We can either choose to be responsible for our existence and our physical body or we can choose *not* to be responsible and ignore it. One responsibility is to *understand* what it takes to maximize our human potential during this lifetime. We then also have a responsibility to *implement* this knowledge so as to maximize our human potential. The choice belongs to each of us and each choice has consequences. We create it all.

If it is true that our spirit, thoughts, and emotions influence what happens in the human body, then we can describe health as the natural expression of this spiritual, psychological, and emotional energy being played out in the body.

PEBBLE IN WATER ANALOGY

Looking at health from a wholistic perspective, we can explain this relationship between the mind, body, and spirit as demonstrated through the simple and familiar "Pebble in Water" scenario.

Imagine a pool of still water. Now imagine throwing a pebble into that still pool. What happens when the pebble hits the surface of the water? Ripples are created. Which way do the ripples move? Ripples move outward, away from the point of entry, in all directions simultaneously. When the pebble hits the water do the ripples ever begin from the outside perimeter of the pool and move toward the center in an inward direction? No. Do the ripples ever start at the shoreline and move in an inward direction to where the pebble struck the water? No. Why do ripples happen and what do ripples represent? The ripples represent the transference of energy from the pebble (that has mass and force) to the water. When the pebble hits the water, the energy of the pebble is imparted into the water and shows up as ripples; the ripples are the flow of energy through the surface of the water. The water itself is not moving outward; it is the *energy* that is moving through the water in an outward direction.

Through this two-dimensional example we can see that every molecule of water on the surface of the pool is affected by the ripples. Now imagine the pool as a three dimensional body of water and the ripples moving outward from the center of a sphere, not merely as two-dimensional circles, but as three-dimensional spheres.

In the same way that the energy of the pebble hitting the water sets up a chain of events—*cause and effect*—that affect every molecule of water on the surface, the energy of our spirit, the energy of our emotions, and the energy of our thoughts create a similar "ripple effect" that is transmitted throughout our entire body, affecting every cell. This energy dynamic, the ripple effect, happens twenty-four hours a day, seven days a week, on an ongoing basis from our first breath to our last.

This perspective leads to a natural conclusion: *since everything in the universe is connected at some level, what we experience at the physical level may have its origins in one of the other energy fields.*

If this is true, our concept of health, how we define it, and how we approach treating illness and disease needs to be expanded to embrace an understanding of the spiritual, psychological, and emotional aspects, as well as the physical aspects, of being human.

All energy, no matter what the source or form, has some effect on the physiology of every cell in the body. A dynamic representation of this wholistic relationship of the mind, body, spirit, and emotion is depicted in Figure 1-1: The Wholistic Health Model.

FIGURE 1-1

THE WHOLISTIC HEALTH MODEL

THE MIND • BODY • SPIRIT • EMOTION CONNECTION

THE WHOLISTIC HEALTH MODEL

When visualizing this static two-dimensional model, imagine it as a target, with the energy moving from the center of the target outward. The center of the target, the bull's-eye, represents the essence or spirit of human life: the energy of love.

The second ring out from the center of the target represents the emotional energy of our feelings, expressed as the level of emotional completeness that exists in our life.

The third ring out from the center of the target represents the mental energy of our thoughts, expressed as our belief systems, those things we hold to be true about ourselves, our health and the world around us.

The outermost ring of the target represents the energy of the physical body and all the factors that comprise our physical environment: the air we breathe, the water we drink, the food we eat, the light we are exposed to, the physical activity we engage in, and other environmental factors that we are exposed to, including chemicals, artificial noise, and electromagnetic force fields.

A WHOLISTIC APPROACH TO HEALTH

What do we mean by a wholistic approach to health? If we acknowledge that human existence is made up of spiritual energy, mental energy, emotional energy, and physical energy, then any comprehensive approach to health and wellness must, by design, speak to the integration of these parts and their relationship to each other and the whole.

A wholistic approach to health and wellness addresses both the physical as well as the non-physical aspects of the human condition. A wholistic approach to health includes all aspects of our interface with the physical environment as well as the sum total of our spiritual, mental, and emotional experience that is being expressed through our physical bodies.

Two energy states of different vibrational qualities—for example, the energy of love and the energy of fear—cannot occupy the same space at the same time. Metaphysically speaking, it is not possible for a person to be out-of-balance in one area of life without imbalance also existing in other areas of life. For example, it is not possible for someone to be suffering from some illness or chronic degenerative disease without some other area of their life—spiritual, mental and emotional—also suffering.

This implies that every physical illness and disease process has its origins at another level of human existence, and because of this dynamic any health approach you pursue that does not take into consideration all aspects of the human condition (mind-body-spirit-emotion) is self-limiting by its very design. If you find yourself stuck in illness and disease and have not been able to find solutions to your health problems at a physical level you may need to look deeper than the physical realm for the answers.

WELLNESS MASTERY™ SUMMARY

Must Know!

1. When trying to solve a health problem, look at the "big picture." The solution to every problem lies in a greater understanding of every aspect of the problem. Sometimes far greater insight into the nature of a problem and its solution can be gleaned by viewing it from 5,000 feet above as well as from under the microscope.

2. Context, or the circumstances in which an event occurs, determines content (meaning and significance).

3. Human beings are comprised of physical energy (body), mental energy (thought), emotional energy (feelings), and love energy (spirit).

4. Wholistic is a term used to refer to the "whole" person and the mind-body-spirit-emotion relationship that describes our true nature.

5. The **Wholistic** medicine (non-medical, holistic, alternative, complementary, natural) approach to illness and disease treats the whole person as well as the symptoms of the condition, utilizing natural therapies to support the body's innate healing ability and strengthen the body's immune response.

Must Know!

6. The **Allopathic** medicine (medical, scientific, conventional) approach is to treat the symptoms of illness and disease utilizing drugs and surgery.

7. Our quality of health is an expression of our spiritual, mental, and emotional energy experience through the physical body.

8. Just as the energy of the pebble hitting the water creates ripples that affect every water molecule on the water's surface, the energy of your spirit, thoughts, and emotions creates a similar ripple effect, generating a chain of events that transmits throughout your entire body, affecting every cell.

9. To be effective, any health and wellness program designed to improve health and quality of life must take into account the spiritual, psychological, emotional, and physical aspects of the human condition.

10. If you find yourself stuck in illness and disease and have not been able to find solutions to your health problems at a physical level, you may need to look deeper than the physical realm for the answers.

CHAPTER TWO

Rules of Health

UNIVERSAL PRINCIPLES THAT GOVERN HEALTH

*Nature never wanted man to leave his body before advanced old age,
and if only everyone would obey the laws of nature from his childhood
on, instead of constantly working against them, the death of human
beings through disease in their youth or middle age would be as rare
as death by violence.*

—**Ramacharaka**, *from Yesudian and Haich, Yoga and Health*

THE NATURE OF THE UNIVERSE

You may be asking . . .WHAT? What does the nature of the
universe have to do with wellness and the quality of the health
we experience on this planet?

Look at it this way: since as humans we are part of the
universe, wouldn't the principles that govern how the universe
works also apply to us? The greater our understanding of these
principles, the more power we have to create the life we desire.
These principles have a direct and immediate impact on every
aspect of our existence, including our health.

Enter quantum physics. Quantum physics is a growing set
of theories that attempts to explain the nature of the universe. It
describes the characteristics of subatomic particles or "quantum"
of matter. A quantum is defined as the basic unit of energy that

is between 10,000,000 and 100,000,000 times smaller than the smallest atom. Quantum physics suggests that as we delve deeper and deeper into this subatomic realm, energy and matter become interchangeable. Therefore at the quantum level, *everything in the universe is energy.*

All energy can be identified as having a specific vibrational frequency. This basic concept applies to all matter—including the cells of our body. The subatomic particles that make up our cells vibrate at certain established frequencies, as do the subatomic particles of the cells that make up a rock, a tree, or a blade of grass. Therefore, any discussion about humanity and health must acknowledge the significant relationship between different energy states and health, illness, disease, and the healing process.

Life force is energy.

It is estimated that our bodies are comprised of between 50 and 100 *trillion* cells. All cells operate within an energy field or energy matrix. At all times the functions of all those trillions of cells are directly influenced by the quality of the energy in that field. Viewed in this way, physical health is merely one expression of what is going on inside of us at a *quantum* energy level.

Health can be described as the unrestricted flow of this energy in the body, and the quality of health we experience is a direct reflection of the quality of the energy fields affecting our bodies.

Universal Principles Rule!

The game of health, like every other game, has a specific set of rules that govern how the game must be played to get a winning outcome. Whether or not we abide by these rules influences the outcome of the game. The rules of the game of health are not rules that you or I make up, or that were created by the healthcare community, the drug companies, our government, or religious institutions. These rules are part of a large collection of Universal Principles, also referred to as universal *truths* or universal laws, which govern how everything in the universe operates. All creation is governed by universal laws.

At one level, Universal Principles govern the expansion of the universe in how the planets in our solar system orbit the sun and how our solar system orbits within the cosmos. At another level, these same Universal Principles govern how electrons orbit around the nucleus of the atoms that make up the cells of our body, and how we experience health. The Universal Principles that we will be discussing are the basic rules of health in the wellness game. They explain how things work in both the physical realm (in the body itself) and in the non-physical realm of the mind, emotion, and spirit.

For the sake of simplicity we will identify these Universal Principles that govern health as falling into two categories: Spiritual Laws and Laws of Nature. Spiritual Laws govern how things happen in the non-physical realm, including things like our thoughts and emotions. The Laws of Nature govern what happens in the physical realm, including things like our body, the food we eat, and how toxic chemicals affect our health. Both operate simultaneously, consistently, and at all times, and influence the quality of health we experience.

The greater our understanding of these laws, the greater our chances of winning at the game of health. When we choose to play by the rules, we increase the likelihood of creating favorable health outcomes. When we violate the rules, either by choice or through ignorance, there are inescapable consequences. So what are these rules of health? How do they operate? And how is our health adversely affected when we break these rules?

SPIRITUAL LAWS & HEALTH

Spiritual Laws refer to those principles that govern the energy dynamics in the non-physical, invisible universe. These energy dynamics in turn determine outcomes in the physical world. "Spiritual" refers to the non-physical, non-material aspect of our being. The universe is comprised of information and energy; although the energy of our thoughts and emotions do not have a physical dimension, these invisible forces greatly influence how we experience the physical world.

We are also comprised of information (DNA) and energy: spiritual energy, mental energy called *thought*, emotional energy called *feelings*, and physical energy called *body*. These spiritual, mental, and emotional invisible forces are expressed in the physical body. We cannot function outside the influence of these Universal Principles. Our physical health does not exist independent of the influence of these non-material factors. Let's take a look at some of the Spiritual Laws and how they relate specifically to health.

THE LAW OF ABUNDANCE

Although we usually hear about this law in the context of creating material wealth on the planet, it also applies to creating health in your life. There are adequate resources in the universe to create all things and these resources flow through the dynamic energy exchange of giving and receiving. If you are in need of something, you must be ready and open to receive it. This implies that you not only have to think it and believe it, but that your actions must also be in alignment with this belief. The universe will recognize your openness and availability to receive and fill it with abundance. By creating visualizations of abundant health you draw this energy into your reality.

THE LAW OF ACTION

Although we may desire optimal health and a life that is pain-free, disease-free, and medication-free, only action that is in alignment with the *truth* about the way the body works as nature intended can make this a reality. All the information and knowledge in the world changes nothing. Your ability to align your actions with the *truth* about health is the only way to create positive change in your life.

THE LAW OF ATTRACTION

This is the basic law of all manifestation. You attract into your life that into which you put the energy of your thoughts. If you desire good health, you can attract it into your life through the positive expectancy of its arrival into your life—but only if your understanding and belief system about health is accurate and truthful. Alternately, you also have the power to attract into your life that which you do not want—illness and disease—by focusing your attention and thoughts on what you don't want, for example, entertaining fearful thoughts about contracting disease, such as "since this disease runs in my family, so I will also get this disease."

THE LAW OF CAUSE & EFFECT

The elemental patterns of nature exist in balance. Disturbances in these patterns (cause) result in consequential alterations of the patterns of nature (effect). When you nourish the body's health you create health. When you starve the body of physical nourishment you create sickness. The same is true on the spiritual, mental, and emotional planes. Nourishment creates health; lack of nourishment creates un-health. To determine why something has come into your life, you simply have to search for the cause of the effect.

THE LAW OF ENERGY

Everything in the universe is Energy. Energy can be directed to create and support or restrict and block an ultimate goal or destination. Energy includes thoughts and feelings. Energy itself has no meaning, quality, or characteristic other than the one you give it. Emotion is one type of energy and, accordingly, has only the meaning you give it. For example, the body's reactions to fear (for one's life or safety) are the same as its reactions to exhilaration (e.g., riding a roller-coaster).

We operate from two primary energies: love and fear. **The Law of Attraction** and **The Law of Cause & Effect** determine the extent to which the outcomes you experience in your life are an expression of either love (expansiveness, abundance, fulfillment, and health) or fear (limitation, lack, unhappiness, and un-health).

THE LAW OF EXPECTATION

Energy follows thought; you move toward but not beyond what you can imagine. If you see yourself as being sickly, universal dynamics will move you toward that direction. If you see yourself as having a strong and healthy constitution, with the power to both heal and prevent illness and disease, universal dynamics will help make that a reality in your life—but only if you are willing to take the appropriate action to support that outcome. Your expectations and beliefs about health color and create your experience of health. By changing your expectations you can change your experience of life, including your health.

The Law of Free Will or The Law of Choice

We each have the opportunity to express our creative energy in the world in either expansive and positive ways or in limiting and negative ways. This decision is ours alone. No matter what our current health circumstances, we have the power to choose a different path. Whether we realize it or not, we create our path in life based upon what we know and what we choose to implement. We can either accept 100% responsibility and accountability for the thoughts, feelings, words, and actions that determine our experience of health, or we can choose to give up our power and accept what others—conventional medicine, drug companies, food manufacturers, governments, and religions—tell us we should do and think about our health.

Are you going through life under someone else's direction or your own? The choice is yours. Who better to make health decision about your body, than you? Who has your best interest at heart? You or someone who is committed to their own personal agenda and self-serving interests? We make our choices daily through the thousands of actions we take. The choices and actions we made in the past are what lead to the circumstances we find ourselves in today.

The Law of Giving & Receiving

The universe operates through the principle of dynamic exchange: as you give to others that which you desire to receive, the abundance of the universe is perpetuated in your own life. Giving and receiving are different aspects of the flow of energy in the universe. Giving and receiving are opposite sides of the same coin of universal dynamics. The energy of each is equal, and the universe will respond to either with a pull of the energy of the other. In our willingness to give that which we seek, we keep the abundance circulating in our lives.

The Law of Healing

When we talk about healing, we are not talking about health care. Health care refers to the mechanical processes used to treat illness and disease: drugs and surgery used by conventional medicine; nutritional supplements used by nutritionists; various techniques of manual manipulation of soft tissue used by massage therapists; manual manipulation of joints by chiropractors; and other mechanically or chemically-based techniques. Healing, in contrast, refers to the shifts in energy that occur in the body that precede any physiological changes.

We all possess the power to heal; healing energy is within us. Subtle shifts in energy and energy flow in the body always precede the physiological changes in cells that *lead to* either health or illness and disease. This law concerns our ability to channel the energy ("Holy Spirit," "chi," "prana") which radiates from the Source we call God.

The purpose of this channeled energy is to improve one's self or another by either removing blockages or instilling the sacred energy which pulsates from the Source. Divine power turns on the healing energy within us to heal ourselves and passes through us to heal others. The brain waves of hands-on healers who are effective in healing have measured 7.8 Hz — the same as the earth's pulse beat. Their brain waves are in sync with the earth's at the time the healing is performed.

Law of Intention

Inherent in every intention and desire is the mechanics for its fulfillment. Intention and desire in the field of pure potentiality have infinite organizing power. When we introduce an intention in the fertile ground of pure potentiality (or the pure ability for something to develop or come into existence), we put this infinite organizing power to work for us. When our intention to cure an illness or disease or prevent disease and create optimal health is genuine, and we take appropriate action that is consistent with the purity of that intention, we activate the energy dynamics of the universe to manifest at a physical level, in our body, that which we desire.

THE LAW OF KARMA OR THE LAW OF CONSEQUENCES

Every action generates a force of energy that returns to us in like kind. What we sow is what we reap. And when we choose actions that are in alignment with the way the body works as nature intended, the fruit of our karma is good health.

This is the natural principle of cause and effect. Every cause has its effect; every effect has its cause. When we engage in thoughts, feelings, and actions that are in alignment with the way the body works as nature intended, we create and support good health. When we eat raw organic fruits, vegetables, nuts, and seeds we support the healthy functioning of the body. When we eat processed and artificial foods and drink synthetic beverages—those products that do not appear in nature and were not intended for human consumption—we create chemical and energy imbalances that stress the body's ability to maintain healthy function.

Karma, in Hinduism and Buddhism, is defined as the effects of a person's actions that determine his destiny in his next incarnation. There are many planes of Karmic causation, but nothing escapes the law. Every action has its consequence, and that consequence is merely an expression of the quality of energy of the action, or series of actions. Everything happens according to this law. There are no accidents in life. Everything has meaning and purpose. Even our illnesses and diseases have meaning and purpose. Is not the physical pain and suffering of an illness or disease merely the universe sending us a message that we are out of sync in some way, that we are doing things that are not working for us, and that we are violating one of its laws?

THE LAW OF PURE POTENTIALITY

The source of all creation is pure consciousness. In pure consciousness lies the seed for pure potentiality. Pure potentiality seeks expression from the unmanifest to the manifest. When we realize that our true Self is one of pure potentiality, we align with the power that manifests everything in the universe. When you discover your essential nature and know who you really are, you can fulfill any desire you have, including optimal health. Every cell in the body is encoded with all the information and instruction (DNA) necessary to function optimally, to repair itself, and to reproduce itself, perfectly, in the natural setting without our conscious intervention. Only when we interfere with the natural order of things do we create health problems beyond the body's natural ability to cope. Every cell in your body has the genetic potential for optimal health.

THE LAW OF RESPONSIBILITY

Everything you experience in your life you create at some level. In some way you have contributed to the creation of every illness and disease that has befallen you other than those that were present at your birth. Inherent in your ability to embrace this understanding lies the empowerment to be able *to recreate* or change anything and everything in your life that is not working for you, including the quality of your health. But this can only happen when you are willing to accept 100% responsibility and 100% accountability, without exception, for everything you experience in your life.

LAWS OF NATURE & HEALTH

The Laws of Nature refer to those principles that govern how things work in the physical, visible world. Laws of Nature include the proven and accepted principles of physics, chemistry, and biology that we use to explain and understand how the human body functions and is *designed* to work. So, "How does the body work as nature *intended*?" Your ability to master the game of health begins with this question. If you can understand how the body works as nature intended, then you have a foundation, a frame of reference, and a starting point for figuring out how to achieve health and prevent illness and disease. This quintessential question opens the door to a cascade of additional questions that must be answered correctly in order to achieve optimal health. "How does digestion work?" "What are we meant to eat based upon how digestion works?" "What foods work well in our digestive tracts?" "Are there certain foods that are more user-friendly to our biological systems than others?" "Which foods should we eat and which should we avoid in order to stay pain-free, disease-free, and medication-free?" These are just a few of the additional questions that will reveal the real insights into how to achieve optimal health.

Everything about our human physical existence is an expression of higher intelligence. If we assume that it took intelligence greater than our own to create us, then we can assume that human design is the creation of a higher source. It appears that our original design is based upon a blueprint for optimal functioning in the natural environment that existed before technology, processed foods, the introduction of synthetic substances into the food chain, pharmaceutical drugs, artificial noise and light, toxic waste, and a lot of other conditions that exist in the present day.

With greater understanding of the design and workings of the human body in the natural setting, we can master the game of health. Once we understand the game and are familiar with the rules, we will be able to recognize when we violate nature's principles. It is these acts that create the chemical imbalances, hormonal imbalances, and nutritional deficiencies that lead to cell and tissue degeneration—the basis for illness and disease.

Our eating, drinking, sleeping, activity, and behavior patterns are either in alignment with the natural order of things and nature's wisdom, or they are in direct opposition to it. The decisions we make and the physical actions we take on this planet either support and promote optimal health and an optimal life or undermine it.

Health is a black and white issue. There is no grey zone when it comes to creating optimal health. Everything we do either works for us or against us. Optimal health can be defined as the natural consequence of being in alignment with the Laws of Nature. Everything that a human being does that is *not* in alignment with how the body works as nature intended violates natural law. All violations over time eventually lead to illness and disease. To put it simply: *all sickness and disease is a natural consequence of breaking the rules of health.*

A living organism does not get sick as long as it lives according to the primitive rules of nature. Health is nothing less than a life under natural conditions. Disease, on the other hand, is a result of unnatural living.

—Selvarajan Yesidian and Elizabeth Haich
Yoga and Health

What Were Humans Designed to Eat?

Given the natural order of things, what are humans designed to eat? What did primitive people eat? What foods work best in the human digestive tract, based upon the physiological and anatomical evolution of humanity in a natural setting?

It is said that 700,000 years ago early humans were hunter-gatherers. They would forage for things to eat in nature, such as wild vegetation and anything else they could catch with their bare hands or find as "road-kill" along the way. Although . . . isn't it more likely that early humans were more of a gatherer-hunter type than the hunter-gatherer theory? Think about it for a moment. It was probably a lot easier foraging and plucking wild plant life such as greens, vegetables, roots, nuts, berries, fruits, and seeds than it was to run down and kill a wild beast with your bare hands and then eat it *raw*. We are talking about very early primitive humans . . . before tools, weapons, and fire.

In the natural setting, wild animals possess far greater speed and superior physical and self-defense attributes than humans. Have you ever thought seriously about what it would be like to hunt down and kill a wild animal with only your bare hands and your physical prowess, let alone kill it and eat it raw? Remember: no tools and no fire. If your imagination is so inclined, I suggest starting with the small prey—birds, rabbits, and squirrels—before taking on a wild pig, deer, bear, or mountain lion. Imagine trying to tear the flesh off a bear, through the hide and the fur, with only your bare hands and your teeth. Good luck! Can you imagine?

Food for thought. Just because early humans started eating meat doesn't necessarily mean that this behavior was in alignment with the natural order of things, even back then. We know historically that humanity has an extensive track record and reputation for exploiting nature and manipulating the natural environment without regard for consequences. Though early humans' total diet may be open to debate, we *do* know that the earliest primitive humans ate nothing processed and nothing cooked. Our earliest ancestors ate organic "live" foods, and they ate them raw, uncooked, and unprocessed. The digestive tract of early humans began with and adapted to a diet that consisted entirely of raw foods found in the wild. Over time humans discovered fire and could cook their food. It was only in the last 10,000 years that humans started to grow things to eat.

For approximately 99% of humanity's existence on this planet, our digestive tract only came into contact with the raw, live, foods found in nature. Today, civilized, Westernized people process almost everything they eat . . . but they are still, essentially and genetically, the same biological and physical creatures as our early ancestors. Anthropologists estimate that it takes between 1,000 and 10,000 generations of evolution of our species for significant genetic changes to take place, and the last 10,000 years only represents about 400 generations. Up until about 10,000 years ago humans lived off the land, eating what nature offered in the form that nature provided. Since that time humans have manipulated their environment and what nature provides, and continue to do so at an ever-increasing rate as we continue to evolve at a relatively slow pace.

It seems obvious, then, that the human digestive tract and body appear to be better suited for a diet of naturally-occurring plant foods — raw, live, unprocessed — rather than artificial foods that are cooked, processed, and do not appear in nature (i.e. cookies, donuts, sodas, ice cream, hamburgers, French fries, etc.).

Consider, too, that human beings are the only animal on the planet (other than domesticated animals or animals grown specifically for human consumption) that eat cooked and processed food. All other creatures on this planet eat *au natural*. Animals in the wild eat their food live — uncooked and unprocessed. They typically eat only one food group at a time and they eat restrictive diets based upon instinct alone.

Herbivores eat raw plants, uncooked and unprocessed. Even carnivores, which eat meat, eat their prey live, uncooked and unprocessed. Humans are considered to be omnivores—animals that eat both plants and animals. Their propensity for both plant and animal may, in part, stem from the fact that they are the only animal on the planet that can manipulate the food chain.

Eat it Raw!

What is this live, raw food thing all about? Could it be that there is some quality or significance about food in its live raw natural state that is missing from that same food when it becomes dead— that is, when it is cooked and processed? Could it relate in some way to our concept of *energy*? All living things, plant and animal, consist of life force energy. Is it possible that the life force energy of a given food contributes in some way to the nutritional quality of that food?

Thanks to the medical research of Dr. Francis Marion Pottenger, Jr. that took place between 1932 and 1942, we gained insight into this question that eventually lead to the identification and understanding of the concept of "enzymes." Dr. Pottenger conducted feeding experiments to determine the effects of heat-processed food on the health of cats. This study demonstrated that the consumption of cooked and processed foods leads to long-term degeneration of body parts, including diminished reproductive ability. It also showed that eating cooked and processed foods creates toxicity in the body that later manifests itself as obesity and degenerative disease when systems start to fail.

Dr. Edward Howell was the first researcher to recognize the importance of the enzymes in food to human nutrition. In 1946, he wrote the book, *The Status of Food Enzymes in Digestion and Metabolism.*

Although the human body does produce metabolic and digestive enzymes, optimal digestion also relies on the presence of the enzymes derived from the foods that we eat. Live, raw foods contain enzymes, an ingredient critical to human digestion that cooked and processed foods do not. We say "live" because enzymes are considered the *life force energy* in food. The absence of these naturally-occurring food enzymes puts a burden on the digestive process and leads to poor digestion. That burden, in turn, is a major contributing factor to compromised immune response and all degenerative disease processes. A more in-depth discussion of enzymes is offered in Chapter 12, Nature's Nutrition.

Cooking plant or animal foods destroys this *life force energy.* Heating foods above 116 degrees kills all enzymes. Therefore, energetically speaking, live, raw foods provide a higher quality of nourishment for the human body than foods that are cooked and processed—dead food.

> *All food is medicine, and the best food is the best medicine. Medical science has made marvelous advances over the past hundred years and we are now at the point where we can do a great deal to help cure diseases like cancer.*
>
> —**Hippocrates,** Father of Medicine

A New Way to Look at Health

All the forces of the universe work together in harmony to produce outcomes that express *truth.* Based upon Universal Principles, health can be defined as the natural consequence of being in alignment with Spiritual Laws and the Laws of Nature. Disease, on the other hand, can then be defined as the natural consequence of violating either Spiritual Laws or the Laws of Nature, or both. Subsequently, healing can be described as that process of getting back into alignment with Spiritual Laws and the Laws of Nature. There's no mystery. No magic. No silver bullet cure-all. You abide by the rules, you create health; you break the rules, you experience illness and disease.

The First Step on the Road to Wellness

So, how can you become pain-free, disease-free, and medication-free? It depends on what you know and understand, how truthful it is, and how much of it you put into practice.

In health as in life, we know only that which we have experienced. Our interpretation of those experiences becomes our reality. That which we have not experienced cannot be part of our reality; that which is not part of our reality cannot be part of our understanding; that which we do not fully understand we cannot change.

Practically speaking, if we do not understand how the body works as nature intended, how can we ever really master health? If we are not aware of the Universal Principles that govern health and healing, how will we ever be able to cure illness or reverse and prevent disease? If we do not understand how spiritual, mental, and emotional energy are expressed in our bodies, how can we hope to create *The Optimal Life*?

What we do know is that the universe always provides outcomes, including health outcomes, that are consistent and in alignment with *truth*. This implies that if we are stuck in illness and disease, we are either not recognizing or not dealing with *truth*.

Because of the human's power to create and freedom to choose, we each have the ability to change anything and everything in our life that is not working. If we hope to achieve and maintain physical and emotional health, then we must face that challenge: the challenge to change.

Wellness Mastery Summary

1. The theory of quantum physics, a set of theories that attempts to explain the nature of the universe, tells us that the more deeply we delve into the characteristics of subatomic particles—particles smaller than an atom—the more we find that *everything is energy.*

2. At an essential level, the universe is comprised of energy: the flow of energy and the exchange of energy. All energy has a vibrational frequency that describes the quality of itself.

3. At the physical level, every cell in the body functions under the influence of an existing energy field. The quality of health we experiences is a direct reflection of the quality of the energy field affecting the body.

4. Health can be described as the unrestricted flow of this energy in the body.

5. There are rules to the Game of Health. These rules are the Universal Principles— Spiritual Laws and Laws of Nature— that govern how we experience health and life on this planet.

Must Know!

6. Spiritual Laws refer to those principles that govern the energy dynamics that describe and define how the non-physical, invisible universe works. These energy dynamics influence health outcomes in the physical world.

7. Human beings are comprised of information and energy: spiritual energy, mental energy called thought, emotional energy called feelings, and physical energy. These invisible forces of spiritual, mental, and emotional energy influence outcomes in the physical body. Man cannot function outside the influence of these Universal Principles.

8. The Laws of Nature refer to those principles that govern how things work in the physical, visible world. Laws of Nature include the proven and accepted principles of physics, chemistry, and biology that we use to explain and understand how the human body functions and is *designed* to work.

9. The operative question is "How does the body work as nature *intended*?"

10. Health is the natural consequence of being in alignment with Spiritual Laws and Laws of Nature. Disease is the natural consequence of violating either Spiritual Laws or Laws of Nature or both. "Healing" is the process of re-aligning our self with Spiritual Laws and Laws of Nature.

CHAPTER THREE

Why People Get Sick

UNDERSTANDING DISEASE

For civilized man who has cut himself off from natural living, there is only one way for nature to make him think of his health— through sickness.

—Selvarajan Yesidian and Elizabeth Haich
   Yoga and Health

HOW WE CREATE ILLNESS & DISEASE

Humans suffer with health problems not because we cannot resolve our health problems, but because we cannot *see* the *truth* about our health problems. What is this *truth* that we cannot *see*? It is that everything we do in our lives either moves us *closer* to optimal health and wellness or moves us *away* from it . . . and therefore closer to illness and disease. When it comes to acquiring optimal health there is no gray zone, no middle ground. There is only black and white.

Everything that we experience in our life, including our current state of health, we have created in some way. Whether we realize it or not, we are each 100% responsible for the health or illness we are experiencing. Each of us determines the quality of our life through our thoughts, feelings, words, and actions.

So why do people get sick? What are illness and disease really all about? If we truly understood the health paradigm then we would possess the understanding necessary to cure any illness and reverse or prevent any disease.

In Chapter 1 we described humanity as being *wholistic*, comprised of spiritual, mental, emotional, and physical energy, and suggested that the quality of health that each of us experiences is merely the expression of these energy states manifested in the physical body. We could say that optimal health is the natural state of a body that is in spiritual, mental, emotional, and physical balance—*homeostasis*.

In Chapter 2 we defined *optimal health* as the natural consequence of being in alignment with Spiritual Laws and Laws of Nature. We learned that sickness and disease are the natural consequences of violating these laws, and that *healing* is therefore the process of returning to being in alignment with these laws. Sickness and disease are indications that the body has lost this balance. Every time we violate a Spiritual Law or a Law of Nature we create a dynamic in the body that leads to some form of physiological and biochemical imbalance that sets the stage for illness and disease.

All of your body's physiological resources are committed at all times to moving the body from a state of imbalance to a state of balance. The greater the imbalance, the harder the body has to work to re-establish equilibrium. When the imbalance is too great and has existed for too long, the body's ability to maintain balance becomes overwhelmed and cells, tissues, and organs systems begin to fail. There are two theories that help explain the illness and disease paradigm from different orientations: the Body-Out-of-Balance Theory and the Toxicity Theory.

THE BODY-OUT-OF-BALANCE THEORY OF DISEASE

There are numerous factors in a person's life that contribute to illness and disease. Because wholistic humanity—mind-body-spirit-emotion—is in a constant state of energy flux, the human body is in a constant state of physiological and chemical flux. In this dynamic state of constant change the physiology of the body continually makes the necessary adjustments to correct the chemical and hormone imbalances that are the underpinnings of most chronic degenerative diseases.

Illness and disease begin as restricted energy flow that creates energy imbalances in different areas the body. These energy imbalances then express themselves in the physiological changes in different cells that we recognize as the symptoms of disease when these cells and the organs systems they comprise begin malfunctioning. Only in a state of spiritual, emotional, mental, and physical balance and harmony can one truly experience optimal health.

The Wholistic Health Model presented in Chapter 1 suggests that being out of balance in one area of a person's life affects to some degree all other areas of that person's life. For example, it is not possible for a person to be in a state of chronic illness or disease at a physical level without some degree of imbalance also existing in their spiritual, mental, and emotional life. Based on this theory, energy imbalances in the body are the primary factor associated with all illness and disease.

THE TOXICITY THEORY OF DISEASE

The Toxicity theory of disease claims that toxins are the cause of all illness and disease. Although this theory is most commonly associated with the physical aspect of human beings, toxicity can also be present at any level of one's existence: spiritual, expressed as a lack of love; emotional, expressed as the emotional incompletions that lead to painful feelings; mental, expressed as inaccurate and limiting belief systems that restrict the body's natural healing potential; as well as physical, expressed as physiological imbalances that lead to physical ailments. Toxicity in one area of our life indicates that other areas of our life are suffering as well. A body that is toxic is a body that is also out-of-balance.

At last the basic cause of disease is no longer a mystery. The basic causes are the habits of improper diet, inadequate exercise, negative mental attitudes, and lack of spiritual attunement which combine to produce toxic conditions and malfunctions in our bodies. The elimination of the cause of illness is the obvious and only way to healing and health.

—**Stanley Burroughs,** *The Master Cleanser*

The mental, emotional, and spiritual aspects of a body that are toxic and therefore out-of-balance will be explored further in Section 2, "What the Body Needs."

At the physical level, the toxicity theory explains that when poisons—including all synthetic chemicals found in drugs, food processing, and the environment—are consumed at a rate faster than they can be neutralized and eliminated, they accumulate in different parts of the body. Over time, these toxins accumulate in the blood, lymph nodes, and other tissues and ultimately saturate the body, creating an opportunistic environment for unhealthy, life-destructive organisms, including harmful bacteria, viruses, parasites, fungi, and other pathogens.

Toxins accumulate everywhere and as they accumulate over time, the adverse effects of these harmful substances to the internal biological environment are expressed in the body as the various symptoms that we experience as illness and disease. In short: we become sick when our internal biological environment becomes toxic. The greater the toxicity, the worse the illness. The greater the imbalance, the greater the health problem. The longer the toxic condition exists, the more progressive the disease.

NUTRITION, GENE EXPRESSION & DISEASE

In our society we are lead to believe that we acquire different diseases such as cancer and heart disease because "it runs in the family" and are therefore "genetic." We know that genes (that carry the information that comprises our DNA) are critical to every one of our biological processes. We also know that genes do not determine disease on their own. Just because we might have a genetic propensity (carry the information) for certain health conditions does not automatically doom us to contract the disease.

Why? Because genes function only when activated, or expressed, and the chemistry of nutrition plays a critical role in determining which genes are expressed. The recent science of "nutrigenomics," or nutritional genomics, is the study of how foods affect our genes and how individual genetic differences can affect the way we respond to the chemical compounds (both natural and synthetic) in the foods and beverages we consume. Research indicates that the chemistry involved with poor nutritional habits has the potential to activate the gene expression for many chronic degenerative diseases. At the same time good nutrition can protect our health genes and prevent the expression of unhealthy genes.

For example, numerous research studies have documented that as people migrate from their native culture to societies with different cultural norms, practices, and behaviors, they assume the disease risk of the country to which they move. They do not change their genes, although they acquire illnesses and diseases at rates that are rare in their culture of origin.

So, what do we need to know about how the body works in order to be in charge of our health destiny and be able to create optimal health?

BODY BASICS

As previously stated, the human body functions at a physical level as a series of chemical reactions controlled by electrical impulses. From a wellness perspective many of the major organ systems of the body—lungs, liver, digestive tract, kidney, lymphatic, and skin—are involved in two major processes:

- ❖ absorbing and assimilating nutrients
- ❖ neutralizing and eliminating wastes (toxins)

In an attempt to convert them into usable nutrients for energy production, cell function, cell repair, and cell replication, specialized cells within specific tissues and organs absorb and assimilate the foods we eat, the liquids we drink, the air we breathe, and the substances we put on our skin and hair.

These same organ systems are also engaged in the never-ending task of neutralizing and eliminating waste byproducts from digestion and metabolic cell activity, harmful bacteria and viruses, and other toxic foreign substances, such as pharmaceutical drugs and synthetic chemicals that are harmful to your health.

Metabolism is the term used to describe the combination of these two continuous processes: **anabolism** (the building-up) and **catabolism** (the tearing-down) of cells in the body.

How Does the Body Get Toxic?

When we think about early humans we can picture them in nature, in the raw. We can see that early humans were designed anatomically and physiologically to function optimally in a setting that looked and felt like clean air, pure water, raw food, natural sunlight, and natural sounds. Early humans lived in alignment with nature. In this natural setting Man is well-equipped to deal with the toxins that are produced from the body's own metabolic processes. But times have changed. Today, most of the population no longer lives under the influences of the purity of a natural setting. Most people live in unnatural environments filled with stale and chemically-polluted air, impure water, synthetic food and drink, non-full-spectrum lighting, and artificial noise.

The Stress Connection

Stress has been identified as the number one risk factor for all chronic degenerative diseases, including cancer, heart disease, diabetes, and many others. According to studies at the National Institute of Health (NIH), approximately 90% of all illnesses—mental and physical—are caused by or aggravated by stress. The World Health Organization (WHO) reports that 90% of chronic illness is related to environmental factors that create chemical and biological stress in the body. Dr. Hans Seyle, a pioneer in stress research, defines stress as a "psycho-physiological (mind-body) event that takes place when our system is overwhelmed by any experience: physical, mental or emotional."

Stressors can be mental, emotional, or physical—*environmental*. Mental and emotional stress involves your mind's interpretation of some event expressed at a physiological level as a cascade of hormonal and chemical activities.

We each create our own level of mental and emotional stress based on how we see things and how we choose to interpret the events in our lives. Sometimes the choice we make is merely a knee-jerk reaction made at a subconscious level, based on our past conditioning.

In addition to mental and emotional stress factors, there are many physical and environmental stressors permeating our lives that are unique to this modern age, which simply did not exist as recently as 100 years ago. Contemporary stressors tend to be more pervasive, persistent, and insidious than what our great-grandparents experienced. Today, our bodies are continually bombarded by all manner and form of environmental stressors, many of which we are unaware of.

Physical sources of stress are primarily environmental: chemical and electrical. Think about the polluted air we breathe, the contaminated water we drink, the chemicals (flavor enhancers, preservatives, pesticide, anti-bacterial and anti-fungal agents) in our commercial food supply, and the industrial chemicals in our household cleaning supplies. Add to that, the bath and beauty products (shampoos, soaps, toothpaste, skin creams, and body lotions) that we bombard our bodies with, the concentrated chemicals in the pharmaceutical drugs we consume, the mercury amalgam fillings that fill our teeth. Now, don't forget about the unnatural fluorescent lighting under which many work, and the electromagnetic pollution, the "electromagnetic smog," in our living and working spaces emanating from anything that runs on electrical current (including televisions, computers, video monitors, cell phones, telephones, beepers, hair dryers, electric shavers, microwave ovens, electric blankets, high-voltage power lines, sophisticated medical diagnostic equipment etc.).

Then there is the noise pollution from the harsh, loud, unnatural sounds we endure from machines, and the visual graphic pollution of unhealthy negative images from our visual media that we call entertainment—magazines, television, cinema—and now from cyberspace, the internet.

The newest source of stress is the "techno-stress" provided by our Information Age—the incessant, all-pervasive influx of new information that we are exposed to each day from electronic gadgetry running 24/7 and the accelerated, constant rate of change we live with. We are an information-saturated society in a chronic state of over-stimulation and sensory overload . . . we are data overfed but soulfully undernourished. We are no longer in sync with the rhythm of nature.

A certain amount of stress is beneficial, because it is in the body's adaptation to stress that causes the body to get stronger. Every stressor moves the body towards a state of physiological imbalance which in turn triggers physiological changes the body makes in an attempt to regain balance. Excess chronic stress causes the body to expend even greater energy to counteract the negative effects of the stressors.

Eventually all stress—mental, emotional, and physical—takes its toll on the body; the "body magnificent" finally reaches a point when it is not able to offset, neutralize, and eliminate the toxic biological, physiological, and chemical effects of the stressors as quickly and as intensely as it is bombarded. Overburdened and overwhelmed, the cells, tissues, organs, and systems of the body start to break down and degenerate. It is then that we begin to experience the chronic, degenerative, "Lifestyle diseases"—the Diseases of Civilized People.

LIFESTYLE DISEASES — THE BABY BOOMER PLAGUE

Lifestyle diseases appear to be in vogue in our current culture. Lifestyle diseases are those chronic degenerative conditions attributed to unhealthy living habits—improper diet, inadequate exercise, and exposure to a plethora of environmental toxins. Early stages of lifestyle diseases show up as weight gain, headaches, indigestion, bad breath, colds and flu, body odor, skin rashes, foul-smelling urine, foul-smelling stool, foul-smelling bowel gas, constipation, diarrhea, and many other unpleasant but relatively minor physical ailments.

The more advanced stages of lifestyle diseases evolve into the chronic degenerative and autoimmune diseases that we know as obesity, diabetes, fibromyalgia, arthritis, cardiovascular disease, cancer, Parkinson's, and Alzheimer's disease.

Statistics indicate that the incidence of degenerative and autoimmune diseases per capita in the U.S. population continues to increase. The leading causes of premature death in America in the over-55 age group are predominantly the chronic degenerative diseases related to lifestyle. See Table 3-1: Leading Causes of Death, United States, (all races, both sexes) from the National Center for Health Statistics (NCHS) Vital Statistics System, 2002, and the *Journal of the American Medical Association (JAMA),* 2000 Jul 26;284(4):483-5.

TABLE 3-1
LEADING CAUSES OF DEATH, UNITED STATES

1. Heart Disease

2. Cancer

3. Drugs, Doctors, and Hospitals*

4. Stroke

5. Respiratory Disease

6. Diabetes (Type 2)

7. Influenza & Pneumonia

Western medicine has been ineffective at successfully treating chronic degenerative disease. Why? Primarily because a drug and surgery approach is employed to treat what is essentially an education and behavior modification problem. Next, the medical healthcare model is a self-limiting paradigm because it is reductionist vs. wholistic: it focuses exclusively on the chemical and mechanical aspects of the physical body at the exclusion of the mental, emotional, and spiritual considerations that are an integral part of health and the human condition. Finally, conventional medicine's approach discounts or ignores the value of a natural lifestyle, minimizes the significance of environmental influences, and skirts the issue of an individual's personal responsibility for staying healthy.

There is a difference between health care and healing. *Health care* refers to the mechanical methods—drugs, surgery, diet, exercise, massage, chiropractic, acupuncture, etc.—employed to treat different health conditions of the physical body. In contrast, *healing* refers to a shift in an energy state that always precedes a change in the physiology of the body. Healing is about treating the life force energy of human beings who have a physical body that represents only one aspect of their existence. Healing is about treating the human person's mind, spirit, and emotions as well as their body.

TOXINS CREATED INSIDE THE BODY

There are toxins that are produced inside the body, by the body, and toxins produced from external sources—environmental toxins. There are two types of toxins that are created inside the body.

The first category of toxins produced inside the body is the waste material that is the normal byproduct of cellular metabolism, like carbon dioxide and lactic acid. Each cell in the human body performs some specialized task. Cells use oxygen and glucose to produce the energy needed to perform their functions, just as an automobile uses gasoline to fuel its engine. And just as an automobile gives off carbon monoxide when burning fuel to create power to run the car, the cells of the human body give off carbon dioxide as one of the normal byproducts of energy production.

Your immune response, made up of the activity of your digestive tract, lymphatic system, and organs of elimination (including your lungs, liver, colon, blood, skin, kidney, and lymph) is designed to neutralize and eliminate normal waste produced by your body on a moment-by-moment basis. Your body was designed to effectively deal with the toxins created from normal metabolism. Your lymphatic system acts as your body's waste management and sewage treatment facility.

The second category of toxins produced inside the body are the waste products of harmful bacteria, such as those found in the digestive tract. These toxins are created inside the intestinal tract, as bacteria breaks down undigested rotting foods, releasing harmful chemicals into the digestive system that, in turn, irritate the delicate mucosal lining of the gut and are then absorbed into the bloodstream to be delivered throughout the body.

Environmental Toxins

Environmental toxins are poisonous substances created *outside* the body that end up *inside* the body. Environmental toxins are created by humans; they include industrial chemicals, pharmaceuticals, pollutants, and pesticides. These harmful synthetic substances find their way into the food we eat, fluids we drink, air we breathe, and health and beauty products we use (including soaps, shampoos, lotions, and make-up) that are absorbed through the skin, as well as the oral hygiene products (such as mouth wash and commercial toothpaste) that are readily absorbed through the mucosal lining in the mouth.

It is ironic that the very substances that were created out of an intended desire to improve our quality of life are actually detrimental to our health, the environment, and all life forms on the planet.

The Chemicalization of Life

A century ago humans had no exposure to 99% of the synthetic chemicals that are found on the market today and that eventually show up in our bodies. Since the end of WWII our planet has been experiencing a chemical revolution. Our existence now depends on thousands of synthetic chemicals that are used to create our modern life. The industries of agriculture, healthcare, energy production, and manufacturing pump out millions of tons of chemicals, most of which are sold to consumers or eventually dumped into the environment. It is estimated that over 11 billion pounds of chemical pollutants were released into the environment in the year 2000 in North America alone.

Every year this number gets larger. In a study by the Environmental Working Group in 2004, 167 chemicals were found in the blood and urine of nine volunteers who do not work in or live near factories. Of the 167 chemicals found, 76 cause cancers in humans, 94 are toxic to the brain and nervous system, and 79 cause birth defects or abnormal development. Only a very small percentage of the chemicals to which humans are exposed have even been tested at all for toxicity, and very few toxins have been studied for their long-term effects when exposure is low.

As greater amounts of manmade inorganic toxins are released into the environment, the body's ability to handle these harmful substances becomes overwhelmed and compromised. The body's natural immune response—its ability to neutralize and eliminate toxins—evolved over tens of thousands of years, and even then was only designed to deal with toxins that occurred in the *natural environment*.

When the body's natural ability to neutralize and eliminate harmful chemicals becomes compromised, excess toxins accumulate in different tissues in the body and cause health problems. How does this happen? The toxins interfere with normal cellular function and create an internal biological environment that supports illness and disease. So what are some of these other sources of environmental toxins?

THE DRUGGING OF AMERICA

Prescription and *non-prescription* medications are a major source of harsh concentrated chemicals that put tremendous stress on the body. A total of 3.5 billion prescriptions were filled in 2004 medicating 129 million Americans, an average of almost a dozen prescriptions for each of 290 million citizens. More than 40% of the population is taking at least one prescription drug every day.

According to Citizen's Health Research Group (CHRG), roughly 1.5 million people are admitted to the hospital each year due to adverse reaction to drugs and of that group, about 100,000 die. A different report estimates that 1/3 of the prescription drugs sold in the U.S. today are sold to deal with the adverse effects of the other 2/3's of the medications in use.

What causes the adverse reactions? The CHRG cited seven reasons, including: the prescribing of a drug for a health problem caused by the adverse reaction or side-effect of another drug; prescribing two drugs that are safe on their own, but harmful when linked together; and prescribing dangerously high doses of one or two drugs within the same class. The message is clear: in many cases prescription and non-prescription drugs are more detrimental to the human body than the illnesses and diseases they are designed to treat.

We are even being drugged through our food supply, both plant and animal. *Pesticides* is the general term used to describe the various methods of controlling (primarily utilizing chemical agents to kill or prevent reproduction of) the pests that interfere with the industrial production of commercially raised or grown food for human consumption. In the 2004 publication *Sustaining the Earth*, by G.T. Miller, it estimated that about a 25% of the pesticides used in the US are used in houses, yards, parks, golf courses, and swimming pools. According to the February 2000 article, "Environmental indicators of pesticide leaching and runoff from farm fields" from the United States Department of Agriculture Natural Resources Conservation Service, 70% of the pesticides sold in the US are used in agriculture (food produced for human and animal consumption). There are numerous classifications of pesticides: insecticides kill insects, bactericides kill bacteria, fungicides kill fungi, miticides kill mites, molluscicides kills slugs and snails, nematicides kill nematodes (roundworms), rodenticides kill rodents, and virucides kill viruses.

Herbicides are used to kill unwanted plants. Widely used in agriculture (a routine part of all fruits, vegetable and grains commercially produced for human consumption) and in landscape turf management, herbicides are also applied in total vegetation control (TVC) programs for maintenance of highways and railroads. Smaller quantities are used in forestry, pasture systems, and management of areas set aside as wildlife habitat. Certain herbicides cause a variety of health effects ranging from skin rashes to death. Exposure to these harmful chemical agents happens due to direct contact by field workers, inhalation of aerial sprays, consumption of commercially grown food, contact with residual soil contamination as well as drinking water that is contaminated by surface runoff. Some of the herbicides in use are known to be mutagenic (causing cell mutations), carcinogenic (causing cancer) or teratogenic (causing non-inheritable birth defects).

It is estimated that 40-50% of all *antibiotics* sold in the United States are fed to animals raised for human consumption, according to the 2001 publication *Hogging It!: Estimates of Antimicrobial Abuse in Livestock*, by M. Mellon, et al. Beef and dairy cattle, hogs, chickens, turkeys, and farm-raised fish are treated with antibiotics to keep them healthy and to step up their weight gain. The problem is that over time the antibiotics given to the animals that we eat give rise to new strains of bacteria that are resistant to current lifesaving antibiotics used to treat humans.

More than 90 percent of all the beef cattle in the United States receive a combination of up to three naturally-occurring and three man-made *hormones*. It's all about the economics. Hormones are given to cattle to fatten them up quickly. Heavier cattle bring more money to the farmer at market. The faster the cattle put on weight, the less money farmers spend feeding and caring for them and the less we consumers pay for meat in the supermarket. Everybody wins, right? I guess it depends on your point of view. Hormones are used in abundance to fatten up almost all animals, birds, and fish raised for human consumption. I'd like to suggest that there might be a high correlation with the following scenario: cattle are fed hormones . . . cattle get fat. People eat cattle full of hormones . . . people get fat. We have an obesity epidemic in America and obesity has been identified as the #2 risk factor (after stress) associated with all chronic degenerative diseases and premature death due to these lifestyle diseases. So, in the overall scheme of things and looking at the big picture, are we really saving any money here?

Recombinant Bovine Growth Hormone or rBGH is a genetically engineered variant of the natural growth hormone produced by cows. It is regularly sold to dairy farmers under the trade name POSILAC. Injection of this hormone forces cows to increase their milk production by about 10%. In cows treated with rBGH, significant health problems often develop, including a 50% increase in the risk of lameness (leg and hoof problems), over a 25% increase in the frequency of udder infections (mastitis), and serious animal reproductive problems, i.e., infertility, cystic ovaries, fetal loss and birth defects. Because rBGH use results in more cases of mastitis, dairy farmers tend to use more antibiotics to combat the infections, the residues of which also may end up in milk and other dairy products (cheese, butter, yogurt, etc.). Currently, the U.S. does not require mandatory labeling identifying dairy products from rBGH treated cows.

In addition to the chemicals that lace most of what we consume and have an adverse affect on our health there are other issues we should be aware of that also adversely affect our health and the quality of what is currently peddled to consumers as food.

BIONIC FOOD?

Something else alarming is happening to the food we eat. The scientific community has been altering the DNA in food through a process called genetic engineering. Genetically engineered foods (also known as genetically modified organisms or "GMOs", biotech foods, bio-engineered foods, gene-altered and transgenic foods, and pharming) are created by splicing foreign genes into a non-related species, thus altering the species' DNA and creating a new organism.

Scientists take an indeterminate amount of genetic information when using this genetic engineering technology. "Junk DNA" is the term used to describe the estimated 97% of genetic material whose role is not yet understood. "Cassettes" is the term used to describe the DNA packages containing the junk DNA that are put into host organisms, thereby creating a new organism.

Why are such processes allowed? The answer is simple: economics. Genetically modified organisms were created to be more pest-resistant, are less costly, and increase the plants' yield with bigger organisms and greater crop outputs per acre. Genetically altered foods are engineered to survive herbicides, produce their own insecticides, or increase shelf life.

While the exact consequences of consuming genetically engineered foods on human and animal health are not yet known, there are reports that genetically engineered crops can decrease soil fertility, create new and more virulent plant viruses, contaminate conventional and organic crops, threaten wildlife, and decrease biodiversity. It has also been indicated that genetically engineered foods are lower in nutrition, cause impairment in immune response, and increase resistance to antibiotics.

Are we not violating the Laws of Nature by this practice? Are we not interfering with nature's design for genetic compatibility between food in its natural form and the human nutritional needs?

Currently, the U.S. does not require mandatory testing or labeling of genetically modified foods. Though genetic engineering has been rejected in many of the countries in Europe and around the world, most people in the U.S. are not aware that they are eating gene-altered foods. The *New York Times* and *Consumer Reports* say lab tests show almost every type of processed food and numerous vegetables and fruits sold to the retail public are genetically altered.

"Caveat emptor" . . . Let the buyer beware!

IRRADIATED FOOD

Radiation exposure is one of the more recent techniques being used to sterilize commercially produced foods. Food irradiation uses high-energy Gamma rays, electron beams, or X-rays to break apart the bacteria and insects that can hide in meat, grains, and other foods. Irradiation of foods creates substances called "unique radiolytic products." These irradiation byproducts include substances that can cause gene mutations, polyploidy (an abnormal condition in which cells contain more than two sets of chromosomes), chromosome aberrations (often associated with cancerous cells), and dominant lethal mutations (a change in a cell that prevents it from reproducing) in human cells. Many mutagens are also carcinogens.

Research also shows that irradiation forms volatile toxic chemicals such as benzene and toluene, chemicals known or suspected to cause cancer and birth defects. Irradiation causes stunted growth in lab animals fed irradiated foods. Irradiation has also been shown to cause the low-level production of furans (similar to cancer-causing dioxins) in fruit juice. The FDA has never tested the safety of these byproducts.

Irradiation also destroys the vitamin content of foods. Irradiated foods can lose from 2-95% of their vitamins. For example, irradiation can destroy up to 80% of the vitamin A in eggs, up to 95% of the vitamin A and lutein in green beans, up to 50% of the vitamin A and lutein in broccoli, and 40% of the beta-carotene in orange juice. Irradiation also doubles the amount of trans fats in beef.

Currently, irradiated food must be labeled as "treated with irradiation" or "treated by radiation"" and must display the irradiated "radura" symbol. But recently the FDA has proposed a new rule that would allow irradiated food to be marketed in some cases without any labeling at all. In other cases, the rule would allow the terms "electronically pasteurized" or "cold pasteurized" to replace the use of "irradiated" on labels. These terms are not used by scientists, but rather appear to be designed to fool consumers about what's been done to their food.

PESTICIDE RESIDUES:
A CASE FOR ORGANIC PRODUCE

Research indicates that consuming commercially grown vegetables and fruits increases the intake of chemical pesticide concentrations, which increases the risk of developing diseases such as cancer and Parkinson's disease. A recent joint study from the University of Hawaii at Manoa and Harvard School of Public Health reported that "consuming lots of [commercially grown] fruits and vegetables appears to increase the risk of Parkinson's disease . . . The culprit is pesticides, plant-borne toxins, or herbicides, not the fruit itself." Many additional studies have linked pesticides with increased risk of cancer, reproductive difficulties, and birth defects.

THE CHEMICALS IN HEALTH & BEAUTY PRODUCTS

Another major source of toxins comes from the daily use of many common health and beauty products, although neither the Food and Drug Administration (FDA) nor any other government agency regulates the cosmetic industry. Instead, in a classic example of the fox guarding the henhouse, the job of regulation falls to the Cosmetic Ingredients Review Panel, the industry's voluntary oversight committee. What this means is that industry insiders are the only ones responsible for overseeing the use of the thousands of chemicals used to preserve, dye, and emulsify most of the personal care products and cosmetics on the market — the very same chemicals that are used in *industrial* manufacturing to soften plastics, clean equipment, and stabilize pesticides.

What's more, a major loophole in federal law dictates that only chemicals developed *after 1976* require health and safety testing, and even then the testing is minimal at best. This allows the cosmetic industry to put untold amounts of chemicals that have been linked to cancer and reproductive harm, and found lodged in human breast and fat tissue, and even in human breast milk, into our shampoos, shaving creams, and hair sprays.

According to Charlotte Brody, executive director of Health Care Without Harm, we have adequate safety and health data for only about 10 to 12% of the chemicals used in our health and beauty products. See Table 3-2: 10 Toxic Chemicals Found in Health & Beauty Products, at the end of this chapter, for a list of the most common external toxins from health and beauty products that we are exposed to on a daily basis.

THE DISEASE PROCESS

In summary, when toxins are introduced into the body at a faster rate than they can be neutralized and eliminated, they begin to accumulate in different parts of the body. Toxins accumulate everywhere—in various tissues, around organs, and in joints. As toxins accumulate over time, the adverse affect of these harmful substances on the internal biological environment is expressed in the body as various symptoms. As the body grows less healthy it passes through five phases to progressive, degenerative illness:

PHASE 1: LOSS OF ENERGY

Everything in the body is designed to work efficiently and effectively . . . as long as it can neutralize and eliminate toxins as they are created. Organs have specific functions. The liver, lungs, kidneys, skin, lymphatic system, and lower digestive tract are responsible for neutralizing toxins and eliminating waste, and these organs can do an effective job of detoxification and waste elimination when we consumes foods as they appear in nature.

When your body can no longer eliminate toxins at least as fast as they are created or introduced into your system, your body begins to store them. When your body becomes a storage facility for waste material undesirable things happen. One of the early symptoms of a body that is toxic is a loss of physical energy. You may feel tired and sluggish.

PHASE 2: THE EARLY WARNING SIGNS & SYMPTOMS

Headaches, body odor, bad breath, constipation, foul smelling urine, foul smelling bowel gas, and foul smelling stool are the early warning signs of a body that is toxic on the inside. You may also experience fever, your body's attempt to burn off the toxins by increasing body temperature, as well as colds and flu symptoms, as your body attempts to carry toxins out of the body in mucous through the respiratory tract. Diarrhea is your body's attempt to eliminate toxins through the digestive tract.

These are all early warning signs of a toxic internal biologic environment. Only a Herculean effort by the body to correct the ongoing unhealthy physiological imbalance can change things for the better . . . and in the meantime, unpleasant and uncomfortable body experiences and symptoms are the universe's direct and simple way of telling us that we are violating Laws of Nature. The body has become a cesspool of accumulated waste.

PHASE 3: PAIN DUE TO INFLAMMATION

Pain is the body's most effective means of communicating that something is wrong. Unfortunately, in our culture pain has gotten a bad rap. Instead of listening to what our bodies are telling us, we have been misguided into believing that pain is a bad thing and that we should focus on eliminating the symptoms related to the discomfort. We have become accustomed to eliminating pain by artificial, unnatural means: medicating with synthetic, highly-concentrated chemical substances like prescription and non-prescription drugs. Yet all drugs are recognized by the body as poisons to the system.

Harmful toxins are irritants to the delicate nature of all cells in the body. Continuous exposure to harmful toxins causes the body to react chemically to the irritation by becoming inflamed, and that inflammation in turn causes additional irritation to pain-sensitive nerve endings. When our joints become inflamed we call it arthritis. When our lungs become inflamed we call it bronchitis or asthma. When our digestive tract becomes inflamed we call it gastritis or irritable bowel syndrome. When our connective tissue becomes inflamed we label it fibromyalgia.

These are just a few of the hundreds of different labels and exotic names we give to toxic environments that "homestead" in different tissues and locations throughout the body. At an essential level, all degenerative and auto-immune disease processes are the body's response to toxicity in the body. We are physically toxic because we eat synthetic, chemically-laced, unhealthy foods, drink poisons and chemically-treated liquids, breathe bad air, take prescription and over-the-counter drugs, and absorb harmful and biologically-destructive chemicals through our skin.

The fact is that all the pharmaceutical drugs in the world will not detoxify you or get your body back into biochemical and physiological balance. In the realm of the chronic degenerative diseases, drugs do not heal anything because they *cannot* heal anything. *The body heals itself.* But it can only do so under the right conditions, when we create a healthy internal biological environment. We create a healthy internal biological environment when we support the body's natural ability to heal itself.

PHASE 4: TISSUE DESTRUCTION

Chronic inflammation eventually leads to tissue destruction. We call tissue destruction in the stomach a gastric ulcer; we call tissue destruction in the cardiovascular system heart disease; we call tissue destruction in the heart a myocardial infarction or heart attack; we call tissue destruction in the brain a transient ischemic attack—"TIA", or stroke, Alzheimer's, or Parkinson's disease; and we call tissue destruction in the lungs emphysema. When our nerves become inflamed and the myelin sheaths protecting the nerves begin to degenerate, we call it multiple sclerosis. We call tissue destruction in the lungs emphysema. No matter what we label it, tissue destruction is the consequence of a long-term, toxic, internal biological environment.

Phase 5: Chronic Degenerative Disease

Cancer, heart disease, diabetes, emphysema, Parkinson's, Alzheimer's, multiple sclerosis, fibromyalgia, arthritis, et al. are chronic degenerative diseases caused by unhealthy lifestyle habits—habits that are not in alignment with what the body requires to be healthy, based upon natural law. All chronic degenerative disease processes are merely a common consequence of a chronic state of excessive toxin accumulation in the body. It does not matter where the "dis-ease" is located in the body. It does not matter what name you give to it. It is all the same basic issue.

Take cancer as an example. In the final stages of this disease, the body is so weak and the immune response so depleted that these "cesspool areas" can no longer be contained; unhealthy cells proliferate uncontrollably. In the cancerous state, the remaining healthy cells can no longer compete for nutrients against the unhealthy cells. The unhealthy cells dominate the environment. The cancerous cells disrupt healthy metabolic processes and the body deteriorates rapidly.

What Can You Do?

Become 100% responsible and accountable for your actions and experience of life. Change your lifestyle. Create new health habits to replace the old unhealthy ones. Change what you eat and drink, get more natural sunlight, spend more time outdoors in fresh clean air and learn to breathe deeper, become more physically active, take a look at the labels of what you are putting into and onto your body. Become aware of the harmful substances you consume. Everything that you put into your mouth is either life-enhancing or life-destroying; everything that you breathe either nourishes the body or pollutes it. Everything that touches your

skin—because *all* substances are absorbed through the skin—
either supports or undermines the health of the body.

As the body becomes more toxic, the immune response
weakens and the body loses its ability to deal with all the harmful
bacteria, viruses, chemicals, fungus, parasites, molds, and other
pathogens that we are all exposed to in our environment on a
daily basis. Our cells become vulnerable. And the only truly
healthy response to this daily assault is cleansing the internal
body—*detoxification*.

Detoxification must be the primary focus for healing to occur.
Detoxification brings the body into balance. Detoxification of our
thoughts, emotions, and spirit, as well as our physical body, is the
foundation for all healing.

In summary, poor spiritual, mental, emotional, and physical
lifestyle habits are all toxic to the body. This chronic toxic
environment eventually leads to compromised immune response,
and compromised immune response facilitates the proliferation
of harmful bacteria, viruses, parasites, fungus, molds, and other
pathogens. Unchecked, these unhealthy pathogens take over
the body. Illness and disease then becomes the common state of
existence.

DETOXIFY: THE CURE FOR ALL CHRONIC DEGENERATIVE DISEASES

If sickness and disease is due to a body out of balance, then the
cure is to regain balance. Detoxification of the physical body is the
process of neutralizing harmful substances in the cells, organs,
and bloodstream, and then eliminating these toxins from the
body. If the origin of all lifestyle diseases is imbalance and toxicity
due to our daily habits, then the solution is to detoxify the body at
all levels and create healthy lifestyle habits that recreate balance
in the body.

At a non-physical level, reversing any disease process requires:

- ❖ healing spiritual imbalances

- ❖ changing inaccurate and limiting belief systems

- ❖ dealing with unfinished emotional business in your life

At the physical level, restoring balance requires:

- ❖ detoxifying & cleansing the internal biologic environment of the body

- ❖ providing the body with the nutrients required for optimal health and performance

THE "BODY MAGNIFICENT"

The body has seven organ systems that all work together in harmony to neutralize and eliminate toxins from the body:

- ❖ **The Liver** neutralizes many harmful toxins that are then carried to the kidneys for elimination in the urine, or dumped into the colon for elimination in fecal matter.
- ❖ **The Kidneys** filter water-soluble wastes from the blood and regulate hydrogen ion concentration (your acid/alkaline pH balance) for elimination in the urine.
- ❖ **The Colon,** defined as the last four or five feet of your digestive tract, eliminates waste material from unusable undigested food particles, neutralizes additional toxins from the liver, and neutralizes other harmful bacteria through the fecal matter.
- ❖ **The Lymphatic System,** which is comprised of lymph fluid and a network of vessels and nodes throughout the body, is a key player in immune response. It neutralizes toxins from cellular metabolic activity and from the blood for elimination from the body.
- ❖ **The Circulatory System,** your blood, blood vessels, and heart pump, carries oxygen and nutrients to the cells and carries away metabolic waste material, including carbon dioxide from the cells, for elimination through the lungs by breathing and the kidneys through urination.
- ❖ **The Skin** eliminates wastes and toxins through perspiration. Many skin conditions, like eczema, are merely the body's attempts to expel toxins through the skin.
- ❖ **The Lungs** help regulate the acid-alkaline pH balance of the body by eliminating carbon dioxide through breathing. The action of breathing also stimulates lymphatic flow in the body, thereby enhancing immune response activity.

If the source of all disease at the physical level is a toxic internal biological environment due to lifestyle habits, then the only true solution is to replace unhealthy lifestyle habits with healthy lifestyle habits that are in alignment with how the body works as nature intended.

Creating healthy habits that detoxify and nourish the body and strengthen immune response is the most powerful way to achieve optimal health. By strengthening the body's natural immune response, we empower it to do what it is already programmed to do: *heal itself.*

Every cell in the body is programmed at birth with all the information and instructions it needs, DNA, to function optimally: to create energy, repair and replicate itself. All 50 to 100 trillion cells in the body have the power to function optimally and to heal themselves without our conscious intervention . . . when we obey the Universal Principles, those Spiritual Laws and Laws of Nature, that govern health.

Sounds simple? *It is.* With this understanding you will have the power to cure any illness and heal and prevent any disease. With this understanding you can become pain-free, disease-free, and medication-free in short order. Your body has tremendous healing potential. Mastering this basic understanding will give you the power, when exercised, to create health from illness and wellness from disease.

SOME GET IT, SOME DON'T

Dr. Phil—or, more formally, Phil McGraw, Ph.D.—has created a masterful, hard-hitting expose on human functioning: *Life Strategies: Doing What Works, Doing What Matters.* In this work Phil states his "Ten Laws of Life." Life Law # 1 states, "You either get it, or you don't," and the strategy is to "become one of those who gets it."

The same applies to creating optimal health and *The Optimal Life*. When it comes to your health, you either get it, or you don't.

❖ If you are ill, you are not getting it.

❖ If you are overweight, you are not getting it.

❖ If you have disease, you are not getting it.

❖ If you are constantly tired and miserable, you are not getting it.

❖ If you are healthy, youthful with vibrant energy, and are pain-free, medication-free, and disease-free, you get it!

Become one who gets it!

The rest of this book is dedicated to helping you become *one who gets it*. Then it is up to you to make it happen. Remember, all the information in the world changes nothing. Action alone creates change.

THE TEN PRINCIPLES OF WELLNESS— A ROAD MAP TO WELLNESS

Part One of this book introduced the wholistic nature of humanity (Chapter 1, Mind-Body-Spirit-Emotion), and The Wholistic Health Model (Figure 1-1), the Universal Principles that govern health (Chapter 2, Rules of Health), and a general overview of the disease process (Chapter 3, Why People Get Sick). You now have a frame of reference and a basic understanding of what you need to know to create a life that is healthy, vibrant, pain-free, disease-free, and medication-free—*The Optimal Life*.

Part Two of this book, What the Body Needs, explores "The Ten Principles of Wellness" based upon The Wholistic Health Model and discusses:

- ❖ *What* you need to know and do to achieve optimal health
- ❖ *Why* you need to do it
- ❖ *How* to do it, including some practical suggestions

Try it, you'll love the results! You can create a healthy vibrant life. By following these principles you can be pain-free, disease-free, medication-free, doctor-free and on the road to creating the optimal life.

TABLE 3-2

TEN TOXIC CHEMICALS FOUND IN HEALTH & BEAUTY PRODUCTS

Your skin has the potential to absorb all chemicals that it comes into contact with. Skin absorption is so potent that an increasing number of medicines are in patch form. Applying creams and oils is no different from eating them, because they enter the bloodstream regardless if they are ingested in the mouth or absorbed through the skin! The following 10 chemicals are the most common toxic chemical agents and synthetic ingredients used in commercially produced skin, oral, and hair products:

1. CHLORINE

Exposure to chlorine and the gassing off of chlorine from tap water, showers, pool, laundry products, cleaning agents, food processing, sewage systems and many others, can effect health by contributing to asthma, hay fever, anemia, bronchitis, circulatory collapse, confusion, delirium, diabetes, dizziness, irritation of the eye, mouth, nose, throat, lung, skin and stomach, heart disease, high blood pressure and nausea. It is also a possible cause of cancer. Chlorine gas is a deadly chemical warfare agent that was used in WWI. Even though you will not see chlorine on personal care product labels, it is important for you to be aware of the need to protect your skin when bathing and washing your hair.

2. DIETHANOLAMINE (DEA)

MONOETHANOLAMINE (MEA)

TRIETHANOLAMINE (TEA)

These chemicals are used to adjust the pH balance of a product. These are commonly found in most personal care products that foam, including bubble baths, body washes, shampoos, soaps and facial cleansers. DEA and MEA are usually listed on the ingredient label in conjunction with the compound being neutralized. Thus look for names like Cocamide DEA or MEA, Lauramide DEA, etc. These are hormone disrupting chemicals and are known to form cancer causing nitrates and nitrosamines. These chemicals cause eye problems, and dryness of skin and hair. DEA has been linked with kidney, liver and other organ damage according to government-funded research. Approximately 200 million pounds of DEA are produced annually in the U.S., most of which goes into personal care products. (USITC, 1990).

3. FLUORIDE

Fluoride is one of the most toxic substances on earth. It has no proven biological use inside the human body, teeth included. Fluoride compounds in water (fluoridation), toothpaste and supplement tablets (including some vitamins) were never tested for safety before approval. In 1997, Environmental Protection Agency (EPA) union scientists and lawyers reviewed the toxicity data on fluoride that had been published since 1985, along with the consequences of fluoride exposure as a result of the public policy of mandatory water fluoridation. This independent research by scientists not associated with dental trade organizations revealed the following: The neurotoxic nature of fluoride has been linked to motor dysfunctions, IQ deficits and learning disabilities in children, hyperactivity, genetic damage, bone pathology (including increased rates of hip fracture in fluoridated cities), and cancer (including increased bone cancer in young men), in addition to dental fluorosis (white spots visible on the teeth of children), a sign that systemic fluoride poisoning is taking place. Review of the studies on the effect of fluoride on dental cavities, including the National Oral Health Survey 1986-1987 published by the National Institute of Dental Research and the World Health Organization's Caries for 12-Year Olds by Country/Area, indicates that there is no meaningful reduction in dental cavities resulting from drinking water fluoridation.

4. FRAGRANCE

Fragrance is present in most deodorants, shampoos, sunscreens, skin care, body care, and baby products. Many of the compounds in fragrance are carcinogenic or otherwise toxic. "Fragrance" on a label can indicate the presence of up to 4,000 separate ingredients. Most of all of them are synthetic. Symptoms reported to the FDA have included headaches, dizziness, rashes, skin discoloration, violent coughing and vomiting, and allergic skin irritation. Exposure to fragrances can affect the central nervous system, causing depression, hyperactivity, irritability, inability to cope, and other behavioral changes. These chemical substances are an inexpensive alternative for real herbal scents.

5. SYNTHETIC COLORS

Synthetic colors are labeled as FD&C or D&C, followed by a color and number such as FD&C Red 6. These highly toxic substances are usually coal-tar based and have been linked as cancer causing agents.

6.   IMIDAZOLIDINYL UREA &

DMDM HYDANTOIN

These are just two of the most commonly used preservatives that release formaldehyde (formaldehyde-donors). Formaldehyde can irritate the respiratory system, cause skin reactions and trigger heart palpitations. Exposure to formaldehyde may also cause joint pain, allergies, depression, headaches, chest pains, ear infections, chronic fatigue, dizziness and loss of sleep. Serious side effects include weakening of the immune system and cancer. Nearly all brands of skin, body and hair care, antiperspirants and nail polish found in stores contain formaldehyde releasing ingredients.

7.   MINERAL OIL

Baby oil is 100% mineral oil. Mineral oil is a petroleum based product. It coats the skin just like plastic wrap. The skin's natural immune barrier is disrupted as this plastic coating inhibits its ability to breathe and absorb the natural moisture and nutrition. The skin's ability to release toxins is impeded by this "plastic wrap," which can promote acne and other disorders. This process slows down skin function and normal cell development causing the skin to prematurely age.

8.   PARABENS
(METHYL, PROPYL, BUTYL, AND ETHYL)

Parabens are used as an inexpensive preservative to extend the shelf life of the product by inhibiting microbial growth. Some combination of these synthetic ingredients can be found in almost every skin and hair product made today. Parabens are known to be highly toxic and cause allergic/skin reactions.

9. PROPYLENE GLYCOL (PG)

This petroleum by-product is the active ingredient in antifreeze and is used as industrial antifreeze to de-ice airplanes. There is no difference between the PG used in industry and the PG used in personal care products. It is used in industry to break down protein and cellular structure (what the skin is made of). It is found in most forms of make-up, hair products, lotions, after shave, deodorants, mouthwashes and toothpaste. It is also used in food processing. This toxic ingredient causes many allergic reactions. Research data states that through skin contact it can cause "liver abnormalities and kidney damage." The government's Material Safety Data Sheets warn against skin contact, as PG has adverse systemic consequences such as brain, liver, and kidney abnormalities.

10. SODIUM LAUREL SULFATE (SLS) &

SODIUM LAURETH SULFATE (SLES)

Used as detergents and surfactants, these compounds are found in car wash soaps, garage floor cleaners and engine degreasers. These highly toxic synthetic substances (used for foaming abilities) cause urinary tract, bladder and kidney infections, genital disorders, eye irritations, skin rashes, hair loss, scalp scurf similar to dandruff, and allergic reactions. Both SLS and SLES are used as one of the major ingredients in cosmetics, toothpaste, hair conditioner and about 90% of all shampoos and products that foam.

The American College of Toxicology states both SLS and SLES can cause malformation in children's eyes. Other research has indicated SLS may be damaging to the immune system, especially within the skin. Skin layers may separate and inflame due to its protein denaturing properties. SLS is a mutagen capable

of changing the information in the genetic material of cells. SLS
easily penetrates through the skin and enters and maintains
residual levels in the heart, the liver, the lungs and the brain.
It is considered one of the most dangerous of all ingredients in
personal care products.

WELLNESS MASTERY™ SUMMARY

Must Know!

1. Lifestyle diseases (degenerative and auto-immune conditions) are those unhealthy conditions that result from a daily lifestyle that is removed from a natural setting.

2. Unpleasant painful body experiences, like illness and disease, are the universe's direct and simple way of telling us that we are violating Laws of Nature.

3. The use of drugs, surgery, and technology—the allopathic approach to treating the symptoms of lifestyle diseases—is inherently a self-limiting paradigm.

4. *Health* is the normal state in nature. Disease, although an unnatural state, is the natural consequence of the lifestyle choices that we make, when those choices violate either Spiritual Laws or Laws of Nature, or both. Man creates his own illnesses; disease is merely a consequence of his actions.

5. Whether we are aware of it or not, we are each 100% responsible and 100% accountable for the health we experience. Our denial or ignorance of natural law will not excuse us from experiencing the *truth* of the consequences for breaking these laws.

6. At a fundamental level, toxicity is the basis for all illness and disease. All disease evolves from a state of physiological and chemical imbalance and toxicity in our internal biologic environment.

7. We can be toxic at any level of existence: spiritual (quality of energy), mental (our thoughts and beliefs), emotional (our feelings, especially about our self), and physical (our body).

8. Toxicity in the physical body is an indication that the other areas in our life—the mind, spirit, and emotion—are also out of balance, are suffering and need attention.

9. Curing illness and healing disease are directly related to our ability to detoxify, cleanse, and nourish the internal biologic environment of the body.

10. The body heals itself. Our primary responsibility is to create an optimal internal biologic environment that is in alignment with Spiritual Laws and Laws of Nature. We accomplish this through healthy lifestyle choices.

WELLNESS MASTERY™ ACTION

Must Do!

1. As you read this book, implement the Wellness Mastery™ Action at the end of every chapter.

2. Make your "self" a priority in your life. Get back into the rhythm of nature.

3. Make your health, happiness, and fulfillment a priority in your life.

4. Take back your power. Start by challenging your own potentially limiting belief systems.

5. Read other books about the wholistic nature of human beings.

6. Knowledge is power. Magnify your power through learning. Search only to discover and uncover and embrace the *truth* about health. Express your power by creating health and wellness in your life and in the lives of those around you. You gave up your power somewhere along the way. Take your power back and never give it up again!

7. Accept 100% responsibility for your health and well being. If *you* don't, nobody else will, because nobody else can.

8. Stop blaming others for what's not working in your life.

9. Read the labels on everything you eat.

10. Become familiar with the toxic chemicals listed in Table 3-1: Ten Toxic Chemicals Found in Health & Beauty Products and read the labels on all health and beauty products.

PART TWO

WHAT THE BODY NEEDS

THE TEN PRINCIPLES OF WELLNESS

Patients carry their own doctor inside. They come to us not knowing
that truth. We are at our best when we give the physician, who
resides within each of us, a chance to work.

Albert Schweitzer, M.D., OM

Theologian, Philosopher, Physician
1952 Nobel Peace Prize

The Ten Principles of Wellness

The following principles for healing illness, preventing disease, and achieving optimal health are based upon The Wholistic Health Model. These 10 principles operate simultaneously at all times and are based upon an understanding of the wholistic nature of humanity (mind-body-spirit-emotion) and the Universal Principles (Spiritual Laws and Laws of Nature) that govern health. To experience *The Optimal Life*, your body needs:

1. **Healthy Spiritual Energy**
   Heal Spiritual Imbalances

2. **Healthy Emotions**
   Take Care of Unfinished Emotional Business

3. **Healthy Thoughts**
   Change Inaccurate & Limiting Belief Systems

4. **Oxygen**
   Breathe Deep

5. **Water**
   Hydrate

6. **Sunlight**
   Bask in Full-Spectrum Natural Light

7. **Acid/Alkaline pH Balance**
   Restore Acid/Alkaline pH Balance

8. **Hormone Balance**
   Correct Hormone Imbalances

9. **Nature's Nutrition**
   Eat "Live" Foods

10. **Physical Activity**
    Move the Body

Each of the following 10 chapters will explore one of these 10 principles.

CHAPTER FOUR

PRINCIPLE #1

Healthy Spiritual Energy

HEAL SPIRITUAL IMBALANCES

> *Spiritual truth is complete within itself as it stands on its own merit.*
> *It is self-evident and requires no external agreement or props of any*
> *kind.*
>
> —**David R. Hawkins, M.D., Ph.D.,** *I, Reality and Subjectivity*

IT'S ALL ABOUT ENERGY!

As discussed in Chapter 2, Rules of Health, quantum physics explains that as we delve deeper into the nature of matter we eventually find that all matter is a form of energy. At the subatomic particle level all energy is described as having a vibrational frequency. This vibrational frequency describes the quality of itself. The subatomic particles in the cells of our bodies vibrate at a certain frequency. The same is true for the subatomic particles of the cells that make up a rock, a tree, a blade of grass, and all matter.

Any discussion about humans and health is incomplete without the acknowledgement that there is a significant relationship between (1) energy and health, (2) energy and disease, and (3) energy and the healing process. Why? Because all 50 to 100 trillion cells of the human body operate within the influence of the energy field occupied by that physical body. The quality of the energy in this field affects the performance of every cell. In a state of optimal energy flow all 50 to 100 trillion cells can function at their optimal potential.

If health is merely one expression of what is going on at the energy level, then illness and disease is also an expression of what is going on inside us at the energy level. All disease begins with energy imbalances and restriction to energy flow in the body. These imbalances and energy restrictions lead to the physiological changes that precede the actual physical manifestation and expression of the disease.

Ayurvedic medicine—a more than 5000-year-old system of preventive medicine and healthcare from India—holds that illness results from distortions in the patterns of quantum vibrations that hold the body intact. In this context, health can be described as the unrestricted natural flow of this energy in the body. Therefore, illness and disease can be described as the result of any restriction to the flow of energy to any part the body.

LOVE & HEALTH

How does the level of spiritual energy of an individual affect his or her health? Many research studies support the notion that the energy of love possesses beneficial and healing qualities to the human body.

In a well-known experiment at Harvard University, psychologist David McClelland showed a group of students a film of Mother Teresa working among Calcutta's sick and poor. The students reported that the film stimulated feelings of compassion. Analysis of the students' saliva after the film found an increase in immunoglobulin-A, an antibody beneficial in fighting respiratory infections.

In another study conducted at the University of Michigan Research Center by James House, investigators found that doing regular volunteer work that involved interacting with others in a compassionate way dramatically increased life expectancy.

In a thirty-year study of a group of Harvard graduates, researcher George Vaillant concluded that adopting an altruistic lifestyle is a critical component to good mental health.

In the 1970s, an Ohio University study of heart disease was conducted by feeding quite toxic, high-cholesterol diets to rabbits in order to block their arteries. Consistent results began to appear in all the rabbit groups except one, which strangely displayed 60% fewer symptoms. Nothing in the rabbits' physiology could account for their high tolerance to the diet, until it was discovered *by accident* that the student in charge of feeding the rabbits liked to fondle and pet them. He would hold each rabbit lovingly for a few minutes before feeding it; this alone seemed to enable the animals to overcome the toxic diet. Repeat experiments, in which one group of rabbits was treated neutrally while the others were loved, came up with similar results.

> *I believe that all disease is ultimately related to a lack of love... for the exhaustion and depression of the immune system, thus created, leads to physical vulnerability. I also feel that all healing is related to the ability to give and accept unconditional love.*
>
> —**Bernie Siegel, M.D.,** *Love, Medicine & Miracles*

Somewhere in our experience of life we may have heard that "love heals all things" and we speak of the "power of love." There is no denying the human experience of love. Although a purely subjective experience, love possesses a quality of energy that is unique unto itself and undeniably different from the quality of the energy we experience with the emotions of pain, such as fear, anger, quilt, shame, and sadness.

CAN WATER REFLECT OUR CONSCIOUSNESS?

Dr. Masuru Emoto's books *Messages from Water, Messages from Water Part 2,* and *The Hidden Messages in Water* document his groundbreaking research into the effect of human consciousness on water. In 1994, in the belief that there must be some correlation between the water that comprises most of your body and your health, Dr. Emoto, a Japanese researcher, and his colleagues at the MRA Research Institute began taking photographs of frozen water crystals after the water was exposed to different forms of energy.

The research illustrates that (1) energy is reflected in the crystalline structure of the water molecules, (2) water easily takes on the vibrations and energy of its environment, and (3) the molecular structure of water can be affected by exposure to pollution, music, photos, words, and even prayer.

After seeing water structures react to different environmental conditions, Dr. Emoto and his colleagues decided to see how thoughts and words would affect the formation of untreated crystals of distilled water. They conducted their experiments by typing words onto paper with a word processor and then taping these papers onto glass bottles overnight. The same procedure was performed using the names of deceased persons. The waters were then frozen and photographed. Consistent with the results of earlier experiments, the crystalline formations for the words "love and appreciation," "thank you," and "Mother Theresa" were dramatically different from the molecular formations for the words "you make me sick," "I will kill you," "Adolph Hitler," and "Satan."

The vibration of good words has a positive effect on our world,
whereas the vibration from negative words has the power to destroy.
—**Dr. Masaru Emoto,** *The Hidden Messages in Water*

Dr. Emoto's work provides factual evidence that human vibrational energy, thoughts, words, ideas and music affect the molecular structure of water. The research also showed that the quality of the vibrational energy of the environment changes the molecular shape of the water. In this sense, water not only has the ability to visually reflect the environment but it also molecularly reflects the environment.

When we reflect on how our bodies are primarily made of water, the implications of Dr. Emoto's work are staggering. Dr. Emoto's rationale was that since the body is comprised mostly of water and water is the medium through which all the cells in the body communicate with each other, in the grand scheme of things, there had to be some significant relationship between the water in our body and our health.

By showing that water is affected by its environment, the natural conclusion is that the cells, tissues, organs, and organ systems of the body (all comprised mostly of water) are equally affected by the same environmental factors.

WHAT DOES LOVE HAVE TO DO WITH IT?

The love we are referring to here is not the romantic love, as in "falling in love," that has been popularized in our Western culture. The love we speak of here is not an emotion. The love we are referring to is that *chosen state of awareness* that Jesus, Buddha, Barclay, the Dalai Lama, and all other spiritual masters practice and speak of. It is a way of seeing oneself and others. It is a way of being in the world. It is the highest guiding principle in the universe.

Love is one form of energy, the quality of which is described by its essence. Love supports life and the unrestricted flow of energy in every biological system throughout the human body. When the body is in the presence of the energy field of love, every cell in the body operates at its highest potential. When cells are operating at their highest potential it is not possible for the body to create or maintain the state of energetic or physiological imbalance that supports illness and disease.

Love in the Buddhist tradition and philosophy is expressed as an *attitude of lovingness* through living a life based upon compassion and non-judgment for all living beings. It is a way of being in the world.

Christians describe it as "agape" love. The word agape—a Greek word for unconditional love—is the purest and highest form of love. It is the quality of love that God demonstrates towards humanity. Agape is considered the noblest form of love. William Barclay (1907-1978), the famous Scottish scholar, theologian, and author, noted that "Agape has to do with the mind: it is not simply an emotion which rises unbidden in our hearts; it is a principle by which we deliberately live."

So how do we manifest and maintain this state of love? Where can it be found? Rumor has it that we all have it, that love is our essence. Spiritual masters believe that there is no lack of love in the universe, and that love is always present although not always chosen.

The energy of love has powerful and interesting dynamics; for example, the more that love is given, the more the capacity of the individual to give love grows. Love is an attitude that transforms one's experience of the world. Love transforms our perceptions of everything in our lives. By its nature, love is the most powerful healing energy in the universe. At an essential level, love is the basis for all healing and all optimal health.

As a man thinketh in his heart so is he.

—Jesus of Nazareth

Spiritual Laws Revisited

Spiritual Laws, introduced in Chapter 2, Rules of Health, Universal Principles that Govern Health, refer to those principles that describe and define how the non-physical (invisible) aspect of the universe works. They embrace those aspects of the universe that do not have physical dimension (such as energy, thought, and emotion) but, none the less, affect the physical world. There are many Spiritual Laws that govern the dynamics of how we experience life. Two of the Spiritual Laws introduced in Chapter 2 that we are concerned with for this discussion on creating optimal health are the **Law of Intention** and the **Law of Action & Consequence**.

The **Law of Intention** states that inherent in every desire and intention is the mechanics for its fulfillment. You can create anything you desire, including optimal health, through the power of intention. This assumes of course that your actions—what you do proactively—are consistent with your intentions, and that your intentions honor that which is in alignment with the natural order of things.

Your desire and intention, in a universe comprised of information and energy, have the power to manifest outcomes in the physical world. This is because every thought that you think is energy that seeks expression in the universe. When you think loving, healthy, life-supporting thoughts, the organizing power of the universe goes to work to manifest a health outcome at a physical level that is in alignment with the quality of the energy of that original thought.

The Law of Action & Consequence, also referred to as "cause and effect," or "Karma," states that every action has specific consequences. Every action generates a force of energy released into the universe that returns to us a consequence of like kind. Loving and compassionate spiritual, mental, emotional, and physical action leads to a balanced healthy experience of life. Unloving action in any of these areas leads to energy imbalance and subsequent illness and disease. The *truth* of this law cannot be avoided.

Based upon these and other Universal Principles (see Chapter 2) the universe can only manifest outcomes that are in alignment with the quality of the input. We may not always recognize the form of the manifestation that the universe provides, but we can rest assured that the dynamics of the principle will always be consistent. As portrayed by the computer-related expression, "garbage-in, garbage-out," the quality of the energy of our spiritual, mental, emotional, and physical actions determines the quality of health we each experience.

SPIRITUAL BALANCE VS. SPIRITUAL IMBALANCE

Spiritual balance is that state of engaging in life with an ongoing *attitude of lovingness*. It is a way of being in the world. When we finally get to a place in our lives where we can maintain a continual state of love in all our thoughts, feelings, word, and actions we will experience peace, joy, fulfillment, health, and happiness. It doesn't mean that living on this planet and dealing with other people is without its challenges. It doesn't mean that we won't have problems and challenges in life. Hey, we're human! It just means that (1) when problems arise we don't stay stuck in them, (2) we don't take on the negative energy of what happens around us, and (3) we don't contribute to the negative energy of what happens around us.

In contrast, spiritual imbalance is the state of engaging in life from a place of fear, anger, guilt, sadness, and shame. It shows up in our personal life as lack of fulfillment, emotional and psychological pain and suffering, as well as illness and disease.

Spiritual imbalance is expressed as impatience, intolerance, lack of compassion, insensitivity, being critical or being judgmental about ourselves and in our personal interactions with others.

In the final analysis, to whatever extent we have not experienced love, compassion, understanding, patience, and tolerance in our own lives, is the extent to which we struggle in the day-to-day game of life to express these qualities in our dealings with ourselves and others. An absence of love in a person's life expresses itself as many different manifestations of mental, emotional, and physical suffering that become the underpinnings for all physical illness and disease.

How Does Spiritual Imbalance Happen?

Our physical structure seems to be suited to feelings of love and compassion. We can see how a calm, affectionate, wholesome state of mind has beneficial effects on our health and physical well-being. Conversely, feelings of frustration, fear, agitation and anger can be destructive to our health.
—**Dalai Lama,** *The Art of Happiness*

So, how does spiritual imbalance happen? It happens due to the absence of having the personal experience of unconditional love in our own lives. This may sound trite and oversimplified but that is how it appears at an essential level. When we are denied an experience of love that is unconditional and nonjudgmental in our formative years, we end up experiencing different manifestations of pain: psychological pain, emotional pain, and eventually physical pain.

All pain is a state of existence where love is blocked, in much the same way as clouds block sunlight. Pain appears to be the essential state of being underlying the feelings of anger, fear, guilt, and shame. Fear expresses itself as lack of confidence, feelings of inadequacy, and low self-esteem. At a deeper level all painful feelings contribute to our formulating a less than loving and accurate perception of ourselves.

Our experience of life at an early age shapes our perceptions. As infants and children we absorb and unconsciously take-on the energy of the environment and those around us. This absorbed energy becomes part of the experiential reality that influences our interpretations of events and our perceptions about ourselves, others, and about life in general. This in turn determines how we think, feel, and behave.

The absorbed energy also becomes part of our physiology and cellular memory. If we experienced kindness, compassion, patience, tolerance, and joy from others when we were very young, we are more likely to develop positive healthy experiences of ourselves, others and the world around us.

On the other hand, if we experienced fear, anger, guilt, shame, and sadness in our interactions with others during our early formative years—from conception through early childhood—our interpretation of our selves and lives can be painful. Every inaccurate perception and limiting belief we hold about ourselves today is due to the emotionally painful experiences that happened in early childhood that we were never able to resolve in our hearts and minds.

The human condition and the dynamics of human psychology are such that we tend to recreate throughout our life, at an energetic and material level, that which we experienced in infancy and early childhood. That which we experienced in early childhood becomes our ingrained frame of reference about how life is, the "box" we are living in that filters our perceptions and subsequent interpretation of life's events and the world around us.

How Do We Heal Spiritual Imbalances?

If spiritual imbalance is due to a lack of love in a person's life, how do we heal this condition? How do we change this state of being? How do we grow beyond the "box"? How do we re-contextualize our experience of life? The short answer . . . with love. With love, an open mind, and a commitment to seek and embrace *truth* no matter how painful it may appear, or what it looks like. Only then will we have arrived at a place in our lives where we have the power to change everything and anything in our lives that is not working for us.

It takes courage to seek out and accept *truth*. It takes a rigorous and constant vigilance to change unloving thoughts, feelings, words, and actions. But without the experience of unconditional love somewhere in our own lives, change can be challenging and difficult, and we tend to stay stuck.

Things will start to change for the better in our lives when we start engaging in life with an *attitude of lovingness*, beginning with how we view and treat ourselves. Easy to identify; tough to implement. "Hitting bottom" in some area of your life helps with the willingness-to-change initiative.

With a healthy dose of humility, a genuine desire to embrace *truth*, an open mind, and a willingness to implement change— do whatever it takes—we can heal any condition in life, any relationship, and any illness or disease in the body. When we are willing to entertain that there may be a health reality that is different from and greater than our understanding at this moment, we raise our level of consciousness. We heal spiritual imbalances through seeking and embracing *truth*. The ultimate *truth* being that we are, and have always been, love.

Truth, although subjective and based upon context, is self-evident and self-revealing. Enlightenment happens when we are open to entertaining realities that may be different from our own.

Enlightenment happens when we surrender the ambitions of the ego. This process will cause us to question our core beliefs and everything we think we know. This can be a tough confrontation. The process of enlightenment begins by accepting total responsibility and accountability for everything we experience in life. Based upon another Universal Principle, **The Law of Responsibility**, once we have gotten to a point in our lives where we are willing to accept total responsibility and accountability for everything that we experience in our lives, we become more available to receive what we need to know—through revelation—that leads to knowledge and a greater understanding of all things. **The Law of Responsibility** states that at some level we have created everything that we experience in our lives (the good, the bad, and the ugly).

In our ability to embrace this concept lies the empowerment of the human spirit to be able to recreate for ourselves, in the present moment, something different and usually something better than that which we created for ourselves in the past. Raising our level of consciousness (enlightenment) is an experiential journey, not an intellectual one.

Spiritual realizations arise spontaneously and not as a consequence of thought processes. They arise in awareness as though coming out of intuition. Truth arises out of subjectivity and is obvious and self-revealing. It is effortless.

—**David R. Hawkins, M.D., Ph.D.,** *I, Reality and Subjectivity*

A SPIRITUAL APPROACH TO LIVING

A spiritual approach to living entails raising our level of consciousness in the pursuit of achieving enlightenment so that we are able to engage in life with this *attitude of lovingness* in everything we do. It includes a search for *truth* without any attachment to what the *truth* may look like.

How do we raise our level of consciousness? We raise our level of consciousness through expanding our awareness of the existence of factors that lie beyond our physical experience, but affect our physical experience of life. We expand our awareness by being open to the possibility of realities other than the ones we are clinging to at this moment.

Spiritual awareness is beyond form. Spiritual awareness embraces an understanding of the principles that govern how the universe works. Greater awareness leads to shifts in perceptions and shifts in how we interpret events. Our perceptions are purely subjective in nature and determine our reality. Shifts in perception lead to shifts in our belief systems. Shifts in our belief systems leads to shifts in our behaviors and consequently what we create for ourselves and how we experience life. Shifts in our own consciousness begin when we entertain the possibility that realities exist that may be different from our own.

How do we achieve enlightenment? Dr. David Hawkins simple formula for achieving enlightenment embraces three key concepts:

1. Be kind to all that exists.

2. See the beauty in all that exists.

3. Be willing to be forgiving and to embrace humility.

INCREASING HEALTH AWARENESS

So, how do we achieve greater knowledge and understanding about health and healing? We start by seeking the *truth* about how the body works as nature intended and we learn rules of the game of health. How do we raise our level of health awareness? First, we must accept total personal responsibility and accountability for the quality of our health at this present moment. Next, we must entertain the possibility that what we currently believe, what we think we know and understand about our health condition, may not be accurate or truthful, especially if we are stuck in disease. Finally, by asking questions with a genuine desire to embrace the *truth*, no matter what *truth* may look like.

Any time we ask appropriate questions of the universe, the answers will eventually be revealed. By asking genuine and responsible questions we open the channels of honest communication with the universe. We also become better receptors for receiving the information and answers that are always available to us. The information for all understanding, including health, already exists in the universe.

Our real challenge is to develop our ability to access this knowledge. An open and receptive mind and heart is the prerequisite to accessing universal intelligence. Seek first to understand *truth*. An open mind and genuine desire to understand the *truth* about any health issue will raise our level of consciousness. From a place of greater awareness we are then empowered to create a pain-free, disease-free, and medication-free life.

HELPING YOUR SELF

Any time we experience a less-than-desirable outcome in any area of our lives, including our health, we have an opportunity for greater understanding. First, ask yourself the following question without passing judgment on your answer, "What is the *truth* about what is really going on in this situation at this moment?" Second, based upon your answer to that question, then ask yourself, "What is the most loving action that I can implement at this moment, based upon the highest guiding principle of love, for the highest good for all concerned?"

One of the most powerful practices for raising our level of awareness and understanding is to take a good hard look at *truth*: the *truth* about ourselves, why we believe what we believe, why we think the way we think, why we feel what we feel, and why we do what we do. Confronting and accepting *truth* is powerful medicine. Every positive and loving action we take in dealing with *truth* is a freeing experience that leads to healing. Our own spiritual, mental, emotional, and physical healing is not contingent upon what anyone else does or does not do. It only matters what we believe and what we do (see Exercise 4-1: Implementations at the end of the chapter).

> *The pathway to enlightenment via radical truth is demanding and requires the surrendering of all belief systems. Only then does the ultimate reality (truth) reveal itself...*
>
> —**David R. Hawkins, M.D., Ph.D.,** *I, Reality and Subjectivity*

HEALING YOUR SELF

"How do I heal myself?" "How do I cure my own illnesses and disease?" "How do I get off medication?" "How do I prevent disease?" "How do I help myself when I get stuck in life?" Another set of million dollar questions! The answers to these questions begin with loving yourself. The degree to which you truly love yourself determines your ability to heal and the speed of your healing. The goal is to exercise love as the highest guiding principle in all your intentions, decision making, words, and actions, beginning with how you take care of your own spiritual, mental, and emotional needs.

Your perceptions determine how you interpret events in your life. These same perceptions frame your belief systems. Your belief systems dictate your thinking processes that determine your behavior. Your actions in turn determine the outcomes you create and experience in your life and your health.

Any action initiated from a genuine attitude of lovingness will create the most loving outcome possible in that situation, at that moment, for all concerned. Metaphysically, it is not possible for an action to be the most loving thing that a person can do for themselves, and for that same action to not also be the most loving for all others involved.

In all decisions, love is always the highest guiding principle and highest expression of *truth*. The energy of love is the most powerful healing energy in the universe and the basis for curing and preventing all illness and disease and restoring optimal health.

Exercise 4-1

IMPLEMENTATIONS

**All the information and knowledge in the world
changes nothing. Action creates change!**

List 10 things you can do right now, today, and this week to create
an experience of life (through your thoughts, feelings, words, and
actions) that are an expression of an *attitude of lovingness:*

1._____

2._____

3._____

4._____

5._____

6._____

7._____

8._____

9._____

10._____

WELLNESS MASTERY™ SUMMARY

Must Know!

1. In a state of optimal energy flow all 50 to 100 trillion cells of the body function at their optimal potential and capacity.

2. The word "spiritual" describes those higher virtues that are an expression of divinity, love, and *truth* as manifested in our thoughts, words, and actions and demonstrated as compassion, patience, tolerance, joy, kindness, gentleness, sensitivity, gratitude, non-judgment, and non-materialism in our dealings with each other.

3. The energy of love has beneficial and healing qualities for the human body.

4. Every feeling, thought, word, and action that is an expression of an *attitude of lovingness* benefits the recipient, the giver, and the entire universe.

5. Love is a chosen state of awareness.

6. Love is the most powerful healing energy in the universe.

7. When the body is in the presence of the energy field of love, every cell operates at its highest potential. When cells operate at their highest potential it is not possible to remain in a state of illness and disease.

8. Spiritual balance is that state of consistently engaging in life from an *attitude of lovingness*.

9. Spiritual imbalance is due to lack of love, and expresses itself as the emotional, mental, and physical suffering that becomes the underpinnings for all illness and disease.

10. With a healthy dose of humility, a genuine desire to embrace *truth*, an open mind, and a willingness to implement change (do whatever it takes), we can heal any condition in life, including health.

WELLNESS MASTERY™ ACTION

Must Do!

1.   Do Exercise 4-1: Implementations at the end of the chapter.

2.   Be kind, gentle, understanding, compassionate, tolerant, and patient with yourself and others.

3.   Create quiet time for yourself daily. Quiet your mind. Meditate. Walk on the beach.

4.   Spend 30 minutes each day outdoors in nature in a peaceful environment.

5.   Ask the universe for a greater understanding of what you seek to know! Then quiet your mind and listen.

6.   Hug yourself three times today and every day.

7.   Hug three other people in your life today.

8.   Perform one random act of kindness daily for the next 30 days.

9.   Share with a loved one all the magnificent qualities you see in them. Every beautiful and desirable quality you see in someone else already exists in you. Metaphysically it is not possible to recognize qualities in others unless you already possess the same.

10. Write down all the ways you are a loving human being.

CHAPTER FIVE

PRINCIPLE #2

Healthy Emotions

TAKE CARE OF UNFINISHED EMOTIONAL BUSINESS

An elderly Cherokee Native American was teaching his grandchildren about life. He said to them, 'A fight is going on inside me . . . it is a terrible fight and it is between two wolves. One wolf represents fear, anger, envy, sorrow, regret, greed, arrogance, self-pity, guilt, resentment, inferiority, lies, false pride, superiority, and ego. The other stands for joy, peace, love, hope, sharing, serenity, humility, kindness, benevolence, friendship, empathy, generosity, truth, compassion, and faith. This same fight is going on inside you, and inside every other person, too.' They thought about it for a minute and then one child asked 'Grandfather, which wolf will win?' The old Cherokee simply replied, 'The one you feed.'

—**Native American Indian Proverb**

THE POWER OF THE MIND

The "mind" we are referring to in this context is not the physical brain and central nervous system, but rather that part of human existence that is comprised of thoughts, attitudes, beliefs, opinions, perspectives, feelings, and emotions. Mind includes both the intellectual, or thinking, and the emotional and feeling phenomena that are expressed through the physiology of the body. The intellect is an expression of the conscious mind, while belief systems and emotions reside in the subconscious or unconscious mind.

There is also an area known as the "critical area of the mind" that processes information and input that comes into the conscious mind through the five senses from the surrounding environment. This critical area of the mind compares this incoming data to what has already been programmed into your subconscious mind, to see whether the new data is in alignment with or contradicts what your subconscious mind holds to be true—your belief system.

This critical area of the mind will tend to reject any input that is contrary to your belief system, the programming that already exists in your subconscious mind. Your conscious mind, your intellect and logic, will only accept additional input that coincides with what's already in your subconscious mind. This is why the most effective way to change a health-destructive behavior —such as smoking, overeating or physical inactivity—is to change the existing programming in your subconscious mind. Conflict arises when you *experience* something at a conscious level that is different than what your subconscious mind is telling you is true or false. Your subconscious mind automatically rejects experiences that are in direct opposition to your current belief system. This disparity creates internal conflict that needs to be resolved.

THE CONSCIOUS MIND

Our conscious minds are our intellectual centers; the home of thinking, reasoning and logic. Some psychologists believe that our conscious minds comprise only 10% of our brain power. This means that we're really doing nothing more than tapping into our five senses (taste, touch, smell, hearing, and vision) to protect our physical well being. We use our conscious minds to process information that is stored in memory as well as the information derived from the physical world around us. It operates by focusing or directing our thoughts (see Chapter 6, Healthy Thoughts). It also reflects our awareness of ourselves.

THE SUBCONSCIOUS MIND

It is believed that the other 90% of our brain power operates in the realm of the subconscious mind. This 90% constitutes our inspiration, creativity, problem solving ability, sense of well being, perspectives and belief systems, and, most importantly, emotions. With 10% of brain power dedicated to logic and the other 90% wrapped up in emotion, which one do you think controls your life?

Even though we might believe that we go through life at the conscious level, making decisions and taking action based upon the activity of our intellect and logic, for most of us our actions, or reactions, to events are a combination of the programming that already exists in our subconscious minds and our emotions that ultimately rule what we think and how we act. Our subconscious minds are essentially the engines that drive our lives.

Our subconscious minds work on auto-pilot based upon what has been programmed there since early childhood. This programming—whether accurate or inaccurate—is what we accepted without challenge at the time of programming as being true. This programming becomes what we call our belief systems, and it is the result of all the accumulated information that we have processed and accepted over time as *truth*. It operates at an automatic subliminal level solving problems and figuring out how to accomplish specific goals, based upon information and beliefs already in the system.

The subconscious mind functions like computer hardware. Similar to the conscious mind, the subconscious mind also acts as the processor. But in this case it only processes the information that already exists in the system. This subconscious mind reflects our true beliefs about ourselves and the external world. It is within our subconscious minds that our self-images exist, the true pictures of how we see ourselves and how we feel about ourselves.

Although our belief systems and self-image are both rooted in the realm of the subconscious mind they will be discussed in Chapter 6, Healthy Thoughts.

Our emotions represent our programming, while our feelings represent how we express those emotions. Our emotions and feelings, whether pleasant or unpleasant, also have a profound impact on our health. Unresolved emotional pain in a person's life — the painful feelings of anger, fear, guilt, shame, and sadness — adversely affect our state of well being.

> *Mind includes your thoughts and emotions as well as all unconscious mental-emotional reactive patterns. Emotion arises at a place where the mind and body meet. It is your body's reaction to your mind — a reflection of your mind in the body.*
> —**Eckhart Tolle**, *The Power of Now*

It is also through our subconscious minds that we have our connections to universal intelligence (all knowledge and wisdom). Our creative intelligence and creative genius is linked to universal intelligence through our subconscious minds.

EMOTIONS & BODY CHEMISTRY

Every emotion we experience is a form of energy and therefore has a specific vibrational frequency. This emotional energy has a physiological effect on changes in brain activity, blood pressure, cholesterol levels, hormone levels, and immune response. We know that painful emotions create undesirable physiological changes in the body.

In 1981 child-development researchers had discovered "psychosocial dwarfism," a disturbingly common syndrome in which an unhealthy emotional atmosphere at home stunts a child's physical growth. They found that when a child experiences hostility and feels rejected by his or her parents, thereby growing up with little self-esteem, the child's brain's emotional center, the limbic system, acts upon the nearby hypothalamus to shut off the pituitary gland's production of growth hormone. In this example what started out as negative emotional energy ended up expressing itself as a physical symptom: stunted growth. The energy of painful feelings produces changes in the physiology of the body that prevent the cells in the body from operating at their optimal potential.

How Emotions Affect Physiology

A 1987 study from Yale, reported by M.R. Jensen, found that breast cancer spread faster among women who had repressed personalities, felt hopeless, and were unable to express anger, fear, and other negative emotions.

In my own case, I was diagnosed with childhood-onset asthma when it was discovered that I was wheezing and had difficulty breathing while in the crib. All through my childhood and teenage years I was treated for the asthmatic condition using the standard medical protocols of that time, with little success. The first noticeable relief from the asthma occurred when I went away to college. The asthmatic condition continued to improve over time in direct relation to the length of time that I stayed away from my family and our family dynamics.

Later, during my own healing journey, I discovered that when I cried and screamed as an infant, my mother would attempt to quiet me because the noise annoyed my father and triggered his anger. Apparently my mother's attempts to keep me quiet were encumbered by the painful energy of her own frustration and fear. Consequently, I grew up in an environment that stifled self-expression and therefore I had been conditioned since birth to repress my feelings. My body subsequently responded and adapted by creating a physiological condition, restricted breathing, which was in alignment with the energy of this emotionally restrictive environment. Simply stated, if I couldn't breathe, it would also be more difficult for me to cry, speak, yell, or express my feelings in any verbal fashion.

Eventually, after identifying, addressing, and bringing completion to the unresolved emotional issues and painful feelings from my childhood, the asthmatic condition resolved itself; no more difficulty breathing, no more allergies, and no more asthma.

> *If you cannot feel your emotions, if you are cut off from your feelings*
> *. . . you will eventually experience them on a purely physical level, as*
> *a physical problem or symptom.*
> —**Eckhart Tolle,** *The Power of Now*

Where Do Painful Emotions Come From?

In *The Power of Now,* Eckhart Tolle describes feelings as "the place where thought meets the physical self." We all have feelings. Every cell in your body has memory of every emotion and feeling you have ever experienced. At one level these feelings are the physical representation of the energy of your thoughts as expressed in your body.

Starting in the womb, at the time of conception, we are exposed to, vulnerable to, and influenced by the spiritual, mental, emotional, and physical energy of the world around us. Since the fetus is literally part of the mother for the first 9 months, it is susceptible to the energy of all her thoughts, beliefs, emotions, and feelings during the entire pregnancy. The fetus experiences every emotion—all the joy, sadness, peace, anger, fear, quilt, shame, and sorrow—that the mother experiences during pregnancy.

The fetus exists within the emotional energy matrix of the mother and shares in all the feelings that the mother experiences during pregnancy. The unborn child is also exposed to all the spiritual, emotional, and psychological energy of the father, although not as directly. All the energy fields that the fetus is exposed to from the mother leaves an imprint on the spiritual, mental, and emotional psyche, as well as the physiology of the unborn child. This emotional imprint becomes part of the "filter" through which the child will interpret events in his life as he grows.

THE CHILD'S EMOTIONAL EXPERIENCE OF LIFE

As the embryo develops it is influenced by the spiritual, emotional, and psychological energy states of the mother, in addition to all the nutritional, chemical, and environmental factors—light, sound and electromagnetic energy—that the mother is exposed to. The DNA in the molecules of the embryo's cells is adversely affected just as easily by painful emotional energy as by the destructive chemical affects of prescription medications, recreational drugs, alcohol, nicotine, caffeine, and refined sugar.

Even after birth, the child continues to absorb the energy of the external world as it is experienced through the ongoing contact (or in some cases, lack of contact) with immediate family members and other human beings. Infants take in the energy of the people around them—mom, dad, brothers, sisters, aunts, uncles, grandparents, nannys, etc.—at a purely *feeling* level, during the alpha stage of brain development. During this alpha state the infant's brain has not yet fully developed its cognitive or thinking processes. As infants we feel the world around us versus thinking or intellectualizing about it . . . that comes later.

As we continue to grow and evolve, the brain next develops its intellectual processes, including thinking, reasoning, and logic. This stage of brain development is known as the beta state. The development of the intellect is superimposed over the pre-existing emotional imprint or emotional bias which evolved during the earlier alpha development. This emotional bias determines how we perceive life to be and how we interpret events based on that perception, whether accurate or not.

This emotional bias exists because as infants and children we did not possess the experience, understanding, knowledge, intellectual or discriminatory power to interpret life's events accurately. We merely absorbed the energy of the feelings surrounding an event without having the ability to discern accurate from inaccurate, and truthful from untruthful information.

Without the discriminating mind at work, we had no choice but to absorb it all. Then, being human, we personalized whatever we felt, both the pleasant and the not so pleasant, and it is the quality of this energy that became part of our emotional energy matrices.

In summary, by the time the beta brain kicks in, a child's malleable psyche has already been imprinted with emotional energy absorbed during the alpha state. Once imprinted into the subconscious mind, this emotional imprint creates a filter for viewing the world and interpreting events. As children we begin to assign meaning (whether accurate or inaccurate) to our internal world (self) and the external world (others) based upon the quality of the emotional energy of our early life experiences. This is due to our attempt as human beings to understand our existence on this planet.

TAKE CARE OF UNFINISHED EMOTIONAL BUSINESS

The painful feelings that we experience as adults—anger, guilt, shame, sadness, and hatred—are merely the result of unresolved emotional pain from our past that is being triggered by some event in the present moment. This unresolved emotional pain represents the unfinished emotional business which still lingers in our lives from childhood.

All painful feelings are based upon the assumption that what you need is outside of yourself. You see yourself as incomplete and therefore unfulfilled. These various painful feelings are all different expressions of common underlying fears; fear of inadequacy, fear of abandonment, fear of rejection, and fear of loss. Although there are many types of fear they all appear to be directly associated with the central theme of "lack of love" somewhere in a person's experience of life.

Since unresolved emotional pain is a significant part of every illness and disease, one path leading to health and healing lies in taking care of the unfinished emotional business that will bring completion to the unresolved emotions. We cannot heal the physical body while we remain in a state of unresolved emotional pain. Although we cannot go back and change the past, we do have the power to change that which is not working for us at an emotional level in the present. We can reframe, or re-contextualize, our understanding and interpretation of the events in our life.

In the present moment we can change our perceptions that form our filters based upon achieving greater awareness and understanding. In the present moment we can choose how we interpret events and how we feel about those events.

To create any permanent healthy change in life we must first become aware that we observe our internal and external worlds through our own unique filters. These filters assign meaning to everything we experience. These filters were already in place from early childhood, before we possessed the ability to discriminate truth from untruth. As children in the alpha brain state we lacked the intellect, awareness, and life experiences to differentiate truth from untruth. As a result, adults interpret events that are filtered through a pre-existing subconscious emotional bias— which they may not be aware of. As enlightened adults we do possess the emotional maturity, intellect, and spiritual ability to understand and resolve every emotional incompletion and heal every emotional wound, allowing each of us to create a healthier, happier, and more fulfilling experience of life, if we choose such a path.

Taking care of the unfinished emotional business is fundamentally about forgiveness and acceptance. It begins with forgiving ourselves for what we believe our transgressions have been and then accepting ourselves as we are. For it is only through absolute forgiveness that we will then be able to accept ourselves, fully and unconditionally. Once we have forgiven, accepted and embraced ourselves as *we* are, then we can effectively forgive, accept, and embrace others as *they* are.

Because every disease process has a direct association with unresolved emotional pain in a person's life forgiveness is therefore an essential ingredient for healing and creating optimal health.

The Ten Principles of Healing

As children many of us were not taught how to deal, in a healthy way, with the emotionally painful events that are a natural part of the human experience of life. Subsequently we have not learned how to work through our emotional pain and how to appropriately express painful feelings; instead, we repress them or act them out. We then inadvertently go through life reacting to events rather than responding to them.

When we bury painful feelings we not only obstruct the development of our emotional intelligence and emotional health, but we also impede the creation of optimal physical health. Emotional intelligence deals with the ability to appropriately process and express feelings and emotions. Unexpressed painful feelings remain unresolved and incomplete. The emotional pain associated with painful feelings—anger, guilt, shame, sadness and hatred—has a quality of energy that adversely affects the physiology of the body. When this happens, the energy that is associated with the emotional pain becomes the basis for the creation of many chronic degenerative disease processes.

Painful feelings from unresolved painful emotions from childhood are carried into adulthood and influence our perceptions, interpretations, and the decisions we make as adults. Every unresolved painful emotion we carry forward from childhood clouds every perception and every interpretation we make as adults.

In the absence of knowing how to effectively deal with what is not working in our emotional lives and in an attempt to "protect" our injured inner child, we avoid painful feelings by distracting ourselves with a myriad of outside activities. We become workaholics, achieve-aholics, food-aholics, extreme athletes, golf-aholics, shop-aholics, spend-aholics, relationship junkies, alcoholics, prescription druggies, recreational druggies, and many other types of "aholics."

Through these distractions we close down the natural expression of our heart energy. We tend to move further away from our authentic feeling self and move more into the direction of our thinking self. Thinking and other intellectual pursuits inadvertently become the popular distraction and avoidance mechanism for feeling. As humans we are well designed to pursue intellectual distraction since we have the most developed brain on the planet.

The following "Ten Principles of Healing" are offered as one approach for challenging the accuracy of old filters and the meaning that we assign to things. These principles are offered as merely one strategy you can use to help you on your own personal journey of healing and self-discovery. These 10 principles can help you create greater awareness and understanding, change your experience of life, and ultimately create a healthier, happier, and more fulfilling life that is pain-free, disease-free, and medication-free.

Healing Principle 1:
Accept Total Responsibility

All true and lasting healing is built on the fundamental principle that we accept 100% responsibility and accountability for our feelings, thoughts, and behaviors at all times, in every situation, without exception. This also includes all things that appear to happen *to* us.

Everything we experience in life we create at some level. Even those things that appear at first blush to happen to us, with greater understanding, can be seen as the consequence of our own creation in some way. If we understand and accept this premise, then by its acceptance we are empowered to create a different life experience. By its acceptance we acknowledge the power we each have to change everything and anything in our life that is not working.

Accepting total responsibility implies a mindful and conscious approach to how we choose to live each and every moment of life. *Mindfulness* describes the ability to respond rather than react to life's situations. *Mindfulness* also implies greater awareness of how the energy of our thoughts, feelings, words, and actions engage with and influences the world around us. Greater awareness allows us to see the *truth* about how things are connected in the universe.

We facilitate our own healing when we stop blaming other people and situations for our circumstances in life. Accepting 100% responsibility, without exception, for everything we experience in life is the basis for all healing. Accepting total responsibility for our feelings and our life's experiences is the foundation for achieving emotional freedom, peace of mind, and physical wellness.

When it comes to our own personal health and well-being, it doesn't matter what anyone else does; all that matters is what *we* do. It only matters what *we* do, what *we* think, what *we* feel, what action *we* take, and how *we* respond to things that happen in our life. Making the commitment to choose personal responsibility, without reservation, in all situations, is the cornerstone of all health and healing and the first step to creating *The Optimal Life*.

HEALING PRINCIPLE 2:

ACKNOWLEDGE THE NEED FOR CHANGE

Before we can create healthy change in our lives we must recognize the need for change. We cannot change that which we cannot see and acknowledge. We cannot change that for which we refuse to accept responsibility. And we definitely cannot change that about which we are in denial.

Adopting an attitude of openness to all possibilities of greater understanding of ourselves is critical to our spiritual growth and personal healing. Every illness and disease we experience we have contributed to in some way. The good news is that if we created it, we have the power to cure it.

Every physical ailment we experience is the body's way of telling us that something is not working. Physical pain and suffering is the universe's way of telling us that we are violating either Spiritual Laws or Laws of Nature, or both. Sickness and disease is the universe's way of telling us, through the discomfort in the body, that we are not paying attention to something that needs to be addressed and possibly changed. Not believing it doesn't change the *truth* about it.

Health is the normal state in nature; illness is the variant. Health is the natural consequence of being in alignment with Spiritual Laws and Laws of Nature. Illness and disease occur as the natural consequence of violating either, or usually both, of these laws. Healing, then, is the process of changing the way we think, feel, speak, and behave to re-align ourselves with these laws. We have the power to change everything and anything in our life which is not working for us, including our health, but only if we genuinely believe that we have this power.

HEALING PRINCIPLE 3:

LIVE IN THE PRESENT MOMENT

All healing happens in the present moment. It is only in the present moment that we can create change. Our power lies in the present moment. As espoused by Eckhart Tolle in *The Power of Now,* the present moment is all we have. We cannot change the past and the future does not yet exist. Therefore, it is a total waste of precious time to dwell on the mistakes, self-limiting thoughts, and painful feelings of the past.

Spending inappropriate mental or emotional energy on past events or on future speculation distracts us from the full experience of what is happening right now. Suffering is merely the unresolved emotional pain from the past that we have carried into the present moment and are projecting into the future.

It is important to accept and release our negative and painful emotional attachments to the past so that we can move forward in health and healing, unencumbered. The value in understanding the past is to enable us to identify and break the conditioning of old patterns and recreate healthier thoughts, feelings, and actions in the present moment.

With a genuine desire to understand how the universe works and the subsequent greater awareness, we can recreate a healthier experience of life starting right now, in the present moment. All healing happens in the present moment. All happiness begins in the present moment. The action we take at this very moment shapes our future. What could you do right now that could change the rest of your life for the better?

HEALING PRINCIPLE 4:

SEEK GREATER UNDERSTANDING & AWARENESS

Seek first to understand. Lack of understanding is one of the greatest impediments to our spiritual growth, emotional healing, and physical health. We must first understand that which we hope to master. The solution to every problem, including health issues, lies in a greater understanding of all aspects of the problem.

Since we are wholistic beings, every health problem we encounter has some mix of spiritual, mental, emotional, and physical elements. Without an understanding of the inter-relationship of all the parts, the whole cannot be mastered. Any approach to healing or health that does not consider all dimensions of what it means to be human is self-limiting by design and therefore can only provide less than optimal results.

Our personal journeys of healing must seek greater understanding of the *truth* about ourselves, including our feelings, beliefs, thoughts, words, and actions. We can only understand others and the world around us to the extent that we have embraced a more accurate, loving, and gentle understanding of ourselves. Greater awareness and greater understanding will reveal the *truth* about any health condition.

Healing, in contrast to what we know as health care, involves matters of the heart: feelings and emotions. Healing involves energy shifts within the body that actually precede any physiological changes that occur. Painful feelings — those unresolved emotional conflicts carried into the present moment from childhood — cannot be resolved at the head level alone using strictly the intellect; they can only be resolved at a heart or feeling level. Since all original emotional pain occurred at a feeling level, metaphysically, it must be resolved at the feeling level before the mind will accept it as complete.

HEALING PRINCIPLE 5:

FEEL & EXPRESS YOUR EMOTIONS . . . APPROPRIATELY

We all have feelings. All feelings, pleasant and painful, are an integral part of the human experience. In the eyes of the universe there really are no "bad" feelings. Whatever we feel was meant to be felt and meant to be expressed. Expressing feelings is a physiological requirement for a healthy mind and body.

Our ability to feel a wide spectrum of emotional energy is what provides richness to the human experience. Positive or joyous emotional energy strengthens the life force energy in the body and strengthens the immune response. Negative or painful emotional energy weakens the life force energy in the body and weakens the immune response, although this same stress is what creates the resistance that provides the opportunity for adaptation and growth.

The unexpressed painful emotions of fear, anger, guilt, shame, and sadness create restriction to the energy flow in the body that adversely affects both body chemistry and cellular physiology. Restriction to cell physiology creates an imbalance that leads to the malfunction and deterioration of the cells, tissues, and organ systems that eventually leads to degenerative disease processes.

All feelings are meant to be expressed. When the energy of painful emotions cannot find appropriate avenues of expression, they accumulate in the body and eventually find inappropriate and unhealthy emotional and/or physical expression. Expressing painful emotions dissipates the negative energy of those emotions within the body and simultaneously dissipates the negative energy effect on the physiology of the cells.

So, what is an appropriate way to process painful feelings? When a painful emotion surfaces, allow yourself to sit with it and *feel* the pain . . . don't deny it. Then observe the emotion you are feeling, as a third party merely witnessing the event, without becoming the feeling. As an observer to your own emotion you have the power and the ability to be able to acknowledge its existence without becoming the emotion or reacting to its influence. In this way you can take charge of the emotion instead of letting the emotion take charge of you.

Once you become aware of and take charge of your painful feelings you can then figure out appropriate ways to express them through actions that are not damaging to yourself and others. The operative word here is *appropriate*. Finding or creating appropriate ways to express negative emotions and painful feelings as they occur facilitates healing. On the other hand, emotional dumping on anyone else, at any time and for any reason, is neither healthy nor responsible. Emotional dumping serves no useful healthy or healing purpose. So, what is appropriate?

Sharing your feelings (only that which is about you) with the appropriate person, at the appropriate time, while accepting full ownership for those feelings, without placing blame on anyone else, is an example of appropriate expression.

By giving yourself permission to feel painful feelings when they surface, you allow that which is unconscious and has been repressed to be brought into the light of consciousness. Once a painful feeling has been brought into the light of consciousness, you can take charge of what you do with that feeling. You now have the power to release painful emotional energy and to re-program the inaccurate and limiting beliefs that dwell in the subconscious mind.

HEALING PRINCIPLE 6:

LET GO OF PAINFUL FEELINGS & LIMITING THOUGHTS

Letting go of painful feelings and limiting belief systems is forgiveness. So, how do you do this? It is possible to let go of the feelings of fear, anger, guilt, shame, and sadness and the limiting thoughts — "I am inadequate," "I am inferior," "I am unlovable," "I am stupid," and "I am unattractive"—since they no longer serve your higher purpose. This is possible because you are in charge of what you choose to feel and what you choose to think. No one can ever make you feel a painful feeling or think a negative thought about yourself that you don't already feel or think about yourself.

Self-limiting thoughts and painful feelings become self-fulfilling prophecies. We become the thoughts and feelings that occupy our minds. The thoughts and feelings that we dwell on become our reality. Appropriate expression is the healthy way to dissipate and release negative energy.

Every self-limiting belief and negative feeling we hold about ourselves is based upon some inaccurate interpretation, misperception, and misunderstanding. Every self-limiting thought and painful emotion we hold is due to a lack of love somewhere in our early experience of life. Until our misperceptions about ourselves—"I am inadequate," "I am inferior," "I am unlovable," "I am stupid," and "I am unattractive"—are confronted and replaced with more accurate and loving perceptions, we will continue to suffer the consequences of low self-esteem.

Until we let go of our self-limiting beliefs and negative emotions and replace them with a more accurate and loving understanding of life we can only continue to recreate life experiences that reflect undesirable and emotionally painful outcomes that contribute to sadness, despair, lack of fulfillment, ill health, and numerous disease processes.

Letting go of painful feelings and limiting thoughts can only happen when we replace them with genuine positive feelings and healthy, appropriate and accurate thoughts.

HEALING PRINCIPLE 7:

GIVE & RECEIVE LOVE

Giving and receiving love are opposite sides of the same spiritual coin. Based upon the **Law of Attraction** and the **Law of Intention**, that which we give, and the quality of that which we give, will attract back to us energy of like kind. If you believe that you are engaging in life in your daily living with an *attitude of lovingness* but find that you are receiving something different in return, think again. It's not possible.

If this has been, or continues to be, your experience in life, first check-in with your motivation behind your acts of giving. Love is pure only when it is selfless. Love is pure only when it is given without expectation of anything in return. In the purest sense anything less is not unconditional love. Unconditional love implies that you have none of your own needs that you are trying to satisfy through your actions. The concept of unconditional love seems easy to grasp intellectually but proves challenging to implement practically. Why? Because we are human and therefore we have needs (mental, emotional, physical, and spiritual) that we are constantly seeking to satisfy at both a conscious and unconscious level.

Love is an action verb. Adopt an *attitude of lovingness* in all that you do. Practice the art of loving in all your relationships and in all your encounters with others. Love can look like different things at different times. The real power embodied in any act of giving is the intention behind the giving and the quality of the energy in the act.

To have love in your life you do not need to go out and look for it. You can attract it into your life. To attract love into your life all you need to do is give love, and by its basic nature you will have initiated the universal dynamic that will attract love back to yourself; it will happen effortlessly and abundantly.

One of the most powerful exercises for facilitating self-healing is to give that which you needed as a child at an emotional level but may not have received, such as compassion, kindness, tolerance, understanding, support, patience, sensitivity, gentleness, loyalty, and honesty. By giving to another, without expectation of anything in return, those expressions of lovingness which you needed, but did not receive, you heal that need within your self. By doing so, you release yourself from the emotional attachment to that need.

Giving love begins by giving to yourself. Every time you give and receive a loving gesture, every time you treat yourself with an *attitude of lovingness*, not only are you one step closer to healing, but the whole world benefits from the energy of your actions. Above all things, be kind, gentle, patient, tolerant, understanding, and loving with yourself, for there is no true and complete healing without love.

Healing Principle 8:

Believe in Yourself

Recognize and embrace your goodness and power. Your parents, or whoever may have raised you, were only brought into the picture to take care of you during the early years. Even then, some of your custodians may not have done such a great job, but hey, they were doing the best they were capable of at the time.

Each of us is an expression of spiritual, psychological, and emotional energy manifested through our physical form. Each of us is an extension of the universal energy of love that created us. All life is energy that originates from one source. All energy is connected. The most powerful energy in the universe is the energy of pure love. The energy of pure love has been labeled God, Source, Divinity, Universal Intelligence, and Great Spirit. If the original source of all creation is the energy of love, then each one of us is a manifestation of that love, and our essence is therefore love.

As children of God and as an expression of the energy of love, each of us, at birth, is bestowed with the power to create and the freedom to choose. No matter how unpleasant or painful our childhood, we were born with the power to create a loving, satisfying, and fulfilling experience of life in the present moment.

The beautiful thing about the human condition is that based upon our power to create and our freedom to choose, each of us has the ability to change anything and everything in our life that is not working for us. We alone have the power to heal ourselves. No one else can do that for us.

Believe in yourself and in your inherent goodness and greatness. Nothing is more powerful for creating positive change in your life than your own belief in your personal power, self-worth, and abilities. As a friend once reminded me, "God doesn't make anything in the universe that is not a reflection of His own goodness and greatness."

Healing Principle 9:

Take Care of Unfinished Emotional Business

With a belief in your power, goodness, and greatness, confront all unresolved emotional issues—fear, anger, guilt, shame, and sadness—as you become aware of them. If painful feelings and emotional suffering keep appearing in your life, it means that there is some unresolved emotional business from your childhood that needs your attention. Any unresolved emotional pain will continue to impede your spiritual growth and block your physical health. Ignoring or avoiding negative feelings only keeps you stuck and perpetuates the emotional pain.

Learn to deal with any unfinished emotional business that may still be lingering in any of your past or present relationships, including and most importantly those involving your biological family. Your biological family offers you the greatest opportunity for healing your emotional pain and facilitating emotional freedom. If you can resolve issues with your biological family you can do it with everyone else.

During childhood we create the behavior patterns that continue to create painful and undesirable outcomes in our adult relationships, both personal and business. Others offer us the greatest opportunity for self-discovery, personal growth, and emotional healing. Consider all of your interactions with people as opportunities to grow both emotionally and spiritually.

Everyone in your life is a gift from the universe and provides you an opportunity to bump up against your own limitations and unresolved emotional issues. Intimate relationships are a special gift from the universe. The more intimate the relationship, the more potential for "bumping." Every interaction with another human being provides a healing opportunity. Relationships are an opportunity to create or recreate something healthy for yourself as well as for the other person.

HEALING PRINCIPLE 10:

RE-CREATE YOUR EXPERIENCE OF LIFE

In the ideal, what would you like your life to look and feel like? How would you like to experience life at this moment and from now on? Whatever that looks like for you, it is possible. The beauty of the human condition is that at any moment in time, if we choose, we can change our experience of life.

We change our experience of life by replacing the old patterns of thoughts, feelings, words, and actions with those that reflect a more accurate, loving, and compassionate perception of self and the world around us. Recreate thinking patterns that express an *attitude of lovingness*, such as compassion, thoughtfulness, kindness, patience, and tolerance.

Every human interaction and every situation in your life is an opportunity to recreate a healthier, more enriching, and more fulfilling experience of life. Practice an attitude of lovingness in all situations, with yourself and others. It starts with being kind, gentle, compassionate, understanding, sensitive, and thoughtful with your self. It is not possible for you to love another human being more than you love yourself.

With an attitude of lovingness in everything you do, you create a new experience of life: a life filled with love, joy, peace, abundance, fulfillment, and health. All the information in the world changes nothing. All the knowledge in the world changes nothing. Action alone creates change. Personal healing is the direct consequence of personal action taken moment-by-moment. Wisdom is the application of knowledge expressed with the energy of Love. Be wise in all things! Begin today!

CLOSING THOUGHT

Healing is a personal journey of forgiveness, self-discovery, and revelation. Each of us is unique in our personal experience and interpretation of life. Each of us is ultimately responsible for our experience of life. In the final analysis, each one of us must figure it out for ourselves.

With a genuine desire to experience health, joy, peace, abundance, and fulfillment, and with a willingness to accept total responsibility for creating it, we have the power to make it happen. On this journey of self-discovery and healing, there are two important self-empowering questions that you can ask in every situation, the answers to which will determine what you create in the present moment. First, "What is the *truth* about what is happening at this moment?" Second, "Based upon this *truth*, what is the most loving thought, feeling, word, and action I can implement at this moment for the highest good for all concerned?"

EXERCISE 5-1

TAKE CARE OF UNFINISHED EMOTIONAL BUSINESS

The next time your "stuff" gets triggered—feeling anger, guilt, shame, sadness or any painful emotion—slow down, take a deep breath, pay attention, write it down, and then explore where and in what situation you remember feeling this way during your childhood. The first step to taking care of the emotional baggage in your life starts with identifying its origins.

1.   **What am I feeling at this moment? What is the emotion?**

   _____

   _____

   _____

   _____

   _____

   _____

2.   **What is it about this current situation that is triggering this feeling in me?**

   _____

   _____

   _____

   _____

   _____

   _____

3. What was the event or circumstance that I experienced this same feeling as a child?

_____

_____

_____

_____

_____

_____

_____

4. What is the *truth* about what is actually happening at this very moment? What is the most loving thought, feeling, word, and action that I can implement at this moment for the highest good for all concerned?

_____

_____

_____

_____

_____

_____

_____

WELLNESS MASTERY™ SUMMARY

Must Know!

1. There exists an intimate and direct relationship between illness and disease and unresolved emotional pain, the unfinished emotional business, in a person's life.

2. Every disease process has it origin in unresolved emotional pain in a person's life.

3. Strong emotions, both joyful and painful feelings, cause changes in the biochemistry of the body.

4. Everything we experience in life we create at some level. Only when we accept 100% responsibility and accountability for our feelings and everything that happens in our lives are we empowered to change our situations.

5. The solution to every problem, including health issues, lies in a complete understanding of all aspects of the problem.

6. We can only understand others and the world around us to
    the extent that we have embraced an accurate, loving, and
    gentle understanding of ourselves.

7. All emotions—the good, the bad, and the ugly—need to be
    expressed, appropriately. This is a physiological requirement
    for a healthy mind, body, and spirit. Unexpressed emotional
    pain eventually finds unhealthy avenues of expression,
    including illness and disease.

8. The self-limiting thoughts and painful feelings we hold
    about ourselves are all based upon misperceptions and
    misunderstandings.

9. Our relationships with our immediate biological families
    offer some of the greatest opportunities for emotional
    healing and emotional freedom.

10. Be open-minded. Greater awareness leads to enlightenment!

Wellness Mastery™ Action

1. Do the Exercise 5-1: Take Care of Unfinished Emotional Business at the end of the chapter.

2. Hug yourself three times today and every day.

3. First thing in the morning and before going to bed at night, look in the mirror and acknowledge what a beautiful, special, and wonderful human being you are.

4. Practice the art of living in the present moment. Practice being 100% present when you are interfacing with another human being.

5. Hugs are healing. Hug every member of your family (biological and chosen) first thing in the morning when you arise and last thing at night before retiring.

6. Find appropriate ways to express negative emotions and painful feelings as they occur within you, without blaming anyone else. Remember, anything and everything you are feeling is only about you. No one can ever make you feel a feeling that you don't already feel about yourself, and that is not already inside you.

7. Take total responsibility for your feelings when sharing them. Emotional dumping on anyone else is counter-productive to your own healing.

8. Avoid negative energy discussions. No gossip! It does not serve your higher self.

9. Take care of all unfinished emotional business, negative feelings, and resentments you harbor in all your relationships, most importantly those involving your biological family.

10. The next time you experience a negative emotion or painful feeling like worthlessness, inferiority, fear, anger, guilt, shame, sadness or hatred, first ask yourself, "What is the *truth* about what I am feeling at this moment?" Second, "Based upon that *truth*, what is the most loving thought, feeling, word, and action I can implement at this moment for the highest good for all concerned?"

Chapter Six

Principle #3

Healthy Thoughts

Change Inaccurate & Limiting Belief Systems

> *As a being of Power, Intelligence, and Love, and the lord of his own*
> *thoughts, man holds the key to every situation, and contains within*
> *himself that transforming and regenerative agency by which he may*
> *make himself what he wills.*

—**James Allen**, British philosophical writer
  As A Man Thinketh

The Power of Mind Revisited

In the previous chapter we described mind as that part of human existence that is comprised of our thoughts, attitudes, opinions, perspectives, feelings, and emotions. We spoke of the mind as including both the intellectual, or thinking, and the emotional and feeling phenomena that are expressed through the physiology of the body. Our thoughts are an expression of our conscious minds, while our emotions reside in our subconscious minds. We explored how the energy of emotions and feelings affects health. We saw the adverse affect that unfinished emotional business and the painful feelings that crop up due to those unresolved emotions has on the physiology of the body and the body's potential to create optimal health and prevent disease. Now let us visit the realm of our thoughts.

THE CONSCIOUS MIND REVISITED

In the previous chapter we also identified our conscious minds as our intellectual centers; the home of thinking, reasoning and logic. Some psychologists believe that our conscious minds comprise only 10% of our brain power. We use our conscious minds to process information that is stored in memory as well as the information derived from the physical world around us. It reflects our awareness of ourselves and it operates by focusing or directing our thoughts.

And although it may be true that our subconscious minds are essentially the engines that drive our lives—because our emotions, feelings, belief systems and self-image reside there—we would find it difficult to reprogram our subconscious mind without the active involvement of the conscious mind to direct our thoughts.

THE CONSCIOUS MIND & THOUGHT

When we direct our thoughts to a specific goal these thoughts become our intention (see **The Law of Intention** in Chapter 4). Intention sets in motion the organizing principles for its manifestation. Intention opens the gate to receptivity to the information that is available at that new level of consciousness. As described by Dr. David Hawkins in *Truth vs. Falsehood*, when you commit to a specific intention, then the thoughts that are appropriate for that field (level of consciousness) are pulled in. It is through this mechanism that we have the ability to affect our bodies' chemistry and physiology to create positive changes in our health and our life.

> *The whole outer world—whether it be the physical body, the common things of life, the winds and the rain, the clouds, the earth itself—is amenable to man's thought, and that he has dominion over it when he knows it. The outer world, far from being the prison of circumstances, that it is commonly supposed to be, actually has no character whatsoever of its own, either good or bad. It has only the character that we give to it by our own thinking. It is naturally plastic to our thought, and is so whether we know it or not and whether we wish it or not. The truth is that the whole of our life's experiences is but the outer expression of inner thought.*
>
> —**Emmet Fox,** Irish "New Thought" spiritual leader
>   *The Sermon on the Mount: The Key to Success in Life*

SELF-IMAGE & HEALTH

Our self-images are the pictures of how we truly see ourselves. They are the result of how we interpret what we experienced as children at an emotional or feeling level— good or bad, pleasant or painful, happy or sad: Mommy hugged me (good, pleasant, happy), my favorite pet died (bad, painful, sad), Daddy yelled at me (bad, painful, sad), the kids at school call me names (bad, painful, sad).

Our self-images are not based on what we have learned intellectually. They come from our perceptions about ourselves based upon how we interpret what we experienced emotionally as children. Our self-images become our mental blueprints. Do you see yourself as wholesome, energetic, and disease-free? Do you see yourself as lovable, powerful, adequate, intelligent, and healthy? Or do you see the opposite picture? Whatever image you subconsciously embrace about yourself forms your belief system— that which you hold to be true.

In the psyche of the child, the validity of the belief system is accepted without question as *truth*. For example, a child may get straight A's on her report card, but if her parents have been "messaging" to her through the energy of their thoughts, feelings, words, and actions that she is stupid and worthless, her real belief about herself might be that she *is* stupid because she *feels* stupid, no matter what she achieves academically or what the factual evidence refutes.

As infants and young children we initially experience the world around us at a purely sensory and feeling level. This happens during the early stage of our brains' development known as the alpha state. The emotional energy we experience is imprinted into our young psyches. As we grow and evolve into our beta states of brain development we begin to "connect the dots," at an intellectual level, in an attempt to make sense of our world. We do this by interpreting our experiences based upon how the world felt to us. We automatically formulate thoughts that support our existing feelings which inevitably become part of our self-portrait.

Current research reveals that an event can only be recorded in memory if there exists an emotional association with that event. Since we were only able to relate to our earliest experiences in life at an emotional energy level, we have many recordings floating around in our subconscious mind from childhood; some of these recordings are accurate and serve us in our understanding of life, and some are not.

For example, if we were psychologically, emotionally, or physically mistreated as children, we may have developed a belief that we are unlovable, insignificant, or stupid. Painful emotional experiences and the associated emotional energy (such as anger, guilt, sadness, and shame) then become the colors we use to paint our self-portrait from that point forward.

Now, how do your early childhood experiences and your self-image relate to your health? It's simple: if you have a poor self-image it might be challenging for you to create a healthy life—spiritually, mentally, emotionally, and physically. The good news is that no matter how you perceive yourself at this very moment, you have the power to change that picture of yourself. You have the power to recreate yourself, to repaint the self-portrait. When you change your self-image, other things consistent with your new concept of self are accomplished more easily and with less stress.

Therefore, if you can see yourself as healthy, if you truly believe that you can be pain-free, disease-free, and medication-free, and if you genuinely believe you have the power to create wellness in your life, it can become your reality. In contrast, if you see yourself as the victim of an environment that you have no control over, this will be your reality and your destiny.

Perceptions & Well Being

Our perceptions create the filters that determine how we see ourselves, others, and the world around us. Each of us sees our world through our own unique filters. The presence of these filters is neither good nor bad. Through our filters—our own unique personal biases influenced by the sum total of our lives' experiences, both pleasurable and painful—we interpret events in the world around us.

Some of the filters that we developed are accurate and beneficial while others are distorted and destructive. Some filters serve our highest good, others do not. Filters influence how we interpret events, respond to situations, and make decisions that determine what actions we take. Our life's circumstances and childhood experiences created our filters.

If we were brought up in a loving and nurturing environment and treated with respect, compassion, understanding, tolerance, patience, and kindness we will see the world as a friendly and safe place. If, on the other hand, we were raised in a physically and/or emotionally abusive and angry environment and treated harshly, we are likely to process our experiences in such a way that causes us to interpret the world as an unfriendly and threatening place.

Our perceptions therefore represent the sum total of all our life experiences as interpreted through our own eyes. For each of us, these perceptions create our reality. Whether our perceptions are accurate or inaccurate, in alignment with *truth* or not, the outcomes we experience are based upon the decisions and actions we take and are always consistent with the *truth* about what is really going on.

Each one of us is a unique individual: genetically, physiologically, spiritually, psychologically, emotionally, and experientially. No one else in the world has had your same exact life experiences. This unique combination and the sum total of your life experiences has formed the basis for your understanding of life, how things work in the world, and the meanings that you assign to everything.

No one else really knows what its like to be you. The meaning that you assign to events that happen in your life is yours alone. When your belief systems, perceptions, and interpretations of events (i.e. your reality) are in alignment with *truth* you stand a better chance of creating *The Optimal Life*. If, based upon past conditioning, your beliefs, perceptions, and interpretation of events are not in alignment with *truth*, you may find life frustrating and you may find creating health to be a real challenge. When you assign inaccurate meanings to events in your life, you inevitably create pain and suffering for yourself.

> *It's not what we don't know that gets us into trouble . . .it's what we are sure we know, that just ain't so!*
>
> —**Mark Twain**, American humorist, satirist, lecturer, writer

Although you may be stuck *in* your perceptions at this moment, you are not permanently stuck *with* these perceptions. You have the power to change your perception at any time. You can raise your awareness and choose to see things differently at any time. With greater love, understanding and awareness you can create a healthier, happier, and more fulfilling life.

If you continue to view the world through the filters created by past painful events, then you are allowing your past to control your present and your future. You can choose, at any time, to change any perception that no longer serves your highest good. You can re-assign a different and more enlightened meaning to every event in your life.

No matter what your circumstance in life, your belief system, perception, interpretation, and response to events are of your own choosing. If your perceptions about health and your interpretations about health-related events are inaccurate, it will be difficult to for you to create health in your life. With accurate beliefs, perceptions, and interpretations about health you can cure illness, reverse any chronic degenerative disease, and heal your body.

THE WELLNESS MIND-SET

We each hold in our subconscious mind a health picture of our self. This self-portrait becomes our wellness mind-set. We either see ourselves as healthy, energetic, disease-free, and in charge of our health destiny or we see ourselves as unhealthy, tired, susceptible to illness and disease, and victims of our environment. Whether we realize it or not we have programmed into our subconscious mind either a wellness mind-set or an illness mind-set.

A wellness mind-set acknowledges our personal power to create health and reflects our belief in our ability to create a vibrant, pain-free, medication-free, and disease-free life. In contrast, an illness mind-set embraces a victim mentality in which individual power has been relinquished to outside forces: from individuals such as parents, peers, teachers, preachers, and doctors to institutions such as religion, government, health care industry, pharmaceutical industry, commercial food interests, etc. What we may not be aware of, and therefore can find challenging to identify and come to terms with, is how as children we inadvertently acquired a victim mentality about many different issues.

> *Our state of mind has an immediate and direct effect on our state of body.*
> —**Bernie Siegel, M.D.**, *Love, Medicine & Miracles*

THE ENERGY OF THOUGHT

The thoughts that we think possess no physical dimension yet influence the chemistry and physiology of every cell in our bodies. As we drift in and out of different mental and emotional energy states the energy fields of our bodies shift thereby causing changes in the physiology of our cells.

For example, joyous and loving thoughts and feelings facilitate the flow of energy in the body that supports optimal cell function. Sad and angry thoughts and feelings create restriction to the flow of energy throughout the body that inhibits optimal cell function.

The beauty and power of the human mind is that through the activity of directed, conscious thought we can influence the physiology of the body. The conscious mind, that which we are aware of, and the subconscious mind, that which we are not aware of, both affect the physiology of the body that determines our level of health. Our thought processes reside in our conscious minds, while our emotional reactions reside in our subconscious minds.

That which we recognize about ourselves we have the power to change. That which we are not aware of controls us. Through greater understanding and awareness we can transition the activity within the subconscious mind to the level of the conscious mind. Once we raise the content of our subconscious mind to the level of conscious awareness we then have dominion.

How do we access and change the programming in our subconscious minds? We can access the programming of our subconscious minds by quieting our conscious minds through various meditation techniques. By accessing our subconscious minds we can bring into our awareness that about which we were previously unaware. In a state of awareness we can then use our intellect and intention at the level of our conscious minds to reprogram the contents of our subconscious minds.

At the level of our conscious minds we have dominion over health and healing. Every thought we think is expressed in some way through our physical bodies. Perfect health is as much an attitude and belief system as it is a physical reality.

Belief Systems & Menopause

Your belief systems—that which you hold to be true—are the foundation upon which you create your reality and experience of life. One example of how belief systems influence the physical body has been the basis for several research studies into the factors that contribute to the symptoms of menopause.

In the United States the current dominant medical view of menopause embraces the hormone deficiency theory. Although there are definite physiological changes that occur during menopause due to changes in the levels of the female sex hormones, cross-cultural research studies indicates that menopause is much more than simply a biological event. The research findings of S.C. Theisen and P.K. Mansfield, reported in an article entitled "Menopause: Social Construction or Biological Destiny?" that appeared in the *Journal of Health Education* 24 (1993), found that social and cultural factors contribute greatly to how women react to menopause.

It appears that in many other cultures of the world, women look forward to menopause because it brings with it greater respect along with other benefits. Achieving an advanced age is viewed as a sign of divine blessing and great wisdom. Studies of menopausal women in many traditional cultures demonstrate that most will pass through menopause without hot flashes, vaginitis and other symptoms common to menopausal women in developed countries.

The results of one of the most detailed research studies on the effects of culture on menopause were reported in 1993 in the *American Journal of Obstetrics and Gynecology* article entitled "Menopause without Symptoms: The Endocrinology of Menopause among Rural Mayan Indians," by M.C. Martin, J.E. Block, S.D. Sanchez, et al. Based upon extensive examination and diagnostic testing of fifty-two postmenopausal rural Mayan Indian women, researchers found that none of the women experienced hot flashes or any other menopausal symptom and none of the women showed evidence of osteoporosis, despite the fact that their female hormone patterns were identical to those of postmenopausal women living in the United States. The researchers felt that the Mayan women's attitude toward menopause was responsible for their symptomless passage. The Mayan women saw menopause as a positive event that would provide them acceptance as respected elders, as well as relief from childbearing.

Studies at the New England Research Institute and the University of Pittsburgh also found that women who anticipate having a hard time during menopause do suffer more negative emotional and physical symptoms than women who expect it to be easier.

Due to our youth-oriented culture, many American women are convinced that menopause marks the end of their best years. But such a negative and pessimistic outlook creates stress which tends to aggravate any physical symptom.

Cross-cultural research clearly demonstrates that the cultural view of menopause is directly related to the symptoms of menopause. Anthropologists who have compared menopause in different cultures find that the society's view of a woman during and after menopause can have a dramatic influence on her experience of it. The healthier the society's view of older women, the less their symptoms.

LIMITING BELIEF SYSTEM

What do we mean by a "limiting belief system?" A limiting belief system is a conglomeration of beliefs that we acquired and hold to be true that (1) are not in alignment with *truth*, (2) typically stem from inaccurate perceptions, especially of ourselves, and therefore (3) prevent us from reaching our true human potential. Inaccurate perceptions result from a lack of awareness and a lack of understanding of the true nature of a thing.

Our perceptions, both accurate and inaccurate, become our reality. No matter what type of family environment we grew up in or believe we grew up in, loving or unloving, we have all acquired some limiting belief systems along the way. Not all the information that we have embraced in our life as *truth* is accurate.

During childhood we are exposed to all types of inaccurate and negative messages and self-limiting thought patterns from our surrounding environment—family, friends, school, church, media, government, and society—which we absorb and accept as "gospel" without ever questioning their validity.

At the core of every unrealized human potential lies a limiting belief system. Limiting beliefs influence every part of our lives, especially when it comes to our understanding of health. The most destructive of all limiting beliefs is the belief that we are not lovable.

At the core of every illness and disease lies a limiting belief that continually chants in the back of our minds that we are not lovable.

EXERCISE 6-1

THINKING OUTSIDE THE BOX

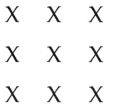

Instructions: Connect all the "X's" using only 4 straight lines, without lifting the pencil off the paper.

How We Acquire Limiting Beliefs

Before reading any further, just for fun, take a moment and do the exercise in Exercise 6-1: Thinking Outside the Box. You will find the solution in Exercise 6-1: Thinking Outside the Box—Solution. So, how did you do? Did you get stuck because you stayed within the confines of the X's based upon the visual and mental conditioning that "boxed you in?" Believe it or not, children outperform adults in this exercise.

As adults, we have been exposed to tens of thousands of negative and un-empowering messages that foster restrictive and self-limiting thinking. However, the negative messaging began for all of us during our earliest childhood years. Our parents, teachers, preachers, politicians, media, and advertisers constantly messaged information to us that molded our thinking and belief systems.

> *Acceptance of illness is often part of a larger acceptance of self that represents a significant mental shift, a shift that can initiate transformation of personality and with it the healing of disease.*
>
> —**Andrew Weil, M.D.**, *Spontaneous Healing*

EXERCISE 6-1

THINKING OUTSIDE THE BOX - SOLUTION

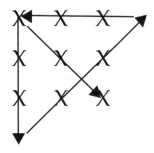

From the time of conception through childhood we absorbed the spiritual, mental, and emotional energy of the people and events that surrounded us. This energy influenced the meaning we assigned to things that happened in our lives. As children we did not possess the intellectual capacity, life experiences, or emotional maturity to interpret events objectively and accurately, or from a healthy spiritual, mental, and emotional perspective.

As children we lacked the knowledge and awareness to differentiate *truth* from untruth. Nevertheless, we did interpret and assign meaning to every experience. Our interpretation of these events, although often inaccurate, formed the basis for our perceptions about ourselves, others, and the world around us. These early interpretations formed the perceptions that we carried into our adult lives. But now as adults, we have the ability to identify perceptions that have never served our higher good or our mental, emotional, spiritual, or physical health, and we can choose to change them.

CHANGING INACCURATE & LIMITING BELIEF SYSTEMS

If inaccurate and limiting belief systems are so detrimental to creating *The Optimal Life*, how do we change them? To change a limiting belief we need to identify and then change our perceptions that we find to be inaccurate. We need to change those beliefs and perceptions that are not in alignment with the *truth* of Spiritual Laws and Laws of Nature (Chapter 2, Rules of Health).

We change our inaccurate perceptions through acquiring greater awareness and understanding about the true nature of a thing, starting with a greater understanding of the true nature of ourselves. Greater awareness and understanding is always accessible when we are genuinely open and receptive to wanting to create positive healthy changes in our lives. See Exercise 6-2: Change Inaccurate & Limiting Belief Systems at the end of the chapter for an exercise to help identify and change those inaccurate and limiting belief systems that are preventing you from creating optimal health. In the final analysis we are as healthy as we believe we can be; we can only be as healthy as our current belief system will support.

> *Whether you believe you can or you can't, you are right.*
> —**Henry Ford,** Founder of Ford Motor Company

The key to creating optimal health begins with the changes we make right now, in the present moment, and then continue to make on a moment-to-moment basis since all healing happens in the present moment. The present moment is the only thing we have to work with. We can begin healing any condition in the present moment based upon right or loving thought, feelings, words, and action.

Out ability to create healing in the present moment isn't limited by what happened to us in the past. Why? Because, in the present moment we have the power (1) to change all of our inaccurate and limiting belief systems, and (2) to resolve all of our unfinished emotional business. When it comes to healing, it doesn't matter what anyone else thinks or does. It only matters what we do. What we create in this present moment determines how we experience the present moment and sets in motion what our experience of life will be in the next moment and into the future.

There are various ways that the power of the mind can be directed to influence the chemistry and physiology of the body. Here are just a few of the research studies that support the premise that the mind, through the power of thought, has a direct and profound influence over bodily processes.

THE POWER OF SUGGESTION

In Japan, two researchers conducted an experiment with 13 young men between the ages of 15 and 17 who had all experienced allergic reactions to a plant similar to poison ivy. After hypnotizing 5 of the subjects and giving "suggestions only" to the other 8, the researchers touched an arm of each subject with a nonpoisonous leaf, but told the young men that it was from the poison ivy-like plant to which they were allergic. All 13 subjects, whether hypnotized or in the suggestion-only group, developed the skin rash associated with the poison ivy-like plant.

Then the researchers reversed the experiment. They touched their subjects with a poisonous leaf but informed them that it was harmless. This time 11 subjects "believed" the doctors. The result: 4 of the 5 who were hypnotized and 7 of the 8 from the suggestions-only group did not develop the skin rash.

HYPNOSIS & BREAST SIZE

In 5 research studies, a total of 70 women used hypnotic suggestion to increase their breast size an average of 1¼ inches in 12 weeks. The women were told to imagine warm water flowing over their breasts, or the sun or a heat lamp shining on them, and to imagine that their breasts "are becoming warm, tingling, pulsating, and that they are growing." They were instructed to give themselves these suggestions of self-hypnosis at home.

The eventual increase in breast size could not be attributed to other physiological changes, including weight gain and menstrual cycle. In one of the studies, nearly half the women lost 2 or more pounds during the 12 weeks.

HYPNOSIS & CANCER SURVIVAL

One of the most publicized medical studies in recent years was conducted by Stanford psychiatrist David Spiegel, who set out to prove that the mental states of patients did not influence whether they survived cancer. Spiegel took eighty-six women with advanced breast cancer (their disease was basically beyond help with conventional treatment) and gave half of them weekly psychotherapy (one hour group sessions) combined with lessons in self-hypnosis. Ten years later, the average survival rate for the group that received therapy was twice that of the group that received none.

ATHLETES & VISUALIZATIONS

Research has shown that the body cannot distinguish between a vivid mental experience and an actual physical experience. Soviet and Eastern European athletic training techniques have utilized this principle for years. The athletes visualized, in full color and complete detail, a winning performance.

This was repeated until the physical act became merely a duplication of a mental act that had already been successfully visualized. Soviet researchers found that athletes who spent as much as three-fourths of their time on mental training performed better than those who placed more emphasis on physical preparation.

SUCCESSFUL VISUALIZATION

The same visualization techniques that are used by world-class athletes to enhance athletic performance can be employed by anyone to improve personal health outcomes, cure illness, and prevent disease. Successful visualization techniques require the following:

1. The image must be chosen by the individual.

2. It must be an image the person can see in the mind's eye as clearly as something seen by the physical eye.

3. It must be an image with which the person feels completely comfortable.

THE POWER OF THE MIND TO HEAL THE BODY

Thoughts and feelings work together in the mind to create the quality of our health. The energy of both thoughts and feelings are expressed in the universe as they occur. The universe then sets in motion the organizing principles necessary to manifest outcomes in the physical world that are in alignment with the quality of the energy of the original thoughts and feelings.

Research studies have repeatedly reported how the body is the servant to the mind. The body obeys the operations of the mind, whether thoughts are deliberately chosen or automatically expressed.

Both disease and health, like circumstances, are rooted in thought. The people who live in fear of sickness and disease are the people most likely to attract sickness and disease into their lives. Those who do not fear disease and who believe in the innate power of their mind and their body to heal and create health, and who also take action that is consistent with that belief, experience health. You can be pain-free, disease-free, and medication-free if you believe it is possible. Be a possibility thinker: think health!

What we really know is possible in our heart is possible. We make it possible by our will. What we imagine in our minds becomes our world.
—**Dr. Masaru Emoto,** *The Hidden Messages in Water*

EXERCISE 6-2

CHANGE INACCURATE & LIMITING BELIEF SYSTEMS

The following personal empowerment exercise can help you identify and change those inaccurate and limiting belief systems that may be holding you back in your own personal journey of healing and creating optimal health. Contemplate the following questions:

1. **What do I have in my life, health, and body right now that I want to change?**

    _____

    _____

    _____

    _____

    _____

    _____

2. **What beliefs do I have about myself, my health, and how my body works that created and supports my current health situation, that may not be accurate?**

    _____

    _____

    _____

    _____

    _____

    _____

3.   What type of life and health do I want to create for myself?

_____

_____

_____

_____

_____

_____

_____

4.   What belief systems would I need to put in place to create
     and support the type of life, health, and body I desire?

_____

_____

_____

_____

_____

_____

_____

The thoughts that dominate your mind—
become your reality!

WELLNESS MASTERY™ SUMMARY

Must Know!

1. Mind includes both mental and emotional phenomena that are expressed through the physiology of the body.

2. You are as healthy as you believe it is possible to be.

3. Optimal health is as much an attitude and belief system as it is a physical reality.

4. The universe simply manifests events in the physical world that are in alignment with the quality of energy of your thoughts.

5. You become the thoughts that occupy your mind.

6. Inaccurate or limiting belief systems about your self, health, and disease limit your body's innate and natural healing abilities.

7. For each of us, our perceptions create our reality.

8. You may be stuck *in* your perceptions, at this moment, but you are not stuck *with* these perceptions. You can change your perceptions any time you choose.

9. All healing happens in the present moment. We can heal any condition in the present moment based upon right or loving thoughts, feelings, words, and actions.

10. Health starts with a picture, held in your imagination, of how you would ideally like to look and feel.

WELLNESS MASTERY™ ACTION

Must Do!

1. Do Exercise 6-2: Change Inaccurate & Limiting Belief
    Systems at the end of the chapter. Challenge your beliefs
    about health and disease. If you lack optimal health, perhaps
    what you have been told about health and disease is not
    accurate or truthful!

2. Open your mind to the possibility that there is a more
    accurate health reality than what you are currently
    experiencing.

3. Describe, with pictures, the ideal healthy you. Hang these
    "healthy" representations of you up on your bathroom
    mirror as a daily reminder of who you are.

4. Create a "Brag List." Brag about yourself. List all your
    wonderful qualities. Don't be shy.

5. Share with a loved one all the magnificent qualities you see
    in him or her. Every beautiful and desirable quality you see
    in someone else already exists within you. Metaphysically, it
    is not possible to recognize admirable and desirable qualities
    in others unless you already possess the same.

6. Read a self-help book. Read a book about Mind-Body Medicine. Read a book about spirituality. Read a book about higher consciousness.

7. Attend a lecture on wellness, mind-body medicine, and spirituality.

8. Participate in a personal empowerment and meditation workshop.

9. Learn and practice at least one visualization technique for creating greater health in your life.

10. Picture yourself in perfect health, energized and disease-free. Create a mental picture of what your life would be like in perfect health. Practice this exercise for 10 minutes a day for 30 days.

CHAPTER SEVEN

PRINCIPLE #4

Oxygen

BREATHE DEEP

THE BODY NEEDS OXYGEN

What is the most important nutrient for the body? Oxygen. In fact, oxygen is not merely the #1 nutrient—it is absolutely vital for human survival, healing, and optimal health. It has been proven that you can live without food for extended periods of time and without water for a couple of days. But, without oxygen you can only exist for a few minutes because oxygen is our primary source of energy and is necessary for all metabolic processes. Every cell in the body needs this energy to carry out its function. Approximately 90% of our energy comes from oxygen, while only 10% comes from food and water.

Think about it this way: every cell in your body is a living, breathing organism. Your cells are busy at work keeping you alive 24 hours a day, non-stop, from your first breath until your last. Even when you are at rest every cell in your body is performing some task, although at a slower rate. Consequently, every cell in your body is in constant need of oxygen. A lack of oxygen to any part of the body, called hypoxia, is detrimental to your health in many ways.

Research studies show that even mild hypoxia increases heart and respiratory rates and places an additional strain on the heart and lungs while prolonged or severe hypoxia results in lung or heart failure. The American Heart Association reports that nearly a million people die of heart conditions every year, and 70% of the population has some evidence of heart problems. Virtually all heart attacks are due to a lack of adequate oxygen supply to the heart muscle and strokes are due to a lack of oxygen to some part of the brain.

THE QUALITY OF OXYGEN IN THE AIR WE BREATHE

According to numerous research findings, several million years ago the oxygen content of earth's atmosphere was 30 to 35%. Today it is about 21%, and due to a variety of environmental factors— including massive pollution of the atmosphere and the ongoing destruction of vegetation on the planet—our oxygen supply is probably not improving. Remember that it is the green plants on the planet that take in carbon dioxide and give off oxygen. As we reduce the amount of green plant life on the planet and increase the human population, I believe that the quality of the air we breathe is declining. Carbon monoxide, one of the toxic gases found in automobile exhaust fumes, is now far more prevalent in our atmosphere than it was before industrialization.

> *When it is known that one takes about 30 cubic inches of air into one's lungs in each inhalation, or about seven times the volume of food and water consumed daily, it can be understood why more people are weakened, devitalized or poisoned by pollution in the air they suck into their lungs, than by all the ingredients in the food they eat and the water they drink.*
> **—H.B. Mellon**

When carbon monoxide is present in the air we breathe it competes with oxygen to attach to the hemoglobin molecule...and wins. Hemoglobin is the molecule in the blood that carries oxygen. Carbon monoxide has a 200 times greater affinity for hemoglobin than does oxygen. Therefore, when carbon monoxide is present in the air we breathe the oxygen-carrying capacity of our blood decreases. This results in lower tissue oxygen levels, lower energy production, lower cellular function, lower glandular function, and greater accumulation of toxins.

Increased oxygen boosts energy, increases endurance, eliminates toxins, promotes rapid healing and recovery from injury, strengthens the immune response, and provides a calming effect on the nervous system.

Oxygen & Disease Prevention

A well-oxygenated internal biological environment is necessary for energy production, disease prevention, tissue healing, and creating a strong immune response. Oxygen needs to be present for the body to burn fat as fuel and could therefore be considered an anti-obesity nutrient. Lack of oxygen in cells lowers their metabolic rate and depresses cell functions. A low level of oxygen in the tissue and the associated depressed cell function are both common in many degenerative diseases. Research has shown that harmful bacteria, viruses, and cancer cannot exist in an oxygen-rich environment. Dr. Otto Warburg won the Nobel Prize in the 1920's for discovering that a 35% decrease in tissue oxygen induced cancer.

The Power of Breathing

If oxygen is the most important nutrient for optimal health, then what is the most important exercise? Breathing. Sounds too simple and too obvious, doesn't it? Many biological activities of the body are closely connected with breathing. Breathing is the mechanism that exchanges carbon dioxide for oxygen in the lungs.

Breathing is also the mechanism for circulating cerebral spinal fluid, the medium for delivering oxygen and nutrients to the central nervous system, brain, and spinal cord. Breathing, along with the milking action of skeletal muscles, helps move lymph fluid throughout the body. The lymphatic system is a major participant in your immune response.

The nervous system is comprised of the brain, spinal cord, skeletal nervous system, and autonomic nervous system (ANS). The skeletal nerves control the operations of all the skeletal muscles that control voluntary movement, while the autonomic nervous system regulates all the activities of the internal organs and all involuntary body processes, including constriction and dilatation of blood vessels. It is the autonomic nervous system that is responsible for controlling blood flow throughout the entire body. Our breathing mechanism—the diaphragm—is unique in that it is governed by both involuntary and voluntary nerve flow.

The autonomic nervous system is made up of sympathetic (arousing) and parasympathetic (relaxing) components that work in harmony with each other to maintain balance in the body. When it is dominant, the sympathetic branch of our autonomic nervous system is associated with tension, restriction, chronic anxiety, stress, and anger. Conversely, the parasympathetic branch of the ANS, when dominant, correlates with relaxation, openness, peacefulness, and serenity. By consciously controlling our breath, we can influence blood flow and oxygen delivery throughout the body.

BREATHING & OXYGEN EXCHANGE

During the breathing process, carbon dioxide, a waste byproduct of normal cellular metabolism, is carried out of the body at the same time that oxygen is picked up by the blood in the capillary beds in the lungs. This blood is then circulated throughout the body by the cardiovascular system—heart pump and blood vessels. During normal breathing, at rest, we are exchanging the gasses that are in the upper two-thirds of our lungs with the gasses of the outside world.

Due to the stress of daily living in combination with a sedentary lifestyle, many people have become "shallow" or "chest breathers." When our breathing becomes shallow, we bring in less fresh air and expel less stale air. Because shallow breathing never fills the lower lungs, it results in suboptimal ventilation of the lungs. Why is it so important to fill the lower lungs with fresh air? Due to gravity, there is a greater volume of blood located in the lower lobes of the lungs than in the upper lobes; consequently, the lower lungs are responsible for supplying 80% of the oxygen to our bodies.

If you are breathing from only high in your chest you are not getting maximum air into your lungs. The stale air and poisonous gases trapped in your lower lungs cannot escape and are therefore reabsorbed back into your blood, to be carried back into your body.

Deep breathing, or breathing from the stomach (where you can actually "see" your stomach expanding outward as you breathe in) forces more air into the lower lobes of the lungs so that greater gas exchange can happen. This minimizes the amount of stagnant air being reabsorbed back into the lower lobes of the lungs.

BREATHING & LYMPH FLOW

Your lymphatic system can be considered the primary sewage treatment and waste disposal system in your body. It is a network of lymphatic vessels and lymph nodes flowing with lymph fluid. Lymph fluid carries nutrients and oxygen to the cells from the blood capillaries, as well as the white blood cells—lymphocytes, monocytes, neutrophils, eosinophils, and basophils—that fight off infections. Lymph fluid also carries waste material away from cells back to the blood capillaries and lymph capillaries to be carried to different organs for detoxification and elimination from the body.

Breathing acts as a suction pump for the lymphatic system. The rhythmical action of breathing, especially deep breathing, moves lymphatic fluid through the lymphatic system of the body. Deep breathing drains lymphatic fluid ten to fifteen times more effectively than any other activity.

BREATHING & DETOXIFICATION

Breathing is the primary mechanism for removing toxic gasses, such as carbon dioxide, from the blood. It is estimated that 70% of the normal day-to-day detoxification of the body happens through the breathing process. Another 20% of the cleansing of the body happens through perspiration/sweating through the skin. An additional 8% occurs through the elimination of urine by the kidneys, and about 2% happens through fecal elimination through the gastrointestinal tract.

BREATHING & HEALTHY-AGING

One of the frequent signs of aging in our culture today is the loss of lung function. According to research studies, our ability to consume sufficient oxygen decreases 5 to 10% per decade between the ages of 25 and 75. As the respiratory tract deteriorates, lung function decreases. Typical lung function at age 70 is only about 60% of typical capacity at age 30. According to the Framingham Heart Study, a reduced lung capacity of 2 liters means that the chance of death is 2.4 times more likely. The Framingham Heart Study was a medical research study initiated in 1948 that employed long-term surveillance of an adult population in Framingham, Massachusetts to study the factors associated with the development of cardiovascular disease.

As lung function decreases, the body's ability to exchange carbon dioxide for oxygen is compromised and the body becomes more toxic and subsequently more acidic. For these reasons, deep breathing becomes even more critical to maintaining optimal health as we age. Deep breathing is one of the best healthy-aging exercises you can do to maintain your vim and vigor.

BREATHING & ACID/ALKALINE pH BALANCE IN THE BODY

Breathing also helps regulate the body's pH balance. pH measures the acid/alkaline relationship in the body. This is important because your body chemistry functions best when the pH is maintained in the neutral to slightly alkaline range. A high acid/low alkaline concentration is reflected as lower pH, while a low acid/high alkaline concentration in the body is reflected as higher pH.

The process of breathing expels carbon dioxide, an acidic gas removed from the blood, from the body. Releasing and removing carbon dioxide reduces the amount of carbonic acid in the blood.

Reducing carbonic acid content in the blood lowers the acidity of the blood. Shallow breathing, also known as "hypoventilation", causes a reduction in oxygen uptake by the cells. Hypoventilating results in a higher acid concentration in the body that is known as "acidosis." Acidosis creates an ideal toxic internal biological environment where opportunistic harmful bacteria, viruses, parasites, fungi, and molds flourish. This acidic condition also accelerates the aging process.

Since the typical American diet is totally acid building— consisting predominantly of cooked and processed foods— anything you can do to lower the acidity and create a more alkaline internal biological environment will facilitate your body's natural ability to heal itself from disease, prevent illness, and maintain optimal health.

BREATHING EXERCISES FOR OPTIMAL HEALTH

What is the best way to get more oxygen to every cell in the body? Slow, deep breathing. As simple as it may sound, deep breathing is the most important and powerful physical activity you can do to improve your health and facilitate greater healing. Slow, deep breathing provides more oxygen to the body and has been proven to be one of the most effective therapies for pain management as well as one of the best ways to relieve mental, emotional, and physical stress. Deep breathing techniques can dissipate the buildup of negative energy anywhere in the body.

The most important aspect of creating any new health habit is getting started. All the information in the world heals or changes nothing, action alone creates change. Start deep breathing this moment. Make it a part of your life. Consider it a gift of love that you give to yourself. Choose a breathing exercise that fits your interest, lifestyle, or need. Start with 5 minutes sessions, 3 times per day. Then add 1 additional minute each week until you are doing deep breathing for at least 10 minutes each session.

> *Slow, deep breathing is probably the single best anti-stress medicine we have. When you bring air down into the lower portion of the lungs, where oxygen exchange is most efficient, everything changes. The heart rate slows, blood pressure decreases, muscles relax, anxiety eases, and the mind calms. Breathing this way also gives people a sense of control over their body and emotions that is extremely therapeutic.*

—James S. Gordon, M.D.
Clinical Professor of Psychiatry, Georgetown School of Medicine
Founder & Director, Center or Mind-Body Medicine, Washington D.C.

When to Practice Breathing Exercises

Deep breathing is the best way to start the day. By breathing deeply first thing upon rising, you will oxygenate your body and set the physiological tone for the rest of your day. Deep breathing first thing in the morning also facilitates the elimination of toxins that have built up in your blood over night while your body was detoxifying itself.

It is also beneficial to take a few moments for some deep breathing immediately before and after lunch to improve digestion. Any time you are feeling tense or angry, do deep breathing to dissipate the negative energy. Do deep breathing immediately before bedtime to relax your body and improve the quality of your sleep; it is one of the quickest and simplest ways to dissipate the mental, emotional, and physical stress that build up in the body throughout the day.

Where to Practice Breathing Exercises

Deep breathing can be performed anywhere, anytime, but ideally in a quiet, relaxing, peaceful place with good air and natural lighting. One of the best places to practice deep breathing is outdoors in nature, around green plants (remember, green plants produce oxygen) and near running water. The negative ions given off by running water have a relaxing therapeutic effect on the mind, body, spirit, and emotions. You can even practice deep breathing in your car – with your eyes open – and anytime you feel stressed.

What Position to Use When Practicing Breathing Exercises

Although deep breathing exercises can be performed in almost any position, unless you prefer the traditional crossed leg yoga position, the ideal position is to sit in an upright balanced position, with shoulders relaxed and head neutral, and feet flat on the ground.

How Long to Practice Breathing Exercises

As a beginner, you can start with a 5-minute session of continuous breath work three times per day, for a total of 15 minutes per day. Practice at this pace for one week. As you get more comfortable with the exercise increase the amount of breath work you do each session. For example, if you add one additional minute per week to each breath work session, within a short period of time you will have doubled the amount of time you spend doing deep breathing exercises. Just by adding one additional minute to each of your daily breathing sessions, by the 6th week you will have doubled your breathing exercise time.

BREATHING EXERCISES

There are many types of breathing exercises. Each one accomplishes something a little different, but all provide tremendous health benefits. The following sample breathing exercises are offered as a basic introduction to different types of simple breath work.

RELAXATION BREATHING

(5 TO 10 MINUTES)

Observe the breath. Sit in a comfortable position with your eyes closed. Focus your attention on your breathing without trying to influence it in any way. Follow the movement of the breath into and out of your body. Let the breathing do its own thing. Do this for at least a few minutes. This breathing exercise is one of the best natural and simple forms of relaxation to relieve tension and stress from the body. This breath observation technique is a simple meditation practice for relaxation.

STRESS-REDUCTION BREATHING

(5 TO 10 MINUTES)

Observe your breath. Again, sit in a comfortable position with your eyes closed. Focus your attention on your breathing without trying to influence it in any way. Follow the movement of the breath into and out of your body. Do this for a few minutes. After a few minutes visualize the movement of the air as colored air currents that you can actually see flowing in and out of your body. When you breathe out, imagine that you are pulling tension from every part of your body and releasing it through the air as you exhale (push) air out of your lungs. As you inhale the next breath, imagine you are breathing in energy that is filling every cell in your body with love, joy, and peace.

PAIN MANAGEMENT BREATHING

(5 TO 10 MINUTES)

Observe your breath. Sit or lie down in a comfortable position with your eyes closed. Focus your attention on your breathing without trying to influence it in any way. Follow the movement of the breath into and out of your body. Do this for a few minutes. After a few minutes visualize the movement of the air as colored air currents that you can actually see flowing in and out of your body. When you breathe out, imagine that you are pulling the tension and pain from those pain areas in your body and expelling it from your body. As you exhale air from the lungs visualize it being expelled as an orange-tinted air current (orange is the color associated with disease in color therapy, green is the color associated with healing energy). Then as you inhale the next breath, imagine you are breathing in green healing energy that is filling every cell in your body with love, joy, and peace.

REVERSE BREATHING

(5 TO 10 MINUTES)

Reverse breathing is a more active breathing exercise than breathing exercises for relaxation, stress management, and pain management. It is designed to increase lung capacity. We tend to think of breathing as a two-step process. We breathe air in (inhale) as the first phase, and breathe air out (exhale) during the second phase. In reality, breathing is a continuous process with no beginning and no end. It is only our perception that differentiates the phases. Practice reversing the process. Think of exhaling air as the beginning phase in the breathing cycle, followed by inhaling air. Reverse breathing is an exercise that will give you more control over your breathing. With reverse breathing you become an active breather rather than merely an observer of the breath. Physiologically you have more muscle control over exhalation than inhalation. Exhalation recruits the voluntary intercostal muscles between your ribs to squeeze the air out of the lungs. These intercostal muscles are more powerful than the muscles used during inhalation. With more control over your breathing when you move more air out of your lungs you will automatically pull more air in, expanding your lung potential.

BREATHING TO INCREASE
LUNG & OXYGEN CAPACITY
(5 TO 10 MINUTES)

This deep breathing exercise is one of the most active and powerful breathing exercising for increasing oxygen potential and oxygen uptake throughout the body:

Step 1:
Once you are in the most relaxed and balanced (seated or standing) position you can find, inhale air through your nose for a count of 5 seconds, expanding the breath into your lungs and belly area. As you breathe air into your lungs you will feel your ribcage expand, and your abdominal area, that area right below your ribcage, protrude outward. As you take in a breath of air your stomach should move outward.

Step 2:
With your lungs full of air and your belly protruding, hold the breath for a 5-second count. Feel yourself relax through this process.

Step 3:

Begin to exhale the air through your mouth, dropping your lower jaw to allow the air unrestricted passage out of your body, continuing to use your stomach muscles to push the air out of your body for a 10-second count.

Step 4:

Once it feels like you have pushed as much of the air out of your body as possible, again hold your breath, this time with your lungs empty, for another 5-second count. (One of the benefits of holding your breath with lungs empty is the negative back pressure that creates a vacuum-like condition in the body that forces the body to get more efficient at using the available oxygen in the system.)

Repeat the pattern continuously for 5 minutes each session, working your way up to 10 minutes a session.

BREATHING AS A SPIRITUAL PRACTICE

The breath has long been recognized in many ancient Eastern cultures as the movement of spirit in the body. At higher levels of awareness the art of breathing becomes a form of spiritual practice. Breath is the link between the body and mind, and between the conscious and subconscious mind. The rhythm of breathing harmonizes the body, mind, and spirit.

How we breathe influences the state of our nervous system. Breathing from a mindful place, or breathing with intention, raises one's level of awareness to the experience of the present moment. Conscious breathing can help re-center and refocus one's attention to the present moment. Being fully available to experience the present moment will lead to an expanded awareness of self, the internal world of your body, and the external world. While you are in the present moment you release yourself from the emotional energy attachments to events of the past, as well as to the projections of past energy into the future.

BREATHING & THE POWER OF THOUGHT

Conscious breath work is also at the center of mind/body integration. Deep breathing can help us gain control over our thoughts. By controlling our breath we can control our thoughts; by controlling our thoughts we can re-create our reality. When we consciously direct our thoughts we have dominion over our internal world. When we are in charge of our internal world we possess a greater ability to influence outcomes in the external world. Our experience of the world around us is merely a reflection of our personal internal world.

BREATHING & THE POWER OF EMOTIONS

> *The single most powerful technique for protecting your health is breathing. I have seen breath control alone achieve remarkable results: lowering blood pressure, ending heart arrhythmias, improving long-standing patterns of poor digestion, increasing blood circulation throughout the body, decreasing anxiety and allowing people to get of addictive anti-anxiety drugs and improving sleep and energy cycles.*
>
> —**Andrew Weil, M.D.**
>   Director of Integrated Medicine, University of Arizona

There is a direct correlation between the physical restriction associated with shallow breathing and emotional restriction. Physical restriction and emotional restriction go hand-in-hand. Psychoanalysts have made a connection between restricted or shallow breathing and the inability to express negative or painful emotional energy (such as fear, anger, guilt, and shame) that is associated with aggressive tendencies. Internalized negative energy is destructive to the body. Deep breathing relaxes the body and facilitates greater energy flow throughout the body. By enhancing energy flow in the physical body we relieve emotional tension and stimulate healthy physiological responses.

WELLNESS MASTERY™ SUMMARY

Must Know!

1. Oxygen is the most important nutrient for the body. It is necessary for healing and for creating and maintaining optimal health.

2. Every cell in the body needs oxygen to carry out its specific metabolic function.

3. Deep breathing is the most important exercise you can do for healing your body and creating spiritual, mental, emotional, and physical health.

4. Seventy percent (70%) of eliminating toxins from the body happens through breathing.

5. Harmful bacteria, viruses, and cancer cannot exist in an oxygen-rich, aerobic environment.

6. Deep breathing techniques can dissipate the buildup of negative energy anywhere in the body.

7. Breath is considered the key to optimal health because of its direct effect on the central nervous system and cell physiology, and its ability to connect the mind, body, and spirit.

8. Deep, slow, full breathing makes the body more alkaline.

9. Deep, slow, full breathing is one of the most effective natural stress management tools.

10. The breath has been recognized as the movement of spirit energy in the body. The breath connects the mind, body, spirit, and emotion.

Wellness Mastery™ Action

Must Do!

1. Take 10 relaxed, slow, deep breaths (inhale and exhale) immediately upon waking, while lying in bed.

2. Begin your day with a 5-minute deep breathing exercise first thing in the morning sitting on the edge of your bed.

3. De-stress with 5 minutes of deep breathing exercises whenever you are stuck in traffic. Remember to keep your eyes open at all times when behind the wheel of your automobile!

4. De-stress with 5 minutes of deep breathing exercises the next time you feel anxious, tense, stressed, or frustrated.

5. Do 5 minutes of deep breathing to energize yourself the next time you feel a lack of energy in the middle of the day.

6. Teach someone you love a deep breathing exercise.

7. If you work in an enclosed and poorly ventilated office environment, with internally-recycled air, whenever possible go outside for fresh air during your breaks and lunch hour.

8. Leave the windows open in your home and office whenever possible.

9. Purchase an air purification system or device for your home and office.

10. End your day with a 5-minute relaxation breathing exercise immediately before bedtime. Share this intimate time with a loved one. Use this time to pull loving healthy energy into your body (breathe in) and to release and remove self-limiting thoughts and feelings out of the body (breathe out).

Chapter Eight

Principle #5

Water

Hydrate

We start out life, at time of conception, being 96 percent water. When we are born we are approximately 80 percent water, and by the time we reach adulthood we are down to 70 percent, where we stabilize. In other words, throughout our lives we exist mostly of water.

—**Dr. Masuro Emoto,** *The Hidden Messages in Water*

The Most Important Fluid for the Body

After oxygen, water is the most important nutrient for optimal health and physical survival. Just as every cell needs oxygen, every cell needs water—quality water—to operate at optimal capacity. It is important that the water we drink gets into each and every cell.

Water is the primary transport medium for carrying nutrients into cells and waste materials out of cells. Water is required for detoxification at a cellular level. Through breath, sweat and urine water carries toxins out of the cells and out of the body. The body needs water to enable it to continually cleanse and flush its cells. Water is also the medium through which all cells in the body communicate with each other.

WATER, WATER EVERYWHERE YOU LOOK!

Planet earth is 75% water. Plant life in nature is 75% water. The healthy adult human body is made up of between 70 and 75% water. Water is the agent that carries oxygen to cells throughout our bodies. Our blood is 90% water. Parts of our nervous system are 90% water. Our brains are composed of 85% water. Our bones are 50% water. Muscles are composed of 90% water.

Water is required for enzymatic activity during all metabolic processes. Water is critical in maintaining proper pH (acid/alkaline) balance in the body. In the ideal, to be in alignment with how the body works as nature intended, we would consume food that is at least 70% water by content. What are the best food sources that contain the highest content of the highest quality water? Fresh, organic, raw (uncooked and unprocessed) fruits and vegetables.

DEHYDRATION & HUMAN PERFORMANCE

It is estimated that 75% of Americans are chronically dehydrated. In 37% of Americans, the thirst mechanism is so weak that it is often mistaken for hunger. A 2% drop in your body's level of hydration can lead to trouble. You may have difficulty performing basic math calculations, foggy short-term memory, and problems focusing on computer screens and printed pages. Chronic dehydration has been identified as a contributing factor to both high blood pressure and asthma.

The body's chronic need for taking in adequate water stems from the fact that your body, under conditions of normal activity, expels about 1 gallon of water per day through the lungs (exhalation), skin (sweat), urinary tract (urine), and digestive tract (fecal matter).

Dehydration is just one of the many problems we attribute to the Standard American Diet, SAD (not to be confused with a term used in the field of psychology—Seasonal Affective Disorder), which is comprised primarily of cooked and processed food with low or no water content. Dehydration, the removal of moisture in foods, is one of the main industrial processing procedures used to preserve the shelf life of food. Foods last longer when the water is extracted. Unfortunately, eating dry processed foods dehydrates the body.

Dehydration has also been documented as a major cause of numerous unhealthy conditions, including obesity, cancer, and arthritis. Lack of adequate hydration has been identified as one cause of daytime fatigue. It has been shown that even mild dehydration slows down body metabolism as much as 3%. Harvard researchers have concluded that up to 99% of all illness and disease would improve with adequate hydration of the body. A University of Washington study showed that drinking just one glass of water shut down midnight hunger pangs in most of the dieters in the study.

How Toxins Affect the Transport and Absorption of Water by Cells

Toxic substances bind to water molecules, changing their molecular structure, and affect how easily they are transported and absorbed within the body. There are two categories of toxins that bind to water molecules over time and thereby affect their molecular structure: endogenous and exogenous. Endogenous toxins are the toxins that are created within the body, by the body, as normal waste products of cellular metabolism. Assuming that we are eating foods that are in alignment with the nutritional requirements of the body as nature intended, our body has the ability to process, neutralize, and eliminate these toxins so that they do not accumulate in the body. Exogenous toxins are produced outside the body and include the synthetic, man-made chemical substances that do not exist in a natural state in nature.

Exogenous toxins include pharmaceutical drugs, pesticides, poisons, industrial chemicals, plastics, and the chemical derivatives of these substances. Exogenous toxins enter our body through the air we breathe (pollution from automobile, truck, airplane, train, boat, and other industrial gaseous fumes), the liquids we drink (chemicals in artificial drinks and the fluoride, chlorine, and other chemicals in our water supply), the foods we eat (pesticides, chemical fertilizers, chemical preservatives, synthetic hormones, antibacterial and antifungal agents, and contamination due to exposure to plastics packaging), the drugs we take (prescription medications as well as recreational drugs), the mercury vapors that escape from the breakdown of amalgam fillings in our teeth (that we inhale or that leach directly into our bloodstreams), and the toxins that come in direct contact with our skin (household cleansing agents, bath and beauty products). See Table 3-1: Ten Toxic Chemicals in Health & Beauty Products for a partial list of chemical toxins to avoid.

Any substance recognized by the body as foreign is considered toxic. Toxins have the ability to bind with water molecules, thereby changing their molecular configuration in a way that can hinder their ability to pass easily through the cell membranes. As we decrease the amount of water that is available in our bodies for our cells, we become dehydrated and more susceptible to a variety of unhealthy conditions.

WHAT YOU SHOULD KNOW ABOUT TAP WATER

More than 700 different chemicals have been identified in our drinking water supply. The Environmental Protection Agency (EPA) reports that our community water supplies are "liberally laced with asbestos, pesticides, heavy metals, arsenic, nitrates, sodium, and a variety of chemicals that are known carcinogens."

Chemical pollution has reached ground water supplies, resulting in contamination of wells. Eight out of ten Americans live near some source of toxic waste. To deal with the contamination problem, our public water supplies are loaded up with chlorine to kill the parasites, viruses, bacteria, algae, yeasts, and molds. The chlorination process itself creates carcinogens. When chlorine combines with other pollutants, or natural organic matter such as decaying vegetation in the water, it forms new harmful compounds known as trihalomethanes (ThMs), i.e. chloroform, bromoform, and carbon tetrachloride.

Studies have shown a direct link between chlorination and increased incidence of colon and bladder cancer. Dioxin, a byproduct of chlorine, has been found to be 300,000 times more potent a carcinogen than the pesticide DDT. Dioxins, which accumulate in fatty tissue in the body, mimic estrogens and disrupt normal hormone function. Plastics found in bottles, food packaging, and drink storage containers are a major source of dioxins. Dioxin has been linked with depressed immunity, endometriosis, diabetes, neuro-toxicity, birth defects, decreased fertility, and reproductive dysfunction in both sexes.

Most recently the highly toxic chemical flouride—in one of its derivative forms as fluorosilicic acid, sodium silicofluoride, or sodium fluoride—is being added to drinking water. These chemicals are industrial waste products from the phosphate fertilizer, aluminum, steel, glass, cement, and other industries. Pro-fluoride experts take the posture that these chemicals are safe because treated toxic waste is ok in small amounts for you. What do you think? Fluoride accumulates in the body and over a period of time can reach toxic levels. Nausea, diarrhea, vomiting, abdominal pain, increased salivation, and increased thirst are some of the early warning signs of fluoride poisoning. A Harvard study found a connection between fluoride levels in the body and a serious form of bone cancer in males under the age of 20. The National Research Council found fluoride can damage the brain, reduce thyroid function leading to loss of mental acuity, depression and weight gain, and diminish bone strength leading to bone fractures.

How Caffeine & Alcohol Dehydrate the Body

Hormones regulate the flow of water into and out of cells. Vasopressin (*vaso* refers to the blood vessels, and *pressin* refers to constriction) is the pituitary gland hormone that regulates the flow of water into and out of the cells and within the cells. Caffeine and alcohol both limit the secretion of vasopressin by the pituitary gland. Less vasopressin means less water moving into and out of cells, which leads to dehydration.

How Pharmaceutical Drugs Affect Hydration

The body in its natural state—healthy, vibrant, pain-free, medication-free, and disease-free—is a body in balance or "homeostasis." Any synthetic, chemical substance introduced into the body is considered foreign and toxic to the body and therefore creates some form of chemical imbalance. Pharmaceutical drugs, both prescription and non-prescription medications, are recognized as foreign substances by the body.

In a state of chemical imbalance the body uses its internal resources in an attempt to deactivate and neutralize the toxic and harmful affects of the foreign chemicals, and then proceeds to eliminate and transport the substance out of the body in an attempt to re-establish homeostasis. Every synthetic chemical substance introduced into the body affects the self-regulation mechanisms which control the delicate balance of water movement between body tissue and different fluid compartments. The introduction of numerous chemicals into the body is a major cause of dehydration.

WHAT YOU MAY NOT KNOW ABOUT THE LIQUIDS YOU DRINK

The active ingredient in Coke® is phosphoric acid; its pH is 2.8 (acidic). Consuming this type of beverage increases the acidity in the body. Any acidic condition in the body puts an excess demand on the body's need for calcium to buffer and help alkalize this acidic condition. If free calcium—the calcium found in circulating blood—is not available to help buffer the acidic biological environment, calcium is leached from the bones (98% of the calcium in the body is in bone material), thus contributing to the potential for osteoporosis, a condition described as the result of loss of calcium from bone matrix.

Did you know that when Coca-Cola® syrup concentrate is transported in commercial trucks it is considered a "Hazardous Material" by the government and classified as a "Highly Corrosive Material?"

NOT ALL WATER IS CREATED EQUAL

Every substance, including water, has a certain molecular configuration. The molecular configuration of water is one of the factors that determine how easily it is absorbed through the cell membrane. How easily water travels through the cell membrane determines the level of hydration of the cell.

There are two types of biological water that have been identified in the human body: "structured" water and "bound" water. Structured water, also known as free, clustered or micro-clustered water, is able to move freely and easily through the cell walls to transport nutrients, remove waste and toxins, and maintain proper communication between cells throughout the body. Bound water has a molecular configuration that has been altered due to factors such as stress and chemical pollution, and therefore does not move as easily through cell membranes.

When we are young, our bodies contain high levels of this structured water. As we age, we are exposed to more and more environmental toxins in the air we breathe, liquids we drink, foods we eat, drugs we consume, electromagnetic energy fields we are exposed to, and the commercial health and beauty products we put on our bodies; unfortunately, each of these toxins alters the molecular configuration of the water in our bodies and adversely affects body hydration.

SO, WHAT IS THE HEALTHIEST WATER TO DRINK?

In the ideal, the healthiest drinking water would come from natural unpolluted sources like underground wells and mountain springs. These sources would also contain important mineral nutrients. But unless you live in a remote, unpopulated, unindustrialized, natural environment good luck finding such a pure source of water. As an alternative, the best water technologies and purification processes include a combination of carbon (charcoal) filtration, steam distillation, reverse osmosis, and ionization. See Table 8-1: Drinking Water Technologies for a summary highlight of the current water technologies that are available on the market and some of their features.

TABLE 8-1

DRINKING WATER TECHNOLOGIES

Technology	Method	Features	Limitation
Activated Carbon	absorption	removes chlorine & volatile organic compounds	fluorides, arsenic, heavy metals remain
Steam Distillation	demineralization	removes minerals & contaminants	lacks minerals & lacks oxygen (acidic pH)
Reverse Osmosis	0.0001 micron membrane filtration	removes minerals & contaminants	lacks minerals & lacks oxygen (acidic pH)
Ionization	electrical ion (+/-) separation through electrolysis	pH-creates acidic & alkaline waters ORP -Oxidation Reduction Potential -anti-oxidizing micro-clustering - creates smaller water molecules for greater absorbability	lacks minerals

Unfortunately, while these purification processes remove harmful toxic contaminants, they also simultaneously remove the naturally-occurring mineral elements as well. Mineral supplementation may therefore be necessary to add back into our diet that which we should be receiving from natural sources, but are not.

The best storage container for pure water or fresh juice is glass, not plastic. Most plastic storage containers leach harmful chemical substances like dioxin into the liquids they store. In addition to drinking lots of pure water, the best way to hydrate the body is to eat the meat of or drink the juice from fresh "live" raw (uncooked, unprocessed, and un-pasteurized) organic fruits and vegetables. The water in raw organic fruits and vegetables is considered structured water. See Table 8-2: Basic Juicing Regimen & Recipes for some simple and basic juicing recommendations.

TABLE 8-2
BASIC JUICING REGIMEN & RECIPES

Purpose: Detoxify, cleanse, alkalize, hydrate, and rejuvenate. All juices are prepared from *fresh, raw, organic* fruits, vegetables and roots.

WATERMELON DELIGHT! (EARLY MORNING - 6AM)

An alkalizing, hydrating, and cleansing drink
Ingredients: (16-20 ounces)
Watermelon (fruit and rind)

LEMON-GINGER BLAST! (MORNING - 8AM)

An enzyme-packed, immune boosting, digestion stimulating, alkalizing, hydrating, and detoxifying drink
Ingredients: (16-20 ounces)
½ lemon (whole lemon including the skin)
1-2" fresh ginger root (peeled)
1 apple (whole)
1 cup pure water
¼ teaspoon cayenne pepper

VEGETABLE JUICE
(MID MORNING -10AM OR MID AFTERNOON - 3PM)

A phytonutrient-packed, antioxidant-packed, mineralizing, alkalizing, hydrating, rejuvenating drink
Ingredients: (16-20 ounces)
Carrot (8 oz)
Spinach (2-3 oz)
Parsley (2-3 oz)
Celery (2-3 oz)

WELLNESS MASTERY™ SUMMARY

Must Know!

1. Water is the 2nd most important nutrient (after oxygen) necessary for optimal health and physical survival.

2. Water is required for the enzymatic activity during all metabolic processes.

3. Water is critical in maintaining proper acid/alkaline (pH) balance in the body.

4. Water helps flush toxins out of cells and helps carry these waste products out of the body in urine, sweat, and breath.

5. The healthy body is 70 to 75% water and, as such, demands that 70 to 75% of our food consumption include high water content foods.

6. The best source of high water content food is fresh "live" raw (uncooked and unprocessed) organic fruits and vegetables. Fruits and vegetables are comprised of 80 to 90% water.

7. The highest quality of pure water content food comes from fresh "live" raw (uncooked and unprocessed) organic fruits and vegetables.

8. Glass is the best storage container for both pure water and fresh, raw, organic juice.

9. Caffeine and alcohol both dehydrate the body by suppressing the pituitary gland hormone, vasopressin, which regulates the flow of water into cells and interstitial tissue.

10. The introduction of synthetic chemicals (pharmaceutical drugs, pesticides, poisons, industrial chemicals, and plastics) into the body causes dehydration.

WELLNESS MASTERY™ ACTIONS

1. Drink one fresh, organic, raw (un-pasteurized, unprocessed, and uncooked) fruit juice in the early morning (see Table 8-2: Basic Juicing Regimen & Recipes).

2. Drink one to two fresh, organic, raw (un-pasteurized, unprocessed, and uncooked) vegetable juices mid-day (see Table 8-2: Basic Juicing Regimen & Recipes).

3. Drink only water that has been purified by reverse osmosis, distillation, and charcoal (carbon) filtering.

4. Store all your juices and water in glass containers.

5. Avoid drinking liquids with your meals. Drinking liquids with meals impedes complete digestion by diluting digestive enzymes. It is okay to drink liquids 30 minutes prior to a meal and 45 minutes after finishing a meal.

6. Do a one-day "juice fast" weekly. Once a week drink only fresh, raw, organic juices.

7. Buy a juicer and learn how to prepare your daily juices. Take a class on "Juicing" at your local health food store.

8. Start snacking on high water content foods: fresh, raw, organic fruits like watermelons, honeydew, apples, oranges, peaches, and pears, and vegetables like carrots, celery, and cucumbers.

9. Avoid both caffeinated and alcoholic beverages because they dehydrate the body.

10. Purchase a water purification system or device for your home and office that includes a combination of reverse osmosis, distillation, and charcoal (carbon) filtering.

CHAPTER NINE

PRINCIPLE #6

Sunlight

BASK IN FULL-SPECTRUM NATURAL LIGHT

Sunshine and fresh air must be considered as good food.

—**Hippocrates**, Father of Medicine

SUNLIGHT & WELLNESS

Sunlight, due to the presence of full-spectrum wavelengths, possesses healing properties. Humans are creatures of the sun. Human history on earth is one of exposure to full-spectrum light rays from the sun. Ozone in the atmosphere acts as a filter that blocks a certain percentage of these rays and allows some UV rays to pass down to us. The thickness of the ozone layer fluctuates over time. Both under-exposure and over-exposure (sunburn) to the different light wavelengths generated by the sun can have harmful effects.

The quality of the light which we are exposed to (i.e. its wavelength composition) influences many physiological functions of the body, including metabolic rate, blood pressure, liver function, brain function, hormone production, immune response, and the maintenance of biological rhythms. Natural and full-spectrum artificial light have been shown to lower high blood pressure and cholesterol, regulate hormonal secretions, and decrease work fatigue and eye strain resulting from artificial lighting conditions.

> *If the human skin is not exposed to solar radiation for long periods of time, disturbances will occur in the physiology equilibrium of the human system. The result will be functional disorders of the nervous system and vitamin D deficiency, a weakening of the body's defense and an aggravation of chronic disease.*
> **— Viktoras Kulvinskas**
>   Co-founder Hippocrates Health Institute
>   *Surviving into the 21st Century*

The best combination of light exposure for optimal health is natural light— sunlight—during the day and total darkness at night. To qualify as full-spectrum lighting, artificial lights must contain the invisible part of the light spectrum (Ultraviolet or "UV" light) as well as the visible parts. It appears that the lack of UV radiation in commonly-used artificial lights is the main cause of the health problems associated with them.

THE LIGHT-EYE-HEALTH CONNECTION

When light enters the eye and hits the photoreceptors in the retina (the internal surface on the back of the eyeball) glandular stimulation occurs. The pineal, pituitary, and hypothalamus glands are activated and produce hormones that regulate other chemical reactions throughout the body.

The pineal gland, located in the center of the skull and commonly referred to as the "third eye," reacts to light. It regulates the onset of puberty, moods, and sleep patterns. The pineal gland produces the hormone melatonin at night as we sleep. The body's *circadian rhythm*—a daily cycle of biological activity based on a 24-hour period and influenced by regular variations in the environment, such as the alternation of night and day—is governed by melatonin and the pineal gland's ability to produce it. This *circadian rhythm*, present in humans and most other animals, is generated by an internal clock, located in the hypothalamus and pineal gland, which is synchronized to light-dark cycles and other cues in the environment. This internal clock accounts for why you tend to wake up at the same time every day, even without an alarm clock. Circadian rhythms can be disrupted by changes in daily schedule. For example, biologists have observed that birds exposed to artificial light for a long time sometimes build nests in the fall instead of the spring. Nighttime causes melatonin secretion to rise, while daylight inhibits it. Light causes the pineal gland to temporarily suspend melatonin production.

Lack of exposure to full-spectrum light prevents the necessary suspension of melatonin production and leads to glandular exhaustion. It has been found that the majority of people over 40 in the U.S. have calcified or atrophied pineal glands. Calcified or atrophied glands lose their ability to regulate melatonin secretion.

Under artificial lighting conditions, adequate glandular stimulation fails to take place largely due to a lack of the necessary ultraviolet "UV" portion of the light spectrum. Glass also screens out UV wavelengths. The glass found in household and automobile windows, eyeglasses, and sunglasses blocks out this vital UV wavelength. Eyeglasses and contact lenses block up to 92% of incoming UV radiation. Sunglasses can be particularly harmful due to their tint, which distorts the color spectrum.

THE HEALING PROPERTIES OF NATURAL LIGHT

When sunlight falls on your skin your immune response is stimulated to increase the number of white blood cells in your system, especially lymphocytes. White blood cells protect the body from harmful bacteria, viruses, and funguses. Lymphocytes are specialized white blood cells that produce immune serums, globin and interferon, that protect the body against infections.

Certain wavelengths of natural light kill harmful bacteria. Known for its bactericidal effects, sunlight was once used as a primary treatment for infectious diseases. Not long ago, daily exposure to fresh air and sunlight was the widely accepted treatment for tuberculosis. This treatment protocol has since been minimized due to the introduction of pharmaceutical antibiotics.

The Adverse Effect of Artificial Light on Health

Commonly used artificial fluorescent lighting presents a distortion of light wavelength patterns that adversely affects the body. A 1980 research study by Dr. Fritz Hollowich monitored changes in hormone secretions in the body resulting from illumination by cool white florescent lighting versus full-spectrum lighting. Exposure to the fluorescent lighting resulted in the release of the stress hormones ACTH and cortisol by the adrenal glands, whereas no such reaction occurred from full-spectrum lights. Based upon the research work of Hollowich and others, Germany banned the use of cool-white fluorescent bulbs in hospitals and other medical facilities.

The research work of Dr. John Ott explored the effects of light on biological systems. He found that fish stopped laying eggs when placed under the artificial light of 40 watt fluorescent tubes. When "full-spectrum" light—natural sunlight or artificial light designed to mimic the wavelength composition of sunlight—was reintroduced, reproduction normalized.

REDUCED SUNLIGHT AFFECTS EMOTIONS

It has been shown that reduced exposure to natural sunlight for extended periods of time also contributes to hormonal changes that lead to emotional imbalances. It is estimated that 2 to 3% of the northern latitude population of the U.S. is affected by a condition known as Seasonal Affective Disorder, or "SAD" (not to be confused with the acronym for Standard American Diet). This condition, characterized by severe depression and fatigue at the onset of winter, has been directly related to diminished exposure to sunlight.

A controlled double blind study done on SAD sufferers was conducted by Drs. Wher and Rosenthal in 1984, as reported in the *Archives of General Psychiatry*. In the study, two groups of patients were treated with light. One group was treated with a yellow incandescent light, the other with bright full-spectrum light. The symptoms vanished in the group exposed to the full-spectrum light, while the group exposed to incandescent light showed no improvement. None of the patients, in either group, were informed of the light to which they were being exposed.

LIGHT IMPACTS MENTAL & EMOTIONAL STATES

Not only is the physical condition of an organism affected by light, but the mental condition is as well. It has been shown that behavior in laboratory animals changes greatly with changes in the lighting conditions. Researchers have long known that it is necessary to remove a male rat from his cage in the laboratory before his pregnant mate gives birth; otherwise he will cannibalize the newborn rats. Under full-spectrum lighting conditions this does not occur. In a sunlit environment papa rat will actually nurture his offspring.

Human experiments were carried out in 1986 in a classroom at Green Street Elementary School in Brattleboro, Vermont, and reported in *The Lancet* (the British Medical Journal) on November 12, 1987. These studies showed that children attending classes in a room illuminated by full-spectrum lights took fewer days off from school due to illness than other students.

In the 1970's Dr. John Ott conducted a similar study with schoolchildren in Sarasota, Florida. When full-spectrum lighting was introduced into a classroom at Gocio Elementary School, it was found that such lighting improved general attendance as well as the behavior of hyperactive children. Their learning ability and concentration were also enhanced.

A Boston study, conducted at a home for the elderly, demonstrated that the rate of calcium absorption by the body increases with exposure to full-spectrum lighting.

From Hunter/Gatherer to Farmer to Factory Worker to Information Worker

When we were hunter/gatherers, getting enough natural sunlight was not an issue, we spent all our waking hours out in nature. When we became farmers, 98% of the population lived in rural areas and we fed ourselves directly off the land. Getting enough natural sunlight was still not an issue because we were still outdoors a majority of our waking hours. As we evolved into an industrialized world we moved off of the farms and into the cities, and changed from spending a majority of our daylight hours outside in nature to spending most of our daylight hours inside factory walls. Today, entrenched in the Information Age, we spend the most time that has ever been spent in human history in environments of artificial, unnatural lighting, and, in some cases, totally removed from natural lighting.

Life on this Earth since the beginning has evolved under the full spectrum of natural sunlight. Abnormal growth responses develop when any part of this natural sunlight spectral energy was blocked from entering the eyes. As people have become more civilized, living under an environment of artificial light, behind window glass, eye glasses and particularly sunglasses of different colors, the balance of the wavelength energy entering the eye has become greatly distorted from that of natural sunlight.

—John Ott, Ph.D.
   Father of Full-Spectrum Light
   Optometric Weekly

Natural light is to the skin what good air is to the lungs! Whether or not we are aware of the adverse impact that the lack of full-spectrum light has on the health of the human body, we will continue to experience health outcomes that are consistent with the *truth* of this situation.

WELLNESS MASTERY™ SUMMARY

1. Natural sunlight and full-spectrum artificial light possess healing properties.

2. The best light combination for optimal health is adequate exposure to natural sunlight during the day and total darkness at night.

3. Underexposure as well as overexposure to sunlight (sunburn) can have harmful health effects.

4. Commonly used artificial (fluorescent) lighting presents a distortion of wavelength patterns that adversely affects the physiology of the body.

5. It is the lack of UV radiation in the commonly used artificial lights that seems to be the main cause of the health problems associated with them.

6. Light coming into the eye regulates specific endocrine gland activity.

7. Eyeglasses and contact lenses block up to 92% of incoming beneficial UV radiation.

8. Sunglasses can be particularly harmful due to their tint, which distorts the color spectrum.

9. It has been shown that reduced exposure to natural sunlight for extended periods of time causes hormonal changes in the body that contribute to emotional imbalances.

10. When natural sunlight falls on the skin the immune response is stimulated to increase the number of white blood cells.

WELLNESS MASTERY™ ACTION

Must Do!

1. Open all the blinds and windows in your home or workplace during daylight hours.

2. Turn off all non-full-spectrum artificial light during daylight hours whenever possible.

3. Replace all incandescent and fluorescent lighting with full-spectrum light bulbs. Full-spectrum light bulbs are considered specialty items at this time, but are available at some health food and specialty lighting stores.

4. During daylight hours spend as much time outdoors as possible.

5. Picnic! Eat your lunch outdoors whenever possible, especially at your workplace.

6. Request outdoor restaurant seating if available whenever you eat out (as long as the outdoor area is not the designated smoking section).

7. Hold business meetings in conference rooms with external building window access.

8. Go for daily walks outside in fresh air during all break times at work.

9. Remove sunglasses periodically when not in direct sunlight.

10. Sleep in total darkness, in rooms with blackout shades, and remove night lights.

Chapter Ten

Principle #7

Acid/Alkaline pH Balance

Restore Acid/Alkaline pH Balance

What's the Big Deal about Acid/Alkaline pH Balance?

The human body functions as a series of chemical reactions controlled by electrical impulses. As you are reading this sentence millions of chemical reactions are occurring simultaneously in your body. Everything that happens in your body—your ability to see, hear, smell, feel, taste, digest food, build and repair cells, neutralize toxins, eliminate wastes, and think—is the result of chemical reactions. These chemical reactions, by design, occur within a very specific pH range and environment.

When your body chemistry is in balance your body is in a state of equilibrium or "homeostasis." Every cell has the opportunity to function at its optimal capacity, and you experience a state of optimal health. When your body chemistry is out of balance your cells are operating at less than their optimal capacity and are expending extra energy in an attempt to regain balance.

When your body chemistry initially drifts out of balance you experience minor symptoms of discomfort, such as headache, sore throats, colds, flus, skin conditions, bad breath, body odor, indigestion, constipation, loss of energy, behavior problems, mood swings, and a whole host of other unpleasant but usually bearable conditions. When your body chemistry has been out of balance for a prolonged period, more dramatic physiological changes occur and you begin to experience the more severe symptoms of the chronic degenerative diseases associated with these physiological changes, such as obesity, diabetes, fibromyalgia, cancer, and heart disease.

Our lifestyles, the things we do to ourselves in combination with what we are exposed to from the surrounding environment, are continually creating chemical imbalances in our bodies. Every cell responds to these imbalances in an attempt to make the necessary changes to re-establish the state of equilibrium we call homeostasis.

All the cells, tissues, fluids, and organs inside the body are part of what we call the internal biological environment. If our bodies' internal biological environments become either too acidic or too alkaline we experience health problems. One way to describe the quality of this internal biological environment is by the measure of the acidity or alkalinity of the chemical environment, expressed as pH.

WHAT IS pH?

pH, the potential of Hydrogen, is the measure of hydrogen ion concentration. Hydrogen ion concentration in the body describes the level of acidity or alkalinity of the body's internal biological environment. pH is measured on a numeric scale ranging from 1 to 14. This scale ranges from acidic (numeric value of 1.0) to alkaline (numeric value of 14.0). The lower the number on the scale, the greater the acidity; the higher the number on the scale, the lower the acidity.

When your body is at its optimal healthy natural state, most of your internal biological environment is maintained at a pH in the 7.0 to 7.4 range, considered neutral to slightly alkaline. Different parts of the body are known to function best at different pH levels as seen in Table 10-1: Optimal pH of Various Body Tissues [Sources: A Bedani, TD DuBose (1995). Cellular and whole-body acid-base regulation in *Fluid, Electrolyte, and Acid Bases Disorders*, Churchill Livingston, NY, pp. 69-103; AC Guyten (1980). Textbook of Medical Physiology (2nd edition). W.B. Saunders, Co., Philadelphia, pp. 457, 803, 853].

TABLE 10-1

OPTIMAL pH OF VARIOUS BODY TISSUES

Tissue	pH
Skeletal muscle	6.9 –7.2
Heart	7.0 – 7.4
Liver	7.2
Brain	7.1
Blood	7.35 – 7.45
Saliva	6.0 – 7.4
Urine	4.5 – 8.0

Because it is possible to measure the pH of the blood and difficult to measure the pH of other tissue, most of what is known and used clinically relates to the acidity and alkalinity of the bloodstream. However, a simple but less accurate way to measure pH of the body is to test the first morning urine with a piece of pH strip paper that is made specifically for testing saliva or urine pH. pH strips are usually available at local pharmacies and health food stores. "First morning urine" is that first elimination after rising but before food or beverage intake. An ideal first morning urine pH is in the 6.5 to 7.5 range.

ACID/ALKALINE pH BALANCE & DISEASE

Why is it important to maintain the right acid/alkaline pH balance? A body that is either too acidic or too alkaline is unhealthy. In this day and age, because of environmental and lifestyle habits, our bodies tend to be more acidic than alkaline.

Research has shown that harmful bacteria, viruses, fungi, cancer, and other pathogens (disease-causing agents) thrive in an acidic environment and cannot survive in an alkaline environment. Dr. Otto Warburg won the Nobel Prize in 1932 for proving that cancer cells do not need oxygen present to derive their energy. What he discovered is that unlike all other cells in the human body, cancer cells do not breathe oxygen. Instead, they thrive in an acidic, low-oxygen (anaerobic) environment. Warburg also showed that cancer cells died once they were removed from an acidic low-oxygen environment and placed into an alkaline, high-oxygen environment.

Your Internal Biological Environment

Every cell in your body is suspended in a liquid matrix that makes up what we refer to as your internal biological environment. The same way that a water balloon holds the shape of the water it contains, your skin acts as the body covering around this internal biological environment. This internal biological environment is either acidic or alkaline. This acid/alkaline relationship is constantly changing based upon a variety of factors, and is mediated moment-to-moment by numerous chemical reactions.

An internal biological environment that is too alkaline is just as dangerous, although much less common, as one that is too acidic. Most of the chronic degenerative diseases we are familiar with (i.e. cancer, cardiovascular disease, stroke, diabetes, etc.) are associated with an underlying acidic condition in the body. A body can become too alkaline, a condition known as "alkalosis," due to decreased carbon dioxide in the blood (due to hyperventilation or any lung diseases that cause shortness of breath) and/or increased bicarbonate levels caused by other metabolic conditions.

Because of the importance of the acid-alkaline balance in the blood and tissues, the body has a number of mechanisms for regulating this balance. Your lungs and kidneys, along with your cardiovascular system (heart, blood vessels, and blood), are the primary mechanisms for regulating pH throughout your body. Your body's internal chemical equilibrium is maintained by the coordinated action of your lungs (through breathing), liver (through toxin neutralization), kidneys (through filtering blood and eliminating waste material in urine), intestines (through digestion and eliminating waste material in feces), skin (through perspiration), and mineral buffering mechanisms throughout the body.

BUFFERING MECHANISMS

Maintaining proper acid/alkaline pH balance is such a critical issue that the body has been designed with several mechanisms that buffer, i.e. normalize by either raising or lowering the pH, conditions when the body becomes either too acidic or too alkaline. These mechanisms work with the help of oxygen, water, and acid-buffering minerals. Acid-buffering minerals, including cesium (pH 14), sodium (pH 14), potassium (pH 14), calcium (pH 12), and magnesium (pH 9), help the body maintain this delicate acid/alkaline pH balance. It is through these acid-buffering minerals that the body also maintains adequate alkaline reserves, which are available at all times to help regulate the pH and keep it in the optimal range.

Acid-forming metabolic wastes, created in the body as a natural consequence of normal cell metabolism, exercise, stress, inflammation, high fat diets, high protein diets, and high sugar diets, are adequately and effectively neutralized only when sufficient acid-buffering mineral reserves are present.

When a slightly alkaline internal biological environment is maintained, the metabolic (tearing down and rebuilding of cells), immunologic (self-defense against harmful pathogens), repair (the body's ability to heal itself) and energy-producing mechanisms of the body function at their best. For the body to maintain optimal pH range it is important to consume foods that contain high organic concentrations of these critical acid-buffering minerals. The best natural source of these organic acid-buffering minerals is fresh, raw, organic vegetables and fruits.

HOW DOES THE BODY BECOME ACIDIC?

Many factors contribute to creating an acidic condition in the body. Shallow breathing (creating a lack of oxygen due to inadequate ventilation of the lungs) lowers the pH of the body. Dehydration (not enough water) contributes to a more acidic internal biological environment. Lifestyle issues such as stress, over-exercising, smoking, alcohol and caffeine consumption make the body more acidic. A diet high in animal protein, refined sugars, and processed foods increase acidity. The waste products from normal cell metabolism, pharmaceutical drugs, and environmental pollutants (harmful man-made substances that do not appear in nature, such as herbicides, pesticides, pharmaceutical drugs, industrial chemicals, and food preservatives) all increase acidity in the body.

The body never rests. Even when we sleep the body, through normal ongoing metabolic processes, generates waste products that need to be neutralized and carried out of the body through the lungs, liver, kidneys, intestines, and skin. Our bodies are continually at work neutralizing and eliminating every toxic substance, whether created by the body or made by man and introduced into the body from the outside environment.

ACID/ALKALINE pH BALANCE & STRESS

Physical, mental, and emotional stresses also create acid-forming metabolites in the body. Physical stressors are created through physical over-exertion, lack of sleep, illness and disease, environmental toxins, lack of oxygen, exposure to fluorescent non-full spectrum lighting, and exposure to electromagnetic forces field. Mental and emotional stressors are the result of how we choose to interpret life's events. Stress, no matter what the source, causes the release of the stress hormones ACTH and cortisol from the adrenal glands, which in turn make the body even more acidic.

Dr. T.H. Holmes of the University of Washington created what he called his Social Readjustment Rating Scale, in which he gave numerical values to many different types of stressful situations. He was able to correlate, with considerable accuracy, the number of stress points a person accumulated in any two-year period. With this information he calculated the degree of seriousness of the disorder which that person was then likely to suffer. The higher the numeric value, the greater the stress. For example, death of a spouse results in 100 stress points, divorce 73 points, death of a close family member 63 points, personal injury or illness 50, marriage 50 points, retirement 45 points, change to a different line of work 36 points, outstanding personal achievement 28 points, and change in residence 20 points. See Table 11-1: Stress Inventory Test in Chapter 11, Hormone Balance, for a list of life events ranked by their stress value. Take the test yourself. The greater the stress in your life, the greater the acidity in your body; and the greater your internal acidity, the greater the chance of illness and disease.

ACID pH, OBESITY, & WEIGHT LOSS

Is there a relationship between fat storage and body acidity? You bet. An overly acidic internal biological environment affects how your body stores and releases fat and extra weight. A problem occurs with the body's natural ability to lose weight and shed excess pounds when the blood pH becomes too acidic. Optimal pH of the blood is one of the critical pH balances that must be maintained by the body at all times for optimal health. When the blood, which must be maintained within a very narrow slightly alkaline pH range of approximately 7.35, becomes acidic, a series of chemical reactions are triggered that actually inhibit the body's ability to lose weight.

In short, obesity is one of the body's responses to over acidification. When your body is acidic, fat cells bind to acids in order to carry them away from the bloodstream to protect vascular walls and vital organs from the damage that would be caused by the increased acidity. Acting out of self-preservation and its own internal intelligence, the body shunts acids away from vital organs to fat stores and keeps them there. Unless one consciously works on alkalizing the blood to a healthy level, the body will not let go of fat or extra water easily. If your internal biological environment is constantly in an acidic state, even reducing calorie intake and increasing aerobic activity will not necessarily shed the pounds. You must alkalize to reduce your size.

FOOD & ACID/ALKALINE BALANCE

Everything we eat is first broken down through digestion to its smallest nutrient form, then carried in the blood stream and distributed throughout our bodies to be picked up by various cells and used for individual cell function.

The terms acid or alkaline ash and acid or alkaline forming are used to describe the pH quality of different foods, but have slightly different meaning. When referring to acid or alkaline ash we are referring to the mineral pH quality of the resulting ash when different foods were burned in a laboratory. Acid ash foods are those that contained the minerals (such as sulfur, chloride, and phosphorous) that form acid compounds in the body. Alkaline ash foods are those that contain the minerals (such as calcium, magnesium, sodium, and potassium) that form alkaline compounds in the body.

In contrast acid and alkaline forming foods refer to how different foods react in the body.

ACID FORMING FOODS

Everything that we eat and drink is either acid forming or alkaline forming when it is broken down and metabolized by the body as shown in Table10-2: Acid/Alkaline Food Chart.

It is primarily the pH quality of the mineral content in foods that influences the acid/alkaline balance within the body. When identifying foods as acid or alkaline forming, we are referring to a food's net affect on body chemistry.

As a general rule of thumb, cooked and processed foods are more acid-forming in the body than the same foods consumed raw and unprocessed. Animal proteins and fats (including beef, chicken, turkey, lamb, eggs, and dairy products) are more acid-forming in the body when metabolized than are most plant life (i.e. fruits, vegetable, roots, nuts, and seeds). Animal proteins and fats contribute to a more acidic internal biological environment because their acid-forming elements are greater than their alkaline-forming elements. Most grains (wheat, rice, oats, and corn) have an acid-producing affect in the body. When processed, this effect increases. Commercially-grown grains have also been shown to be more acid-forming than traditional, organic, or biodynamic grain sources.

TABLE 10-2

ACID/ALKALINE FOOD CHART

The following chart is a partial list of common foods categorized by their acid or alkaline effects on body chemistry once they are broken down through digestion. This chart is reconstructed from the "Food & Chemical Effects on Acid/Alkaline Body Chemical Balance" chart prepared by Dr. Russell Jaffe at ELISA/ACT Biotechnologies.

ALKALIZING FOODS

FRUITS

Apple
Apricot
Avocado
Banana
Blackberry
Blueberry
Cantaloupe
Cherries
Currants
Grapefruit
Grapes
Honeydew
Lemon
Lime
Mango
Nectarine
Orange
Papaya
Peach
Pear
Persimmon
Pineapple
Raspberry Raisins
Strawberry
Tangerine
Watermelon

NUTS/SEEDS (PROTEIN)

Almonds
Cashews
Chestnuts
Seeds, flax
Seeds, poppy
Seeds, pumpkin
Seeds, sesame
Seeds, sprouted
Seeds, sunflower
Soy, tempeh
Soy, tofu
Spirulina

SWEETENERS

Agave
Molasses

VEGETABLES

Alfalfa
Asparagus
Barley grass Beets
Broccoli
Brussel sprouts
Cabbage
Cauliflower
Celery
Chard
Chlorella
Collard greens
Cucumber
Dandelions
Dulce
Eggplant
Garlic
Jicima
Kale
Lentil
Lettuce, Butter
Lettuce, Romaine
Mushrooms
Mustard Greens
Onions
Parsley
Parsnips
Peas
Peppers
Pumpkin
Rutabaga
Spirulina
Sprouts
Squashes
Sweet potato
Wheat grass
Wild greens
Yam

FATS & OILS

Avocado oil
Coconut oil
Cod liver oil
Flax oil
Olive oil

SPICES/ SEASONINGS

All Herbs
Chili Pepper
Cinnamon
Curry
Ginger root
Miso
Mustard
Sea Salt
Tamari
Turmeric

ORIENTAL VEGETABLES

Dandelion root
Kombu
Maitake Reishi
Nori
Sea veggies
Shitake

Wakame

OTHER

Bee pollen
Egg, duck
Egg, quail
Ghee (clarified butter)
Grain, oat
Juices, fresh fruit
Juices, fresh veggie
Kombucha
Lecithin
Milk, human breast
Probiotic cultures
Tea, dandelion
Tea, ginger
Tea, ginseng
Tea, green
Tea, herbal
Vinegar, apple cider
Water, mineral

ACIDIFYING FOODS

FRUITS
Coconut
Cranberries
Dates
Dried Fruits
Figs
Guava
Plum
Pomegranate
Prune
Tomato

DAIRY
Butter
Cheese, cow
Cheese, goat
Cheese, sheep
Cheese, soy
Cottage cheese Cream
Ice cream
Milk, cow
Milk, goat
Yogurt

VEGETABLES
Carrot
Chutney
Rhubarb
Spinach
Zucchini

NUTS & BUTTERS
Brazil nut
Hazelnut Peanut
Peanut Butter
Pecans
Pine Nut
Tahini
Walnuts

SWEETENERS
Aspartame
Honey
Maple Syrup Saccharin
Stevia
Sugar

ANIMAL PROTEIN
Beef
Carp
Clams
Egg, chicken
Fish
Lamb
Lobster
Mussels
Oyster
Pork
Rabbit
Salmon
Shrimp
Scallops
Tuna
Turkey
Veal
Venison
Whey protein

FATS & OILS
Almond oil
Canola oil
Chestnut oil
Corn oil
Cottonseed oil
Grape seed oil
Hemp seed oil
Lard
Palm kernel oil
Safflower oil
Sesame oil
Sunflower oil

BEANS & LEGUMES
Beans. black
Beans, kidney
Beans, lima
Beans, pinto
Beans, red
Beans, white
Peas, chick
Peas, green
Peas, snow
Soy milk, Soybeans

DRUGS & CHEMICALS
Chemicals, food
Drugs, medicinal
Drugs, psychedelic
Pesticides
Preservatives, food
Herbicides

BEVERAGES
Alcohol/Liquor
Beer
Coffee
Sodas
Spirits
Tea, black
Wine

GRAINS
Amaranth
Barley
Buckwheat
Corn
Hemp seed
Millet
Oats (rolled)
Quinoi
Pastas
Rice (all)
Rye
Spelt
Kamut
Wheat

OTHER
Nutmeg
Potatoes, white
Vinegar, balsamic
Vinegar, distilled
Wheat germ

In summary, highly refined and processed foods are more acidic to the body than the same foods eaten raw (unprocessed and uncooked). In general, animal protein (meat and dairy), refined sugars, and starches are more acidic in the body than fruits, vegetables, roots, nuts, and seeds. Cooked foods are more acidic in the body than the same foods in their raw state.

ALKALINE FORMING FOODS

In general, raw fruits, vegetables, roots, nuts, and seeds contain higher proportions of alkaline-forming elements than other foods as shown in Table 10-2: Acid/Alkaline Food Chart. Uncooked and unprocessed fruits and vegetables also have a greater alkaline affect on the body than the same fruits and vegetables when cooked or processed.

While naturally-occurring raw, organic, plant-based foods, uncooked and unprocessed, tend to create the greatest alkaline internal biologic environment, a healthy body needs a balance of high quality nutrients from high quality food sources from both acid and alkaline forming food categories . . . the operative word being quality. Table 10-3: Acid/Alkaline Foods Summary is a synopsis of acid/alkaline food basics.

TABLE 10-3

ACID/ALKALINE FOOD SUMMARY

More Alkaline	More Acidic
Plant-based (fruits, vegetable, nuts, & seeds)	Animal-based (meat & dairy)
Live—raw (uncooked & unprocessed)	Cooked & processed
Made by nature (naturally occurring)	Made by man (synthetic & artificial)

WELLNESS MASTERY ™ SUMMARY

Must Know!

1. At a fundamental level, the body is nothing more than a series of chemical reactions controlled by electrical impulses.

2. When the body's acid/alkaline pH chemistry is in balance, every cell functions at its optimal potential.

3. When our bodies are in their natural healthy states, our internal biological environments are maintained at a pH around 7.0.

4. For the body to maintain optimal pH it is important to consume foods that contain high organic concentrations of critical acid-buffering minerals: cesium (pH 14), sodium (pH 14), potassium (pH 14), calcium (pH 12), and magnesium (pH 9).

5. The body never rests. Even when we sleep all body processes are functioning and waste products are being created and then neutralized to be carried out of the body through the lungs, liver, kidneys, intestines, and skin.

6. Harmful bacteria, viruses, fungi, cancer, and other pathogens (disease-causing agents) thrive in an acidic environment and cannot survive in an alkaline environment.

Must Know!

7. External toxins (exotoxins) include the chemical substances found in pesticides, herbicides, pharmaceutical drugs, industrial chemicals, plastics, and processed foods.

8. Exotoxins get into the body through the air we breathe (air pollution), the water we drink (water pollution), the food we eat (processed and genetically altered substances), and other things we put in our mouth (such as toothpaste), on our hair (such as hair care products), and on our skin (such as beauty products).

9. When broken down by digestion, animal protein (meat and dairy), refined sugars, and starches (grains) leave a residue ash that is more acid forming in the body than "Live" raw fruits and vegetables.

10. Naturally-occurring, live, raw organic plant-based foods, uncooked and unprocessed, provide the greatest alkaline internal biologic environment.

WELLNESS MASTERY™ ACTION

Must Do!

1. Practice deep breathing exercises 2 to 3 times per day, in order to raise the body pH.

2. Drink plenty of quality water daily to help cleanse the body and eliminate neutralized and eliminate toxins.

3. Eat more fresh, live, raw (uncooked and unprocessed) organic fruits and vegetables.

4. Squeeze fresh organic lemon juice (highly alkalizing) in drinking water and on all foods.

5. Drink one fresh raw organic fruit juice (watermelon) in the early morning to cleanse, hydrate and alkalize to body.

6. Drink one fresh raw organic vegetable juice in the late morning or early afternoon to hydrate, nourish, and alkalize the body.

7. Take acid-buffering vitamin C and acid-buffering mineral supplements (sodium, potassium, calcium, and magnesium) daily to increase your body's alkaline reserves.

8. Participate in some form of cardiovascular activity (e.g. walking, swimming, rowing, rebound trampoline) to get your heart rate up for 20 to 30 minutes a day, every day.

9. Eat more live, raw foods and less cooked and processed foods.

10. Meditate for 10 to 20 minutes daily as an effective stress reduction program.

Chapter Eleven

Principle #8

Hormone Balance

Correct Hormone Imbalances

Why Are Hormones So Important?

Everything that happens in your body—your ability to see, hear, smell, taste, touch, digest food, circulate blood, make love, move, and think—is the result of a series of chemical reactions controlled by electrical impulses. All metabolic processes of the body are mediated by chemicals. Therefore, any chemical imbalance contributes to the creation and perpetuation of mental, emotional, and physical health problems.

Hormones, a special class of chemicals produced by the endocrine glands and released directly into the blood stream, are the master chemicals that regulate all other chemical reactions and cellular activity in the body. The word "hormone" means "to excite," and that is exactly what hormones do. Hormones are the chemical messengers that stimulate the body's ability to deal with constant change.

One example of hormones at work is how sugar gets from the food we eat into the form of glucose and then into the cell. Every cell in the body requires glucose (a sugar) for energy to function. When you eat a carbohydrate it is broken down in the digestive tract into glucose and is then absorbed into the blood stream. Through a series of neuro-chemical processes this increase of glucose in the blood "excites" the pancreas and induces it to produce the hormone insulin. Insulin then activates specific receptor sites on the cell's outer membranes that transport the glucose into the cell. Amazingly, the pancreas only produces and releases the exact amount of insulin it needs to get the job done, no more or no less than what is required. Although the pancreas has the ability to produce both insulin and glucagon—both of which work in harmonious tandem to regulate sugar metabolism and the amount of glucose in the blood—in this instance only the pancreas' ability to produce and release additional insulin is "excited."

The hormone insulin is also responsible for transporting proteins, fats, and sugars into cells and lowering blood glucose levels. In contrast, the hormone glucagon is responsible, through activity of the liver, for raising blood glucose levels. Insulin also promotes the conversion of excess sugar into fats for fat storage, while glucagon stimulates the breakdown of glycogen, the stored form of glucose, fats, and proteins for energy.

YOUR ENDOCRINE SYSTEM & HORMONES

Hormones, the master chemicals of the body, are produced and secreted by the various endocrine glands. Working together, hormones regulate every chemical reaction that happens in the body. There are nine master glands that comprise the endocrine system, and each one of these glands has a specific function (see Figure 11-1: The Endocrine Glands).

Collectively the endocrine glands, through hormone activity, work in harmony to maintain biochemical and physiological balance in the body. Each gland manufactures and releases a precise amount of a specific hormone when instructed by the brain to do so. The endocrine system is an auto-regulated system that keeps itself in constant balance through an elaborate and sophisticated information feedback network.

In addition to specific endocrine glands, we also have: patches of glandular tissue on organs, such as the heart and intestines, that release hormones; some individual cells, such as those in the immune system, that release hormone-like substances called parahormones; and the brain and nerves, that release neurotransmitters that also act as hormones. Endocrine glands and other tissue produce more than 200 different types of hormones that regulate every chemical reaction in the body to maintain homeostasis.

ENDOCRINE GLANDS

The endocrine glands (and associated primary hormones) that make up your endocrine system include:

Hypothalamus (hypothalamic releasing factors) – a grape-size structure located in your brain that is considered the "master gland" that regulates the activity of all other glands, especially the pituitary gland, regarding regulation of your body temperature, biological rhythms, water balance, and emotions.

Pineal (melatonin) – a gland located in your brain that regulates your "biological clock" and your wake/sleep cycles.

Pituitary (anterior pituitary—growth hormone, and posterior pituitary—vasopressin and oxytocin) – a pea-sized gland located in your brain that secretes at least nine major hormones, including hormones that stimulate your thyroid.

Thyroid (thyroxine, triiodothyronine, and calcitonin) – a butterfly-shaped gland located in your neck that regulates your metabolic rate and energy production in every cell in your body. It tells your body how fast to work and use energy.

Parathyroid (parathormone) – a gland located near your thyroid that helps regulate calcium balance throughout your body. It is involved in the ongoing process of bone remodeling, the breaking down and building of bone tissue.

Thymus (T-lymphocyte) – a gland located at the base of the neck that is active in establishing immune response in infants.

Adrenal (cortisol, aldosterone, DHEA, epinephrine, and nor-epinephrine) – small pyramid-shaped glands located on top of each kidney. Nicknamed the "stress glands" because during times of stress they activate the "fight-or-flight" response.

Pancreas (insulin and glucagon) – a gland organ located near your stomach and small intestines that regulates blood sugar levels.

Ovaries and **Testicles** (estrogen, progesterone, and testosterone)– the female and male sex glands that regulate reproductive-related activities.

Your endocrine glands and their associated hormone production may be adversely affected by any number of mental, emotional, or physical factors (including over-exertion, lack of sleep, improper nutrition, pharmaceutical drugs, and foreign chemicals), When your body is under stress and you are experiencing the chemical imbalance that is caused by stress, your endocrine glands will initially ramp up activity to produce and

FIGURE 11-1

THE ENDOCRINE GLANDS

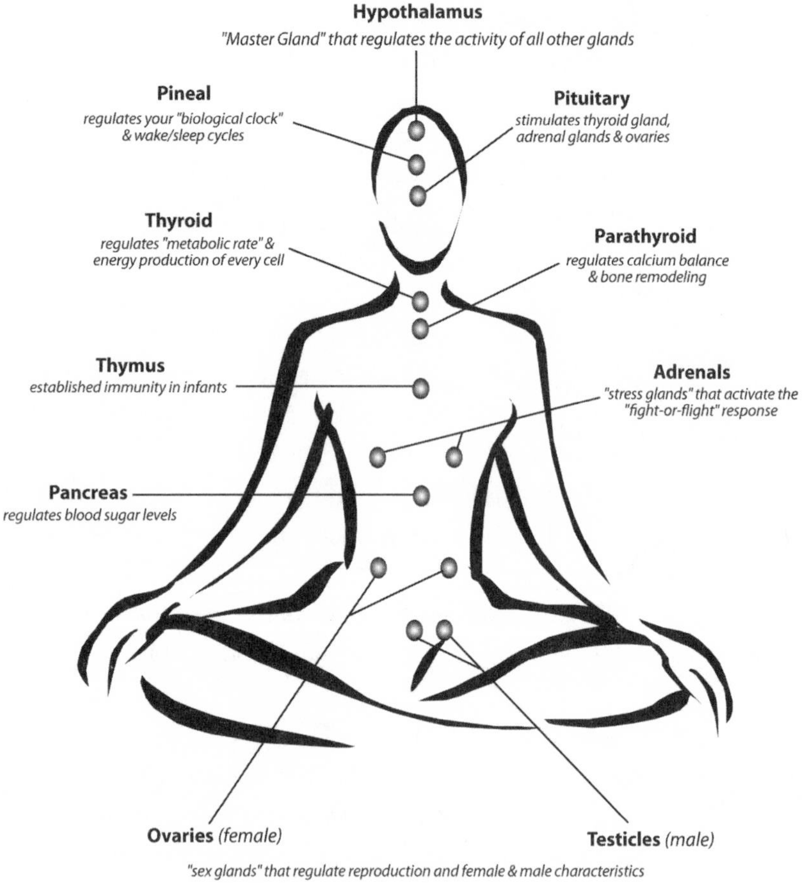

Hypothalamus
"Master Gland" that regulates the activity of all other glands

Pineal
regulates your "biological clock" & wake/sleep cycles

Pituitary
stimulates thyroid gland, adrenal glands & ovaries

Thyroid
regulates "metabolic rate" & energy production of every cell

Parathyroid
regulates calcium balance & bone remodeling

Thymus
established immunity in infants

Adrenals
"stress glands" that activate the "fight-or-flight" response

Pancreas
regulates blood sugar levels

Ovaries *(female)*

Testicles *(male)*

"sex glands" that regulate reproduction and female & male characteristics

secrete hormones in an attempt meet the challenge of the stress and bring your body back into a state of chemical homeostasis.

When stress—mental, emotional, or physical—becomes chronic, these same glands that initially ramped up to meet the short-term demand eventually fatigue due to continual overexertion. Once they fatigue, their hormone-producing ability starts to drop. Once hormone production drops you will start to experience the symptoms of hormone and chemical imbalances. Two of the most common health conditions that affect endocrine/ hormone balance are stress and blood sugar metabolism. Stress affects the adrenal gland, while blood sugar metabolism issues are typically associated with thyroid imbalances.

THE STRESS & ADRENAL CONNECTION

Stress, considered the number one risk factor associated with all chronic degenerative diseases, triggers a cascade of hormone releases by several endocrine glands. Under stress, the hypothalamus, tucked in the center of the brain, releases corticotrophin-releasing hormone (CRH). CRH stimulates the pituitary gland to release adrenocorticotropic hormone (ACTH). ACTH in turn prompts the adrenal glands to release cortisol, considered to be the major stress hormone.

At the same time the adrenal glands are pumping out cortisol, they are simultaneously releasing two other hormones, epinephrine and norepinephrine, that activate the fight-or-flight responses. Although epinephrine and norepinephrine activate this stress response, their effects are short-lived, lasting for only a few brief moments. The most damaging health effects come from cortisol, because it promotes more long-lasting responses to stressors.

Excess cortisol: suppresses your immune response, making you more susceptible to colds, flus, and infections; increases your risk of high blood pressure and heart disease; is associated with insulin resistance and Type 2 diabetes; and affects the hippocampus area of the brain that is responsible for memory recall of names, faces, words, and dates.

The Adrenal "Fight-or-Flight" Response

The human body has the ability, through the release of cortisol, to divert its energy resources, in times of perceived danger, to enhance physical performance for short periods of time. This mechanism is part of the human body's evolutionary blueprint designed to help humans deal with immediate physical danger through enhanced physical performance.

For example, early humans, who existed in a totally untamed natural environment and lived among the beasts, may have been confronted at any moment by a hungry carnivorous animal, such as a saber-toothed tiger. At that precise moment of heightened excitement, their body, through an elaborate chain of hormonal chemical events, immediately diverted it resources to enhance muscular performance, thus improving the ability to fight or run away.

A stressful event stimulates the adrenal glands to produce more of the hormone cortisol, as well as epinephrine and nor-epinephrine. Additional sympathetic nervous system responses and a cascade of other chemical reactions, all designed to instantaneously enhance physical performance, are stimulated by this elevated level of cortisol and the release of epinephrine and norepinephrine into the bloodstream. For example, as a result of a stressful event the liver will start converting glycogen into glucose to provide the body with more blood sugar for energy, and blood flow will be diverted from the interior organs of the body to the muscles, instantly providing more oxygen and glucose for increased energy for physical activity.

As exemplified in the confrontation with the saber-toothed tiger, human physiology evolved over thousands of years with this enhanced capability for "on-demand" peak performance based upon dramatic changes in body chemistry. Although extremely beneficial when needed, this design feature was meant for short-term application only!

For early humans, whose life was about day-to-day physical survival in a potentially harsh and unforgiving environment, it appears that the greatest source of stress was physical and short-term. Today's stress is usually a combination of physical, mental, emotional, and environmental, and it is long-term. Table 11-1: Stress Inventory Test is an adaptation from the stress inventory scale developed by Holmes and Rahe to investigate the relationship between social readjustment, stress, and susceptibility to illness. They found that a person with a score of 200 to 250 during a one-year period has a 50% chance of developing illness or health change. With a score of 300 or more, a person's chances increase to 80%. The stress inventory scale is reprinted from the *Journal of Psychosomatic Research*, Volume 11, T. H. Holmes and R. H. Rahe, "The social readjustment rating scale", 1967, with permission from Elsevier.

Look over the events listed in Table 11-1: Stress Inventory Test. Place a check in the box if you have experienced this event within the last twelve months. Then tabulate the results for a total score and interpretation.

TABLE 11-1

STRESS INVENTORY TEST

Instructions: Check off each event that you have experienced in the last 12 months. Then add up the numerical values to arrive at a total score.

- ❑ 1. Death of a spouse (100)
- ❑ 2. Divorce (72)
- ❑ 3. Marital separation (65)
- ❑ 4. Death of a close family member (63)
- ❑ 5. Personal injury or illness (53)
- ❑ 6. Marriage (50)
- ❑ 7. Marital reconciliation (45)
- ❑ 8. Change in health of family member (44)
- ❑ 9. Pregnancy (40)
- ❑ 10. Gain of new family member (39)
- ❑ 11. Job change (38)
- ❑ 12. Change in financial status (37)
- ❑ 13. Death of a close friend (36)
- ❑ 14. Increase in arguments with significant other (35)
- ❑ 15. Mortgage loan for major purchase (home, etc.) (31)
- ❑ 16. Foreclosure of mortgage or loan (30)
- ❑ 17. Change in responsibilities of your job (29)
- ❑ 18. Son or daughter leaving home (29)
- ❑ 19. Trouble with in-laws (29)
- ❑ 20. Outstanding personal achievement (28)
- ❑ 21. Spouse begins or stops work outside the home (26)

❑   22. Revision of personal habits (24)

❑   23. Trouble with boss (23)

❑   24. Change in work hours or conditions (20)

❑   25. Change in residence (20)

❑   26. Change in sleeping habits (16)

❑   27. Change in eating habits (15)

❑   28. Vacation (13)

❑   29. Christmas (12)

❑   30. Minor violations of the law (11)

Total: _____

Interpretation: Drs. Holmes and Rahe have shown the relationship between recent life changes (exposure to stressors) and future illness. Listed below are the score categories and the related probability of illness for a person in that range. It is estimated that it will take 1 year to replenish the energy used to adjust to any of the changes described in the scale.

0-149	**no significant problem**	
150-199	**mild stress**	**35% chance of illness**
200-299	**moderate stress**	**50% chance of illness**
300+	**major stress**	**80% chance of illness**

It is the long-term unrelenting stress that creates a chronic condition. Chronic stress causes the adrenal glands to work beyond their intended design and capacity. During extended periods of chronic stress the adrenal glands are forced to work overtime.

When any gland or organ of the body is forced to work overtime for a long enough period of time, it eventually reaches a point of failure and begins to shut down. Overworked adrenal glands initially increase cortisol production, a state of hyper-function, in an attempt to meet the excess demand, then eventually fatigue and under-produce cortisol, a state of hypo-function, and in extreme cases shut down all together.

The Stress & Blood Sugar Connection

Along with the typical adrenal response to stress there is also a blood sugar response to stress. Triggered by stress, the adrenal glands release cortisol while at the same time additional glucose is released into the blood through a series of chemical reactions by the liver. Glucose is the primary and most easily converted energy fuel available to all cells. The release of additional cortisol and glucose stimulates the pancreas to release additional insulin into the blood stream.

Every cell has specialized insulin receptor sites that are responsible for glucose uptake by the cells. When insulin binds to insulin receptor sites, the mechanism is enabled for transporting glucose from the bloodstream across the cell membrane and into the cell to be used as fuel for energy. The net effect of additional glucose and insulin in the blood is greater glucose uptake by the cells, for use as additional energy. In the absence of insulin or when insulin receptor sites are not activated, glucose cannot be transported into the cell to be used for energy production . . . with one exception: during physical activity. During physical activity, muscle cells have the ability to uptake glucose in the absence of insulin. This is the reason that daily physical activity is a critical and primary treatment strategy for reversing Type 2 diabetes.

Under normal conditions, the more insulin available in the body, the more receptor sites can be activated to bring more glucose into the cell. More glucose into the cell means greater energy potential. This mechanism provides the cell with a greater source of fuel to create even more energy for greater physical performance.

The problem begins when prolonged cortisol output, caused by chronic stress, leads to prolonged insulin output, which eventually causes desensitization of the insulin receptor sites on the target cells. Once this happens the cells lose their ability to uptake glucose from the blood as fuel for energy production. This constant increase in blood sugar levels and subsequent increase in insulin secretion contributes to insulin insensitivity (when insulin receptor sites deactivate) and hyperglycemia (increased blood sugar), both symptoms of a pre-diabetic state. In this way chronic stress can contribute to the development of diabetes.

"On-demand" enhanced physical performance was a great survival advantage in the time of early humanity. But today's technologically-based culture requires more brain and less brawn. We live in an information age, where the brain is exercised more than the body. In today's world, unless you are a professional or high-performance athlete, your survival and success is predicated more on your intellectual abilities than on your physical prowess. At the same time that we have become less physically active, emotional and mental stress appear to be on the rise. This is a dangerous combination to contend with on our journey to creating optimal health.

THE THYROID & DIABETES CONNECTION

There are two types of diabetes: Type 1 or juvenile-onset/insulin-dependent and Type 2 or adult-onset. Type 1 diabetes is due to a malfunction in the pancreas' ability to produce adequate insulin, which typically shows up during infancy or early adolescence. On the other hand, Type 2 diabetes is due to either "insulin resistance," the desensitization of insulin receptor sites on the cells, or the "absent first-phase insulin release," where the initial release of insulin in response to elevated blood sugar is impaired (a consequence of a lifestyle issue: prolonged ingestion of large amounts of refined sugar). As of this writing, Type 2 diabetes is the 6th leading and the fastest-growing cause of premature death among baby-boomers and seniors in the U.S. It is *the* number one disorder of blood sugar metabolism.

In Type 2 diabetes the cells' ability to uptake glucose from the blood for energy has been compromised, even though there may be enough glucose in the blood stream. Adult-onset diabetes is attributed to two important factors: (1) a lack of adequate and regular physical activity, and (2) a poor diet typically consisting of long-term consumption of excessive refined sugar and processed carbohydrates in combination with low and poor-quality fat intake. The most important of these two risk factors for Type 2 diabetes is not how much sugar you eat, but how much extra fat you are carrying around. It appears that weighing too much and moving too little makes our cells more insulin resistant.

The lack of adequate and ongoing physical activity leads to a gradual slowdown in body metabolism; we become less efficient at burning calories, and the excess intake of processed sugar, processed carbohydrates, and greater calories consumed leads to greater fat storage in the body. Our lack of awareness of this inactivity, diet and blood sugar metabolism connection may compromise our ability to accurately diagnose and effectively treat adult-onset diabetes.

THE THYROID & BODY ENERGY CONNECTION

The thyroid produces hormones that affect energy production in every cell of the body. The main hormone secreted by the thyroid gland is thyroxine (T4). T4 is the inactive pre-hormone form that is protein bound in the bloodstream until acted upon by enzymes, primarily in the liver, and converted to triiodothyronine (T3), the active form of the hormone that is responsible for 90 percent of thyroid action in the body.

The most common thyroid condition is an under-active thyroid, hypothyroidism. Some of the symptoms of hypothyroidism include difficulty getting out of bed in the morning, general drowsiness, apathy, loss of enthusiasm, "sluggish" thinking, headaches, loss of interest in sex, unexplained weight gain, and difficulty losing weight. In contrast, some of the symptoms of an over-active thyroid, hyperthyroidism, include protruding eyes, anxiety, insomnia, mood swings, elevated blood pressure, unexplained weight loss, and difficulty gaining weight. Even if your body makes enough T4, chronic stress, nutritional deficiencies, certain medications, and imbalances in estrogen levels can inhibit the conversion of T4 to T3.

OTHER WAYS WE MESS UP OUR HORMONE BALANCE

Smoking drains estrogen levels in women, both before and after menopause. Studies show that women who smoke experience menopause one to two years earlier than those who don't, and in another study women who smoke were shown to have two to four times more risk of breaking a bone due to osteoporosis. Numerous research studies link smoking with increased risk of developing breast, ovarian, and cervical cancer in women, as well as lung cancer in both men and women.

Caffeine, found in coffee, tea, soft drinks, "power drinks," diet aids, and many medications, interferes with the activity of the brain chemical called adenosine. Adenosine is a neurotransmitter that normally slows the activity of other neurotransmitters, in order to maintain brain activity balance. Caffeine blocks adenosine from connecting with the adenosine receptor sites on brain cells.

Caffeine also speeds up brain activity, causing ongoing uncontrolled firing of neurons that transmit nerve impulses. This causes the pituitary gland, also located in the brain, to secrete ACTH (adrenocorticotropic hormone), which signals the adrenal glands to release more cortisol, a stress hormone. The sympathetic nervous system is then activated to release epinephrine and nor-epinephrine, two more stress hormones, that activate the fight-or-flight response, including an increase in heart rate and blood pressure.

It is believed that caffeine can also reduce nighttime levels of melatonin, the light-sensitive hormone produced by the pineal gland, thus interfering with the biological clock and natural sleep/wake cycle. Any form of sleep deprivation causes additional physical, psychological, and emotional stress on the body.

Alcohol can also be a problem. Some experts say one drink of alcohol per day is okay (when one drink equals one 12-ounce can of beer, one 5-ounce glass of wine, or a mixed drink containing 1.5 ounces of 80-proof alcohol), but consume anything more than one drink per day and any supposed health benefits disappear. Chronic heavy drinking, which increases estrogen levels, raises the risk of breast cancer in women. It is believed that alcohol disrupts bone remodeling by interfering with the parathyroid (PTH) and calcitonin hormones involved with the bone remodeling process. Since alcohol acts like a concentrated sugar in the body, it can adversely affect blood sugar metabolism and is believed to affect insulin secretion and insulin resistance, both significant factors in Type 2 diabetes.

Medications that are commonly prescribed to treat conditions such as allergies and asthma, high blood pressure, depression, and infections also alter hormone balances.

Pesticides, developed to kill insect pests, are toxic concentrated chemicals that are sprayed on commercially-grown fruits and vegetables as well as dairy and beef cattle, chicken, and hogs in large industrial food raising operations. Some pesticides are what we call hormonally active agents (HAAs) or xenoestrogens. These xenoestrogens mimic the action of the female and male hormones (estrogens and androgens) that alter natural human hormone function and balance.

Herbicides, developed to kill unwanted plants, are toxic concentrated chemicals that are sprayed on commercially-grown fruits and vegetables. Certain herbicides cause a variety of health effects, ranging from skin rashes to death. Problems can arise from: improper application resulting in direct contact with field workers; inhalation of aerial sprays; consumption of herbicide-contaminated food; and contact with residual soil contamination. Due to surface runoff, herbicides can contaminate distant surface waters, thereby creating another pathway of ingestion when we drink these waters. Some of the herbicides in use are known to be mutagenic, carcinogenic, or teratogenic (able to disturb the growth and development of an embryo or fetus).

Recombinant bovine growth hormone (rBGH) is given to dairy cattle to increase milk production. More than 90% of all beef cattle in the United States receive a combination of up to three naturally-occurring and three manmade hormones: estradiol, progesterone, testosterone, trenbolone acetate, zeranol, and melengestrol acetate. Why? To fatten them up quickly. Think about it. The rBGH given to dairy cattle ends up in the milk and is consumed by us. The hormones given to beef cattle, hogs, chickens, turkeys, and farm-raised fish to fatten them up remain in the meat after the animals are slaughtered to be consumed by the public. So, what do you think the consequence might be for humans who are consuming the same hormones used to fatten up beef cattle, hogs, chickens, turkeys, and farm-raised fish? These hormones also raise estrogen levels, which have been associated with increased risk of developing cancer in both men and women.

EMOTIONS & THE HORMONE CONNECTION

Your emotions also stimulate hormone activity in your body. Your limbic system, located in the brain, is considered the "Feeling Center" between your ears. It is made up of two almond-shaped structures, called the amygdala. Computerized imaging techniques have identified the amygdala as the area of the brain that is activated when anger or fear is registered, while another part of the brain, the nucleus accumbens, lights up when registering the sensations of pleasure, happiness, and comfort.

When any of the five sense organs (eyes, ears, nose, mouth, and skin) are stimulated the sensations register in the amygdala and nucleus accumbens areas of the brain, while the emotional information simultaneously accesses the memory and thinking areas of the brain. This complex series of events triggers hormone release and electrical discharges that are targeted toward different organs in the body, which produces the physiological reaction we associate with whatever we are feeling, such as sweaty palms or "butterflies" in the stomach when we are feeling nervous or anxious.

Overworked Endocrine Glands

Any organ system of your body that is continually overworked eventually breaks down. This includes your endocrine glands. The typical pattern of endocrine gland failure is (1) initial gland hyper-activity for greater hormone production due to chronic over-stimulation, followed by (2) gland hypo-activity with under-production of hormones due to exhaustion and subsequent failure.

With hormone imbalances that are due to endocrine gland malfunction, management of the associated health conditions warrant special nutritional consideration based upon the specific endocrine glands involved. The stress/adrenal and diabetes/thyroid connections previously discussed are some examples of how different systems in the body contribute to the chemical imbalances that lead to chronic degenerative disease conditions.

Improving Your Hormone Balance

The things that whack your hormone balance include prolonged mental and emotional stress, lack of adequate sleep, exposure to different frequencies of electromagnetic energy from devices such as cell phones and computers, exposure to unnatural light, physical inactivity, unhealthy eating, the consumption of caffeine, nicotine, alcohol, medication, pesticides, and the synthetic hormones and other chemicals in our food supply. If stress is the #1 culprit, the simplest and most effective strategies for balancing your hormones include stress-reduction activities such as laughter, deep breathing exercises, meditation, yoga, relaxation techniques, visualization techniques, and communing with nature. Go ahead, treat yourself to a weekly massage!

Other strategies for maintaining proper hormonal balance include limiting or giving up caffeine, nicotine, and alcohol intake. When it comes to nutrition, stick with the three fundamental basics for creating optimal health: eat more live, raw, foods and less cooked and processed foods; eat more plant life (fruits, vegetables, nuts, and seeds) and less animal products (meat, dairy); eat more organically-grown products and less commercially-grown. In addition, eat only *quality* protein, *quality* fats, and *quality* carbohydrates. Get healthy and you won't need the medications!

WELLNESS MASTERY™ SUMMARY

Must Know!

1. Every function of the body is regulated by chemical reactions and electrical impulses.

2. Hormones are the master chemicals that regulate all other chemical reactions.

3. Hormones are produced by nine endocrine glands throughout the body.

4. When the endocrine system malfunctions, your body experiences physical health symptoms that are a result of chemical imbalances caused by hormone imbalances.

5. Optimal health cannot be achieved or maintained in the presence of hormone imbalance.

6. Chronic stress eventually leads to hormone imbalances in the body.

7. The adrenal glands are the primary glands that take a hit due to prolonged mental, emotional, and physical stress.

8. Harmful chemicals (pharmaceutical drugs, pesticide, herbicides, and industrial chemicals) can cause hormone imbalances in the body.

9. Endocrine glands will make adjustments in hormone production to correct chemical imbalances in the body for as long as possible, even at their own expense.

10. When continually overworked for prolonged periods of time, any gland, organ, or system of the body will eventually fatigue and fail.

WELLNESS MASTERY™ ACTION

1. Consider the possibility of an undiagnosed hormonal imbalance (adrenal, thyroid, and male or female) if you are experiencing a chronic health problem that is difficult to treat or does not resolve itself with standard nutritional treatment protocols.

2. Consider the possibility of adrenal gland involvement if you are experiencing sleep disorders or having difficulty losing excess weight.

3. Consider the possibility of adrenal gland malfunction if you have been diagnosed with any of the blood-sugar metabolism disorders (hypoglycemia, hyperglycemia, and diabetes).

4. Consider a natural alternative treatment to Hormone Replacement Therapy (HRT) for the symptoms of menopause.

5. Participate in daily physical activity to de-stress the body.

6. Meditate for 10 to 20 minutes each day as a stress reduction therapy.

7. Practice yoga 2 to 3 times per week for 30 to 60 minutes per session. There are specific Yoga positions that stimulate different glands and organs of the body.

8. Eat fresh, live, raw, organic foods to nourish the glands of the endocrine system.

9. Consider a natural nutritional supplement regimen (herbs, vitamins, and minerals) to nourish malfunctioning glands, in lieu of prescription medications to treat glandular conditions.

10. Reduce or eliminate caffeine, alcohol, and tobacco consumption. These substances contribute to chemical imbalances in the body that prevent optimal health. Also consider reducing or eliminating prescription and non-prescription medication consumption, with the help of, or under the care of, a physician familiar with natural remedies.

CHAPTER TWELVE

PRINCIPLE #9

Nature's Nutrition

EAT "LIVE" FOOD

All food is medicine, and the best food is the best medicine.
—**Hippocrates,** Father of Medicine

WHAT TO EAT?

Overfed and undernourished. As a society we suffer from "over-consumption malnutrition." What should we eat? The obvious answer is whatever keeps the body healthy. Maybe the more appropriate question should be, "Based upon how we are designed by nature and how our digestion system works, what are we intended to eat?" There are many choices. Humans have been classified by anthropologists as omnivores, a species that eats both plant and animal—a trait that has provided humans the versatility to survive, adapt to many environments, and manipulate the food chain.

Humans, their bodies, and their digestive tracts—evolved on this planet over the course of tens of thousands of years within the context of the earth's natural environment. This early natural environment was free from any synthetic or artificial substances, manmade poisons, or environmental toxins, including unnatural sources of light, sound, and electromagnetic energy. In fact, it has only been in the last few hundred years of the history of humans on the planet that humanity has unleashed into the environment factors that are destructive to health and the human condition. In the most recent of times, humans have continued to move even further away from the food choices, lifestyles, and behaviors that are aligned with the wisdom of nature.

Many factors harmful to health have been unleashed by humans into our world without a complete understanding of, or a responsibility to, the impact and consequences of such actions on the environment—including our own health. In understanding how our bodies function as nature intended, and in letting that awareness guide our health and eating decisions, we possess all we need to know to be disease-free and create optimal health. Our experience of life is the sum total of all of our actions; every action we take on this planet either supports life and health, or does not. When it comes to creating health and quality of life there is no middle of the road, no gray zone.

HUMAN—DESIGNED BY NATURE!

Everything in nature, as in the universe, has meaning and purpose. Everything in nature has a design that is intimately and directly related to its function and optimal performance. With an understanding of how the body works as nature intended, we stand a better chance of creating optimal health and well-being, and, through mindful and responsible action, preventing most illness and disease.

Every part of the human digestive tract—every organ and every cell—has a specific design, purpose, and function, as programmed in our genetic profile (which has evolved over the history of humankind). By studying the human animal in relation to other animals in the natural setting we can arrive at an accurate picture of what food nature may have intended, or not intended, for human consumption.

When we study the performance, design features, and habits of animals that live in a purely natural setting we gain insight into human existence and health requirements as well. Which animals are genetically the most similar to humans? The higher primates, apes and chimpanzees. Humans and primates are 99% genetically identical. So, what are the similarities? What can we learn from this? All the bones in the skeletons of the higher primates and humans correspond to each other. The chemical structure of the blood corresponds. The nerves, brain, liver, skin, and hair are all the same. Unlike any other animal, the length of the umbilical cords is the same. Only humans and apes have mammary glands that are located on the chest; all other mammals have breasts located on the abdomen. Primates and humans are the only species with opposing thumbs that enable the hands to have the ability to grasp. Our teeth (arrangement, number, structure, and size) are identical to that of primates. Our digestive tracts are similar. What do these higher primates eat? They eat mostly plants.

MAN: MEAT EATER OR PLANT EATER?

Based upon the power and intelligence that designed human beings, are we intended to eat meat, or plants, or both? We know from anthropological findings that early humanity, 40,000 years ago during the Paleolithic period, was a hunter/gatherer: our ancestors hunted wild game and gathered wild plants. Twenty thousand-year-old Cro-Magnon cave paintings show bison with spears piercing their chests and flanks. The 10,000-year-old fossil remains of 300 buffalo were excavated at an archeological site near the Arikaree River in Colorado. These buffalo were trapped by being driven down sloping ice banks into a streambed filled with drifts of snow, where they were slaughtered and their bones arranged in an orderly fashion . . . suggesting that the Paleoindians may have had an assembly line for butchering.

We also know that early humans lived in small, semi-nomadic bands that moved with the seasons, following wild game, water, and wild, uncultivated vegetation. Research indicates that with few exceptions, a higher percentage of the food consumed by early humans came from what was gathered rather than from what was hunted.

So here's the million dollar question: are humans designed to eat meat, plants, or both? It's true that hunting and gathering was the context in which humans evolved. But just because early humans hunted and ate meat, are we to deduce that animal flesh is what humans are intended to eat?

Granted, the wild game consumed by early humans was organic in the purest sense: hormone-free, antibiotic-free, totally chemical-free, a pure grazer or carnivore, and of course, never corn fed. As compared to the animal flesh that we eat today, this wild game was also lower in fat and provided a higher concentration of omega 3 essential fatty acid. As was pointed out in *The Paleolithic Prescription: A Program of Diet and a Design for Living*, by S. Boyd Eaton, M.D., Marjorie Shostak, and Melvin Konner, M.D., Ph.D. if we look at the evolution of humans over time, we find that vastly more generations have depended on hunting and gathering than on any other way of life. If you compare the hunting/gathering period of about 2,000,000 years to agriculture (about 10,000 years), industrial manufacturing (about 200 years), and computer technology (about 30 years), you'll see that hunting/gathering was the context in which humans evolved.

Because of this evolutionary context we must therefore also take into consideration what possible genetic adaptations may have transpired due to the natural selection process that favored this eating behavior. But the question remains, in the ideal, if there is an ideal, are humans really designed as omnivores, part carnivore (meat-eating) and part herbivore (plant-eating)? Also consider that humans are the only animal on the planet that manipulate food selections. Why? Because we can.

In a publication entitled *What's Wrong with Eating Meat?*, the author, Vistara Parham, points out several thought-provoking differences between carnivores and humans, as well as the similarities between herbivores and humans. Sharp front incisors and canine teeth combined with an exceptionally strong jaw are found in carnivorous species. Why? Having sharp front teeth makes catching, killing and ripping animal flesh easier in the wild. On the other hand, herbivores and humans both possess well-developed flat back molars that are ideally suited for grinding plant foods.

Humans and most plant-eating animals also have well-developed salivary glands, alkaline saliva, and secrete ptyalin (a starch-splitting enzyme) in the saliva. This design is perfectly suited for predigesting grains, tubers, and other vegetable matter. Because cats and other carnivores do not have grinding teeth and therefore do not chew their food, large pieces of non-predigested flesh are gulped down and enter the stomach. This explains why the hydrochloric acid concentration in the stomach of carnivores is 10 to 20 times stronger than in herbivores. Hydrochloric acid is quite effective at breaking down the fibers of connective tissue and muscle that is found in this non-predigested meat. In comparison, humans, like the plant eaters, produce only weak amounts of stomach acid. The primary purpose of stomach acid in humans is to lower the pH in the stomach in order to facilitate enzyme activity and convert pepsinogen into pepsin for breaking down protein.

Claws, another carnivorous characteristic, are not found in herbivores or humans. Claws are an asset for meat-eating hunters, but are of little use to plant eaters. Carnivores do not possess skin pores for the release of body heat; they perspire through their mouths, while breathing or panting. In contrast, herbivores utilize millions of porous openings in the surface of the skin as a mechanism for releasing body heat.

Perhaps the most striking difference between flesh eaters and plant eaters is the length of the intestinal tract. Herbivores and humans have intestinal tract lengths of 10 to 12 times trunk length (i.e., distance between the base of the neck at the shoulder and the bottom of the pelvis); carnivores have intestinal tracts that are only 3 times their trunk length. Why? A shorter digestive tract means shorter transit time. A shorter transit time minimizes the putrefaction potential (rotting) of the slower-moving meat matter that is more easily broken down by digestive microflora in the gut due to lower water content.

In humans, slow-moving cooked and dehydrated animal protein clogs the colon. Placing cooked meat into the longer human digestive tract means longer intestinal exposure time to harmful bacteria and their more harmful waste-product toxins. Longer digestive tracts, possessed by plant-eaters and humans, are more ideally suited for plant food breakdown, which needs more gut transit time to absorb nutrients from rapidly-moving (due to higher water content), fiber-filled plant foods. This comparison is summarized in Table 12-1: Similarities and Differences between Carnivores, Herbivores, and Man.

TABLE 12-1

SIMILARITIES AND DIFFERENCES BETWEEN

CARNIVORES, HERBIVORES, AND MAN

CARNIVORES (MEAT EATERS)	HERBIVORES (PLANT EATERS)	MAN (OMNIVORE)
Claws	No Claws	No Claws
Sharp pointed front teeth	No sharp pointed front teeth	No sharp pointed front teeth
No flat back molar teeth	Flat back molar teeth	Flat back molar teeth
No pores on skin	Pores on skin	Pores on skin
Small salivary glands	Well developed salivary glands	Well developed salivary glands
Acid saliva	Alkaline saliva	Alkaline saliva
No ptyalin* in saliva	Ptyalin* in saliva	Ptyalin* in saliva
High hydrochloric acid concentration in stomach	Hydrochloric acid in stomach 1/20th the concentration of meat eaters'	Hydrochloric acid in stomach 1/20th the concentration of meat eaters'
Short intestinal tract - 3 times trunk length	Long intestinal tract - 10-12 times trunk length	Long intestinal tract - 12 times trunk length

*Ptyalin is a digestive enzyme for breaking down starches (carbohydrates).

Source:
What's Wrong with Eating Meat? by Vistara Parham,
PCAP Publications, Corona, New York, 1981, pp.3-11.
Reprinted with permission.

Looking at other physical attributes of humans, in the context of the wild natural environment and in comparison to typical carnivores in the same setting, we find that humans are slower, weaker, have poorer night vision, less peripheral vision, a less acute sense of smell, and inferior hearing. It would appear that humans are better equipped for gathering and digesting vegetation than hunting and eating meat. Just because early humans *became* hunters doesn't qualify the condition as being in alignment with nature's original intention. Were we meant to eat meat, or was this the first in a series of many acquired behavioral aberrations departing from nature's design, even though these habits may have been acquired and adopted for survival purposes? So, again the question is posed: although we can eat meat, were we intended to do so? What do you think?

ANIMAL FLESH VS. PLANT LIFE

When we compare a multitude of live, raw (uncooked and unrefined) foods across a variety of nutritional content parameters (calorie composition, vitamin, and mineral) we discover that raw animal flesh is higher in calories, higher in fat content, higher in protein, lower in complex carbohydrates, lower or non-existent in essential vitamins and minerals, and higher in cholesterol than unprocessed plant foods; raw animal flesh is also void of fiber. In comparison, unprocessed plant foods are lower in calories, lower in fat, lower in protein, higher in complex carbohydrates, higher in essential vitamins and mineral, void of cholesterol, and rich in fiber.

THE IMPORTANCE OF ENZYMES

What are enzymes? Why are enzymes important to digestion and critical for optimal health? To understand the significance of enzymes to optimal health we must first understand the concept of enzymes, the value of enzymatic action, and the process of digestion. It is probably easiest to explain that there are three types of enzymes necessary for optimal health and wellness. Without an adequate enzyme supply in any one of these areas, the body will eventually experience health problems. Why? Earlier we described the functioning of the human body as a series of chemical reactions controlled by electrical impulses. Enzymes are the critical ingredients, along with certain vitamins, that facilitate or mediate every chemical reaction in the body. In the absence of enzymes, chemical reactions come to a standstill. In the absence of enzymes, life ceases to exist.

THE POTTENGER CAT STUDY

What we know about the value of enzymes in human digestion and optimal health we owe to the research work of Dr. Francis Pottenger, a medical research scientist. Between 1932 and 1942, Dr. Pottenger conducted a feeding experiment to determine the effects of heat-processed food on cats. His ten-year study was prompted by the high mortality he was experiencing among his laboratory cats that underwent adrenalectomies (surgical removal of the adrenal glands) for use in standardizing the hormone content of the adrenal extract he was making.

He created this feeding study because he wanted to know why cats stayed healthier on a diet of raw (uncooked and unprocessed) foods than on a diet of the same foods when cooked. What Dr. Pottenger learned during this landmark study became the foundation for future research that lead to the discovery of enzymes as the critical substance present in live, raw foods, which is non-existent in cooked and processed foods.

This study clearly demonstrated that the consumption of cooked and processed foods leads to long-term degeneration of body parts, including immune response and reproductive ability, and, when systems start to fail, manifests itself as degenerative disease and obesity due to toxicity. The study made clear the distinction between the power of "live" (uncooked & unprocessed) foods and the dangers of "dead" (cooked & processed) foods. This distinction is at a foundation level even deeper than the common way of dividing foods simply into proteins, fats, and carbohydrates. The problem with processed and cooked foods comes on a level previously not considered by most people.

Although it was Dr. Pottenger's work that first opened the door for a greater understanding and appreciation of the importance of enzyme activity in animal digestion, it was Dr. Edward Howell who conducted the first research to recognize the importance of enzymes in food to human nutrition. In 1946, he wrote the book, *The Status of Food Enzymes in Digestion and Metabolism*. To better understand their value to human health, lets look at the three categories of enzymes: metabolic, digestive, and food.

METABOLIC ENZYMES

Metabolic enzymes are found throughout the body in every system and mediate every chemical reaction and cellular function in the body. They are manufactured within the body by the liver, pancreas, and other organs and cells. Our ability to see, hear, smell, taste, feel, think, make love, digest food, walk, skip rope, and more is all enzyme mediated.

We are born with the ability to produce a finite number of metabolic enzymes during our lifetime. Studies from the 1940s prove that this ability varies in each of us, and is dependent on our individual DNA. When metabolic enzyme reserves are depleted, the potential of our immune response (i.e., our defense against illness and disease) is compromised. The quality of our immune response, our body's protection mechanism against harmful bacteria, viruses, funguses, parasites, and other pathogens, is determined by the available metabolic enzyme pool. A depletion of metabolic enzymes leads to a variety of chronic degenerative health problems.

Digestive Enzymes

Digestive enzymes are produced and released along the digestive tract in the mouth, stomach, pancreas and small intestines to aid digestion. Their primary purpose is to break down food into smaller nutrient particles for absorption, and waste byproducts for elimination. Different digestive enzymes are released at specific times along the digestive tract as the food moves through the system.

Any disruption to the production or availability of digestive enzymes leads to incomplete digestion and the health consequences associated with incomplete digestion. For example, undigested protein, carbohydrates, and fats in the small intestines have the ability to pass through the intestinal walls into the bloodstream, triggering inflammatory and autoimmune reactions throughout the body.

FOOD ENZYMES

Food enzymes are the enzymes present in every live, raw (uncooked and unprocessed) plant and animal food product we put into our mouths. They are released from the cells of the live foods we eat by the mechanical action of chewing and the chemical action of saliva in the mouth. Food enzymes help break down the food we eat and facilitate pre-digestion in the stomach.

For example, when we take a bite out of a fresh apple, banana, or avocado and then let the remainder of the fruit sit for awhile, it is the activity of these enzymes within the food that causes the browning affect that we are all familiar with. This is caused by the activity of the enzymes released and subsequently exposed to the oxygen in the air.

Although our body manufactures metabolic and digestive enzymes, our digestive tract is designed and operates on the premise that the food we eat possesses the necessary enzymes to aid in its own breakdown during early digestion. Our body relies on the consumption of live raw foods to provide the critical enzymes needed for the complete digestion of foods into smaller nutrient particles.

HEAT DESTROYS FOOD ENZYMES

The main problem with cooked, processed, pasteurized, and flash-pasteurized foods and beverages is that all food enzymes are killed when a live, raw food or beverage is heated above 115 to 118 degrees Fahrenheit. Some sources report that the destruction of enzyme activity actually begins above 104 degrees. Lack of adequate enzymes in the foods we eat burdens digestion, taxes the digestive enzyme potential, and leads to incomplete digestion.

Digestion is such a high-priority function of the body that without adequate food enzymes available, the body will divert enzymes from the metabolic enzyme pool to aid in digestion. The continual robbing of metabolic enzymes to do the work of digestion eventually lowers metabolic enzyme reserves. As the metabolic enzyme reserves are depleted, critical metabolic processes of the body, including immune response, are compromised.

DIGESTION, THE KEY TO OPTIMAL HEALTH

Health begins in the gut. The strength of your immune response is directly connected to the efficiency of your digestion. The primary purpose of the digestive tract is to break down the food we eat (through mechanical and chemical processes) into smaller nutrient particles that can be easily absorbed through the intestinal walls into the bloodstream. Once in the bloodstream, these minute particles are taken to the liver for processing. Once the liver performs its numerous functions, newly-formed nutrients are dumped back into the bloodstream to be carried to all the cells throughout the body, to enable these cells to perform their individualized and specialized functions.

The process of digestion begins in the mouth as soon as food hits the palate and continues into the stomach, small intestine, and large intestines until finally we eliminate what has not been absorbed and what we cannot use.

The human digestive tract operates under the assumption (genetically encoded) that the foods we eat not only contain the nutrient values of quality protein, carbohydrates, and fats, but also include the water, vitamins, minerals, anti-oxidants, phyto-nutrients, fiber, enzymes, and friendly bacteria necessary to prevent illness and disease and create optimal health.

At a fundamental level, the body is simply a series of chemical reactions and electrical impulses. Enzymes are the chemical catalysts that mediate every chemical reaction in the body. Without adequate "food" and digestive enzymes, the digestion process is impeded and the body cannot heal itself, create or maintain a state of optimal health.

INCOMPLETE DIGESTION LEADS TO HEALTH PROBLEMS

Complete digestion can only occur when the quality foods we eat are completely broken down to the proper particle size necessary for easy absorption and assimilation. Incomplete digestion is the basis for a wide range of health problems and autoimmune reactions that create painful symptoms in the body. Anything that inhibits the chemistry of digestion slows the movement of food through the gut. In the warm, moist, bacteria-laden, tropical climate within the digestive tract, undigested proteins putrefy, undigested carbohydrates ferment, and undigested fats turn rancid; this is where the problems start.

LEAKY GUT SYNDROME

Through a cascade of events, undigested food leaving the stomach and passing into the small intestines causes irritation and inflammation to the delicate mucosal lining of the small intestines. This inflammatory response causes increased permeability of the mucosal lining, which allows the food particles, which have not been broken down completely, to be absorbed into the bloodstream. In other words, these partially digested food particles "leak" into the bloodstream. Partially digested food that makes its way into the bloodstream is consequently recognized as foreign to the body, triggering an autoimmune reaction in which the body's specialized immune response cells attack what is foreign, causing an autoimmune reaction.

Symptoms of Incomplete Digestion

How do you know if you are not digesting food completely or effectively? The initial symptoms of incomplete digestion typically look like gastric distress syndromes: bad breath, belching, esophageal reflux, acid indigestion, sour stomach, bloating, intestinal cramping, foul smelling bowel gas, foul smelling stool, diarrhea, and constipation.

Constipation also slows down food transit time through the bowel tract. Increased transit time means that putrefied protein, fermented carbohydrates, and rancid fats remain in the colon longer. This leads to re-absorption of toxins (harmful bacteria) back into the bloodstream, to be circulated throughout the body. This self-poisoning condition is called autointoxication. Toxins reintroduced back into the body from the digestive tract cause numerous health problems.

One study reported in the British medical journal *The Lancet* found that women who are frequently constipated are 4 times more likely to develop breast cancer. Headaches are a common symptom of the autointoxication that is associated with the Standard American Diet. Slow transit time in the bowel also causes the accumulation of toxic material on the lining of the intestinal walls. This toxin build-up in the folds of the mucosal lining impedes the absorption of nutrients, causing malabsorption. Lack of energy and depression are typical symptoms of digestive malabsorption syndrome.

STAGES OF DIGESTION

The following non-scientific and oversimplified description of digestion is offered as a basic understanding of what happens within the digestive tract when we eat something.

DIGESTION IN THE MOUTH

Digestion begins in your mouth at both a mechanical level, through chewing, and at a chemical level, as the enzymes in the food you are eating (if you are eating live foods) are released, and the enzymes in your saliva start breaking down starches. While food is in your mouth your brain transmits instructions to specific cells and glands in your stomach, pancreas, and small intestines as to what enzymes and hormones need to be synthesized and released for proper digestion. As you swallow the chewed food (called the "bolus") it travels down your esophagus and enters the first part of your stomach where the next phase of digestion begins.

PRE-DIGESTION IN THE STOMACH

When the bolus of food first reaches your stomach it is held there initially to allow the food enzymes and the digestive enzymes from the saliva to continue decomposing the food (pre-digestion). The food is held here for up to 60 minutes— assuming there are no digestive slowdowns due to lack of food enzymes, improper food combining, or the presence of artificial chemicals that interfere with enzyme activity.

This initial stage is responsible for up to 80 to 85% of the digestion that takes place in the stomach. At the same time that pre-digestion is happening in the upper part of your stomach, specific glands in your stomach are receiving instructions to synthesize specific amounts and concentrations of hydrochloric acid and the chemical pepsinogen, in preparation for the continued digestion that will occur.

DIGESTION IN THE STOMACH

Upon completion of pre-digestion, hydrochloric acid and pepsinogen are released into your stomach. In the presence of hydrochloric acid, pepsinogen is converted into the enzyme pepsin. Pepsin is the enzyme that chemically breaks down protein into smaller particles through the process of proteolysis, the splitting of proteins. This splitting of proteins happens by hydrolysis—the splitting of a compound by the addition of water. Once digestion has been completed in your stomach, this soupy mixture travels to your small intestines for further breakdown of proteins into amino acids, fats into essential fatty acids, and carbohydrates into glucose for absorption into the bloodstream.

THE PANCREAS' ROLE IN DIGESTION

While digestion is occurring in your stomach, your pancreas is receiving instructions to synthesize and release specific amounts of additional enzymes and hormones. Your pancreas produces and releases the enzymes protease (for the breakdown of protein into amino acids), lipase (for the breakdown of fats into essential fatty acids), and amylase (for the breakdown of starches into simple sugars) into your small intestines as the food mixture arrives.

Your pancreas also produces and releases the hormones insulin and glucagon into the bloodstream in response to blood glucose levels. These hormones work together to regulate carbohydrate and fat metabolism for the creation of energy at the cellular level and the maintenance of appropriate blood glucose levels.

DIGESTION IN THE SMALL INTESTINES

As the food exits your stomach and enters your small intestines, additional pancreatic digestive enzymes and bile salt from your gall bladder (for fat emulsification) are released. Broken down food particles are then ready to be absorbed through the wall of your small intestines as the mixture continues to move down your gut canal. Additional digestive enzymes are also present in the lining of your small intestines. These additional enzymes facilitate the final breakdown of proteins into amino acids, carbohydrates into glucose, and fats into essential fatty acids as these nutrients pass through the walls of your small intestines into your bloodstream. Once in your bloodstream these nutrients are carried directly to your liver for processing, and are then released back into your bloodstream for distribution throughout the body.

ACTIVITY IN THE LARGE INTESTINE

Your large intestine, more commonly referred to by its Greek name, the colon, is the last part of your digestive system. At this stage, your large intestine's function is not digesting food but absorbing the remaining water from indigestible food matter, storing the unusable food substances (wastes), compacting the feces, and then eliminating the feces from the body. Food is not broken down any further in this stage of digestion. Your large intestine simply absorbs water and vitamins that are created by the bacteria that inhabit your colon.

Your large intestine also houses over 700 species of bacteria that perform a variety of functions. Your large intestine absorbs some of the products formed by the bacteria inhabiting this region. These bacteria also produce small amounts of vitamins, especially K and B, for absorption into the blood. Although this source of vitamins generally provides only a small part of your daily requirement, it makes a significant contribution when dietary vitamin intake is low.

NATURE'S WISDOM

So the question remains: what are we meant to eat based upon nature's wisdom? Are we eating in alignment with the Laws of Nature? Think about it. Humans are the only animal on the planet—excluding domesticated companion animals (dogs, cats, etc.) or animals raised for human consumption (cattle, pigs, chickens, fish, etc.)—that eats cooked, processed food, and synthetic or artificial food. Maybe it is no accident that humans are also the only animal on the planet that suffer from a plethora of degenerative and autoimmune diseases.

Metaphysically speaking, there are no accidents in life. Every other species on the planet, in their wild natural settings, consumes only live, raw foods (plant and animal). Even carnivores eat the flesh of other animals raw, never cooked. It appears that humans are the only animal on the planet that have developed feeding habits that are not in alignment with what nature intended.

Got Milk?

Consider the following observations and then arrive at your own conclusion. Are you aware that:

1. Humans are the only creatures on the planet that drink the milk of another animal as part of our regular diet.

2. Humans are the only mammal on the planet that drink milk beyond infancy and after weaning, except in the case of some domesticated animals where humans have interfered with their natural food selection as dictated by instinct.

3. Human babies in the natural setting drink only mother's milk and are able to derive all the nutrients and energy they require to survive and thrive from that milk, which contains the milk sugar lactose. This is because the healthy human baby produces the enzyme lactase necessary to break down lactose. At about year one, the natural gene expression for the production of lactase, the enzyme necessary for breaking down milk sugar, is turned off in the human infant.

Common sense would dictate that nature's wisdom probably intended cow's milk for baby cows, dog milk for baby dogs, horse milk for baby horses, human milk for baby humans, and . . . get the picture?

Food Combining for Optimal Digestion — Diet Mastery

Optimal digestion is influenced by the way we combine the foods we eat. Why? Because the human digestive tract is designed to be most efficient when handling one food type at a time. So, what is the ideal? For optimal digestion, in the ideal, every food (proteins, carbohydrates, and fats) would be eaten alone, separately and independently, as happens in the natural setting for all animals in the wild. For variety, humans, and only humans, eat foods from different food groups at the same time.

The concept of food combining for optimal digestion is based upon the principle that there are specific and different chemistry requirements for each different category of food as food moves along the digestive tract. Proteins, carbohydrates, and fats, based upon their different individual chemical compositions, each require somewhat different chemistry mediums for efficient digestion. Each type of food is acted upon by different digestive chemicals and enzymes (proteases for proteins, amylases for carbohydrates, and lipases for fat) that break food substances down into different chemical compounds in different areas along the digestive tract (mouth, stomach, and small intestine).

Protein digestion begins in the stomach, based upon initial enzyme activity, and is completed in the small intestines where proteins are broken down into amino acids, based upon additional enzymes activity from enzymes released from the pancreas. Carbohydrate digestion begins in the mouth through the mechanical action of chewing and the chemical action of the enzyme ptyalin in the saliva, and is completed in the small intestines where carbohydrates are broken down to simple sugars for easy absorption. Fat digestion does not occur until the fats reach the small intestines at which time the bile acids, which chemically break down the fats, are released by the gall bladder.

Based upon this chemistry of digestion there is an optimal way of combining the proteins, carbohydrates, and fats for efficiency and ease of digestion. Based upon the principles of food combining for optimal digestion, the basic food groups are: proteins and fats (usually appear together in nature), fruits (carbohydrate), non-starchy vegetables and greens (carbohydrates), and starches (carbohydrates). See Figure 12-1: Diet Mastery, Basic Food Combinations.

FOOD COMBINING MADE EASY

Based upon these general guidelines outlined in Figure 12-1 we can delve deeper into effective food combining for proteins & fats with non-starchy vegetables and greens (wild king salmon with broccoli and a green salad), and starchy vegetables and grains with non-starchy vegetables and greens (potato or whole grain rice with broccoli and green salad). See Figure 12-2: Diet Mastery, Optimal Food Combinations. The least desirable food combining practices include proteins & fats with starchy vegetables and grains (meat with potato or rice), proteins & fats with fruit (wild king salmon with oranges), and starchy vegetables and grains with fruit (potato with strawberries).

How should fruits be combined when eaten? For optimal digestion fruits should always be eaten separately. For the purists at heart, even within the fruit category there are four subcategories: melons (watermelon, cantaloupe, etc.), acid fruits (oranges, grapefruits, pineapple, etc.), sub-acid fruits (apples, pears, peaches, etc.), and sweet fruits (banana, figs, dates, etc.). Figure 12-3: Diet Mastery, Optimal Fruit Combinations suggests the best ways to combine fruits to achieve optimal digestion. Melons should also be eaten alone. Of the remaining three subcategories, optimal digestion is achieved by adhering to the following food combining guidelines: acid fruits with sub-acid fruits (oranges with apples), and sub-acid fruits with sweet fruits (apples with bananas). The least desirable combination is acid fruits with sweet fruits (oranges with bananas). The rule of thumb when eating fruits is "eat them alone, or leave them alone."

FIGURE 12-1

DIET MASTERY
BASIC FOOD COMBINING

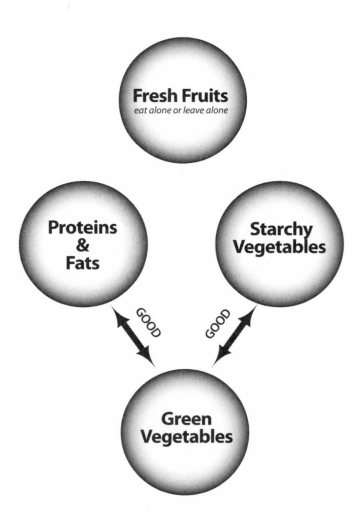

FIGURE 12-2

DIET MASTERY

OPTIMAL FOOD COMBINING

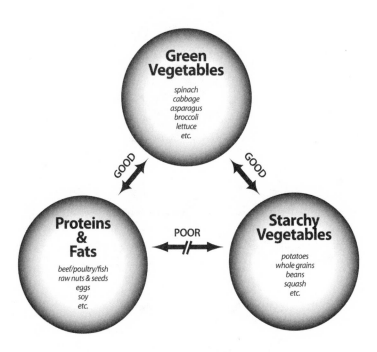

Figure 12-3

Diet Mastery
Optimal Fruit Combining

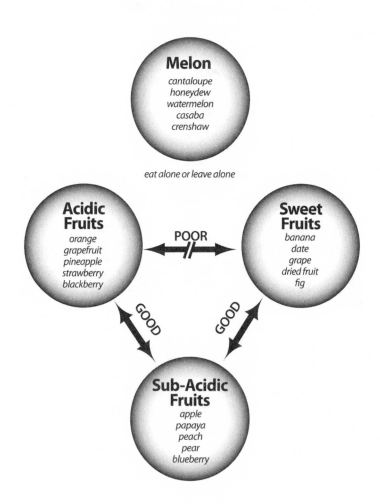

Following these simple guidelines will improve your digestion, strengthen your immune response, and minimize digestive stress and gastric discomfort.

ORGANIC VS. NON-ORGANIC (COMMERCIAL)

Organic refers to natural (non-synthetic, non-chemical, and ecologically-balanced) methods of growing (farming and ranching), processing, and labeling foods throughout the entire food processing cycle, beginning with soil consideration. Non-organic refers to any chemical-based or synthetic method utilized at any stage of the food processing cycle.

Effective October 21, 2002, the U.S. Department of Agriculture (USDA) established official "organic standards." Only foods that have been produced in compliance with these standards are granted the federal stamp of approval as "organic." Organic growers create farm systems that protect and enhance the biodiversity of species, use natural methods suited to the land and the region (such as crop rotation, cover crops, and beneficial insects), and conserve resources (including soil and water). Rather than using synthetic fertilizers to provide plant nutrients and synthetic pesticides for insect and weed control, organic farmers concentrate on building healthy soil that is naturally nutrient-rich, pest-resistant, and disease-resistant.

Organic methods of food production strive to create foods that have the highest nutritional value and are in alignment with the natural environment. The only problem is that with the recent popularity and increased consumer demand for organic, more industrial farming methods are being adopted within organic guidelines to qualify as organic. At the same time, organic guidelines are being redefined based upon underlying economic considerations. The result is that the original integrity of what organic used to stand for has become compromised. Caveat emptor! Let the buyer beware! Because of this trend you may actually be able to find a higher quality of organic produce from local growers in your area, who, although are not legally allowed to present themselves as officially organic because they have not been granted federal approval, may be in even greater alignment with the purity of the original intention of the organic movement than the much larger industrial agricultural machinery in America.

THE ESSENTIAL NUTRIENTS OF WELLNESS

Essential nutrients are necessary for survival and optimal health. These nutrients are not produced by the body and therefore need to be obtained through outside sources. The wellness building blocks of the human body include air (see Chapter 6), water (see Chapter 7), light (see Chapter 8), and food (see Chapter12). In the food category, the body requires energy (derived from carbohydrates, proteins, and fats), 8 essential amino acids (10 for children, 11 for premature infants), 2 essential fatty acids (EFA's), 20 minerals, and 14 vitamins.

Although technically not classified as essential nutrients, other substances have been found to provide great health benefits. These non-essential elements include antioxidants, phytonutrients, digestive enzymes, probiotics (good bacteria in the digestive tract), and fiber (soluble and insoluble).

The following discussion is an introduction to the value of each of these groups of substances, and is therefore limited in scope. When making food choices, the quality of the nutrient should always be considered. "Natural foods," (foods as they occur in nature), possess greater health benefits than foods that have been altered in any way through processing.

CARBOHYDRATES: GLUCOSE

The primary need of the body is for energy. The body needs energy to perform every function and run every system. Carbohydrates (from fruits, non-starchy vegetables, starchy vegetables, and grains) are the primary source of this potential energy. All carbohydrates are broken down during digestion into glucose (blood sugar) and then absorbed into the blood from the small intestines. Glucose is the specific and most efficient energy form used by cells. The body's need for energy is such a high priority that in the absence of glucose and in the depletion of glycogen reserves (the stored version of glucose), the body has mechanisms in place to immediately convert fats and proteins into glucose as a back-up energy source.

The brain has been called a "glucose hog" because it consumes as much as 70% of the glucose in the bloodstream for the thinking process and for running all the others body functions when we are physically inactive.

The best sources of quality carbohydrates for the body are fresh, live, raw, organic fruits and non-starchy vegetables. Whole grains are also a good source of carbohydrates for the body when sprouted and eaten raw (uncooked and unprocessed).

PROTEINS: AMINO ACIDS

Every cell in the body is made up of protein, and amino acids form the building blocks of all protein tissue in the body. Cell membranes are comprised of protein and fat. Enzymes are protein molecules. Without adequate quality amino acids available in the body, the cells are unable to repair and reproduce.

The best source of quality amino acids is derived from sprouted fresh, live, raw nuts and seeds. Certain animal and fish proteins

also provide quality amino acids and are the most nutritionally
beneficial when prepared in ways that preserve enzymes. Please
refer to Table 12-2: Quality Protein Sources for a partial list of
protein sources, and Table 12-3: Protein Drink Recipes for several
protein smoothie recipes.

TABLE 12-2

QUALITY PROTEIN SOURCES

PLANT SOURCES	ANIMAL SOURCES
(fresh, raw, organic)	(fresh, organic, hormone-free, antibiotic-free, range-fed, or wild)
Almonds & almond butter	Eggs (poached, soft boiled)
Brewer's Yeast	Halibut (wild)
Cashews & cashew butter	Lamb
Peanuts & peanut butter	Salmon
Walnuts	(wild, Pacific Northwest)
Pumpkin seeds	Tuna
Seaweed (spiralina)	Turkey
Sesame seeds & sesame butter (tahini)	
Soy (non-GMO)	
Spinach	
Spirulina	
Sunflower seeds	

TABLE 12-3

PROTEIN DRINK RECIPES

RECOMMENDED:

One protein drink per day is a good source of amino acids as a breakfast, lunch, or dinner replacement. Brewer's yeast is one of the best sources of plant-based amino acids. Rice bran protein is a plant-based source of amino acids. Whey protein is a byproduct of milk (cheese making) and therefore an animal-based amino acid source. Use *fresh, raw, organic* fruits whenever possible. Blend in a blender or Vitamix.

BENEFITS:

Quality protein provides the body with the amino acids to: (1) rebuild body tissue, (2) enhance protein synthesis in the liver, (3) enhance immune function, and (4) protect cells against free radical damage.

ORANGE-BANANA BONANZA

16 oz orange juice (base)
1 banana
2 tablespoons brewers yeast or whey protein powder
2 tablespoons essential fatty acids (EFA'S)

SOY MILK DELICIOUS

16 oz soy milk (base)
1 banana
2 tablespoons brewers yeast
½ cup fresh/frozen blueberries, peaches or strawberries
¼ cup raw (not toasted) almonds
¼ cup raw (not toasted) sunflower seeds
2 tablespoons essential fatty acids (EFA'S)

RICE DREAM DELIGHT

16 oz rice milk (base)

1 banana

2 tablespoons brewers yeast or whey protein powder

½ cup fresh or frozen blueberries, mango or papaya

¼ cup raw (not toasted) almonds

¼ cup raw (not toasted) sunflower seeds

2 tablespoons essential fatty acids (EFA'S)

FATS: ESSENTIAL FATTY ACIDS (EFA's)

Fats or lipids are found in every cell and are integrally involved in cell membrane structure, blood and tissue structure, enzyme reactions, the synthesis and use of certain hormones, and are an important source of stored energy for the body. Fatty acids are the molecules that make up fats and are the main component of hormones, nerve myelin sheaths, cell membranes, and membranes surrounding sub-cellular organelles.

There are healthy dietary fats (natural oils from plants, certain wild fish, and wild game animals) and unhealthy fats (processed oils from plants and processed fats from domesticated animal sources).

The body requires healthy oils and fats in the form of essential fatty acids (EFA's) on a daily basis: omega-3, omega-6, and omega-9 fatty acids. Cold water fish oils and flaxseed oil are a primary source of omega-3 essential fatty acids. Plant oils from vegetables, seeds, grains, and even bean seeds (flax and soybean) are the primary source of omega-6 and omega-9 essential fatty acids.

It is estimated that up to 80% of the people in America are deficient in essential fatty acids, particularly omega-3. In addition, the United States has the lowest consumption of omega-3 in the world and the highest consumption of omega-6.

Current wisdom suggests that omega-6 and omega-3 are said to work the best in the human body from a 1:1 to 4:1 ratio, but even this ratio is argued among the experts. Research indicates that the Paleolithic diet of our prehistoric relatives contained foods in the 1:1 omega-6 to omega-3 ratio. Today, the typical American consumes a ratio of between 10:1 to 20:1, with some indications that we may be consuming these fats at ratios as high as 40:1 to 50:1. The problem with this high consumption ratio of omega-6 is that an overabundance of omega-6 has an inflammatory effect on the body, and interferes with the body's ability to use omega-3.

The highest quality EFA's are organic and cold processed, and for optimal benefit should be refrigerated once opened and consumed at room temperature. Heating damages the quality of all oils.

Years ago, scientists were perplexed about the healthy arteries of the Eskimos, who had low to non-existent incidence of coronary vascular disease, although their diet was rich in fatty foods such as salmon, whale, and seal meat. It was discovered that the oils in these foods, (raw and unprocessed), were rich in the omega-3 essential fatty acids which promoted healthy heart, brain, nerve, eye, joint, skin, and immune function. Farmed fish (compared to wild fish) may be lower in omega-3 and higher in omega-6 if they are fed grain products instead of their natural marine foods.

The brain is comprised of approximately 60% fat, 1/3 of which is EFA's, 1/2 of the 1/3 (approx 10%) being omega-3. Having an adequate supply of quality omega-3 and omega-6 EFA's in the diet is critical to optimal brain function and disease prevention. See Table 12-4: Quality Essential Fatty Acids for a partial list of quality EFA sources.

TABLE 12-4

QUALITY ESSENTIAL FATTY ACIDS
(RAW, ORGANIC, COLD PROCESSED)

Omega-3	Omega-6	Omega-9
Flaxseed oil	Flaxseed oil	Olive oil
Salmon	Eggs	Canola oil
Mackerel	Grape seed oil	Vegetable oils
Sardines	Safflower oil	
Tuna	Sunflower seed oil	
Walnut oil	Turkey	
	Wheat germ oil	

MINERALS

The body requires 20 minerals to maintain healthy electrolyte balance. Our bodies are comprised primarily of water and minerals, both of which are essential to every function. Minerals are the main components in teeth and bones, and they serve as building blocks for other cells and enzymes. Minerals also help regulate the balance of fluids in the body and control the movement of nerve impulses.

Some minerals also help deliver oxygen to cells and help carry away carbon dioxide, thereby regulating acid-alkaline pH balance in the body. An excess or deficiency of any one mineral can throw the body out of it's delicate health balance, setting the stage for illness and disease.

Minerals are categorized based upon daily requirements: major (more than 250 milligrams per day) and minor (under 20 milligrams per day). Calcium, phosphorus, magnesium, sodium, potassium, sulfur, and chloride are considered major minerals because adults need them in larger amounts. Trace minerals—chromium, copper, fluoride, iodine, iron, manganese, molybdenum, selenium, and zinc—are required by the body in smaller amounts.

Size matters. The ability of a mineral to be utilized by the body is primarily a matter of size and absorbability. When the particle size of the mineral is small enough, there is better absorption and assimilation at the cell level, which is the key to fully utilizing the health benefits of minerals. If the mineral particles can be reduced to a small enough size they can be absorbed by the body without the need to be broken down into a less usable form through the process of continued digestion.

Current research indicates that "chelated" and "angstrom-sized" minerals provide greatest absorbability in the body. Chelation refers to the process of binding a mineral to an amino acid. Research indicates that this chelated form of minerals possesses greater uptake and usability by the body's cells. An angstrom is 1/10,000th of a micron, which is a millionth of a meter. Previously, only plants, with help from the sun and organisms in the soil, had the ability to reduce minerals to angstrom-sized particles; now we can do it with technology.

Fresh, live, raw, organic non-starchy vegetables are the best source of minerals for the body. Humans get their minerals from plants and plants derive their mineral content from the soil. Therefore, the richer the soil, the greater the mineral content in the plants.

VITAMINS

The body requires 14 vitamins for optimal health. Vitamins are organic compounds required by humans in small amounts. An organic compound is considered a vitamin if a lack of that compound in the diet results in overt symptoms of deficiency. For example, a lack of vitamin A causes night blindness, a lack of vitamin B1 causes beriberi, a lack of vitamin C results in scurvy, and a lack of vitamin D results in rickets.

Vitamins are needed for a variety of biologic processes, including growth, digestion, mental alertness, and resistance to infection. Vitamins enable the body to use proteins, carbohydrates, and fats, because they also act as the catalysts, along with enzymes, to initiate or speed up certain chemical reactions. Though vitamins are involved in converting food into energy, they supply no calories.

Vitamins are either water-soluble or fat-soluble. Water-soluble vitamins include Vitamin C, biotin, and the seven B vitamins: thiamin (B1), riboflavin (B2), niacin (B3), pantothenic acid (B5), pyridoxine (B6), folic acid (B9), and cobalamin (B12). Water-soluble vitamins dissolve in water and aren't stored in your body in any significant amounts. Any water-soluble vitamins that you consume in excess of your body's immediate needs are excreted in your urine. Fresh, live, raw, organic fruits and vegetables are the best natural source of water-soluble vitamins.

Fat-soluble vitamins require the presence of fat to dissolve. Fat-soluble vitamins include A, D, E, and K. Any extra fat-soluble vitamins not used by your body immediately after ingestion are stored in your body fat and liver. Excess fat-soluble vitamins can accumulate in your body and become toxic at extremely high dosages. We are especially sensitive to excess amounts of vitamins A and D. Vitamins E and K affect blood clotting. Be careful if you take any supplements that contain either of these vitamins when taking a blood thinner, such as warfarin (Coumadin), or if you are undergoing any surgical or medical procedure that causes bleeding. Fresh, live, raw, organic nuts, seeds, grains, and certain fish oils are the best source of fat-soluble vitamins.

Antioxidants

At the molecular and cellular levels, antioxidants serve to deactivate harmful particles called free radicals. A free radical is a molecule with an unpaired electron. This unpaired electron, created as a by-product during normal cellular metabolism, can damage other cells. Any molecule can become a free radical by either losing or gaining an electron. Molecules containing these uncoupled electrons are unstable and highly reactive.

Free radicals can also be created through exposure to various environmental factors, including tobacco smoke and radiation from microwave ovens. Free radicals can damage cell walls, certain cell structures, and genetic material (DNA) within the cells. In the worst-case scenario, over a long period of time, such damage can become irreversible and contribute to disease processes. If left unchecked, free radicals contribute to heart damage, cancer, cataracts, and a weakened immune system.

Antioxidants work by (1) binding to the free radicals, thereby transforming them into non-damaging compounds and (2) repairing cellular damage. Antioxidants come in a variety of forms and include Vitamins A, C, and E, the Carotenoids (a pigment that adds color to many fruits and vegetables), and Selenium (a mineral). Fresh, live, raw, organic fruits and the non-starchy vegetables are the best source of natural antioxidants. The highest concentrations of antioxidants are found in the most deeply or brightly colored fruits and vegetables (dark green spinach, bright orange carrots, red bell peppers, green bell peppers, red tomatoes, etc).

PHYTONUTRIENTS

Phytonutrients are one type of antioxidant. The terms phytonutrient and phytochemical are used interchangeably to describe those plant compounds which are thought to have health-protecting qualities. Phytonutrients are concentrated in the skins of many vegetables and fruits, and are responsible for their color, hue, scent, and flavor. They are pigments, or, more precisely, the biologically-active constituents of pigments. To a lesser extent, phytonutrients are also found in grains and seeds.

Broadly defined, phytonutrients are any chemical or nutrient that is derived from a plant source. However, in common usage they have a more limited definition. The term phytonutrient is usually used to refer to compounds found in plants which are not required for normal functioning of the body, but that have a beneficial effect on health or an active role in improving disease. Thus, they differ from what are traditionally termed nutrients in that they are not necessary for normal metabolism and their absence will not result in a deficiency disease.

Phytonutrients are thought to be destroyed or removed by many modern food processing techniques, possibly including cooking. For this reason, it is believed that industrially-processed foods are less beneficial (contain fewer phytonutrients) than unprocessed foods. Fresh, live, raw, organic fruits and vegetables are the best natural source of phytonutrients. Foods rich in phytonutrient include tomatoes, red onions, green tea, grapes, red cabbage, broccoli, parsley, spinach, raspberry, blackberry, and garlic.

ENZYMES

Please refer to the discussion on enzymes presented previously in this chapter.

PROBIOTICS: FRIENDLY BACTERIA

There are hundreds of different bacteria (microflora) species that inhabit the human digestive tract; some cause disease, while others have health benefits. Probiotic refers to the "friendly" or beneficial bacteria found in the human gut that enhance digestion and immune response. The term "probiotic" is derived from the Greek word meaning "for life." Probiotics have been defined as "any viable organism in a supplement or food form that exerts health effects on the host when ingested on a consistent basis."

Although the intestines of the fetus are free from bacteria, the bacterial colonization within a newborn's intestines starts immediately upon delivery through the birth canal, and then through continuous ingestion of mothers' milk during nursing. The composition of intestinal bacteria varies from one person to another depending on the person's age, diet, medication, emotional and mental stress levels, and psychological state.

The concept of probiotics was introduced in the early 1900s. However, scientific studies on the health benefits of probiotic bacteria did not begin until the 1960s. Today numerous scientific research studies demonstrate that both probiotic bacteria and foods fermented with beneficial bacteria have a variety of health benefits. Probiotic bacteria favorably alter the intestinal bacterial balance, inhibit the growth of harmful bacteria, promote good digestion, boost immune function, and increase resistance to infection.

People with flourishing intestinal colonies of beneficial bacteria are better equipped to fight the growth of disease-causing bacteria. Lactobacilli and bifidobacteria maintain a healthy balance of intestinal flora by producing organic compounds—such as lactic acid, hydrogen peroxide, and acetic acid—that increase the acidity of the intestine and inhibit the reproduction of many harmful bacteria. Probiotic bacteria also produce substances called bacteriocins, which act as natural antibiotics to kill undesirable microorganisms.

Why take probiotics? Many degenerative disease conditions can be linked to intestinal toxemia and our inability to properly eliminate them from the body. Harmful bacteria that are allowed to remain in the body for an extended period of time will begin to affect all bodily functions. Autointoxication occurs when accumulated toxins are re-absorbed back into the body before they can be excreted.

The body's ability to maintain proper intestinal flora equilibrium becomes compromised due to the over-use of antibiotics coupled with the consumption of chlorinated water, alcohol, and preservatives in food. Without beneficial bacteria, the natural defenders that guard against pathogenic organisms, we can become susceptible to a wide range of health problems that affect all other bodily processes. By replenishing the healthy intestinal flora on a regular basis, we help the body fight off invading bacterial and viral organisms, and improve our overall quality of life.

Antibiotics destroy unfriendly as well as friendly bacteria in the gut. It is therefore important to recolonize the intestinal tract during and after antibiotic use. Probiotic supplementation has been shown to replenish the beneficial bacteria, preventing up to 50% of infections occurring after antibiotic use. Probiotic bacteria also secrete enzymes that aid digestion. Probiotics are found in fermented foods such as yogurt, Kefir, and cheese, as well as fortified foods and supplements.

FIBER

Fiber is a complex carbohydrate found in plants which is not broken down or absorbed in the digestive tract. Fiber is not a single food or substance. Fiber in itself has no calories because the body cannot absorb it. Fiber substances move through the digestive tract, cleaning the digestive tract as they go. High-fiber foods that are low in fat, such as fruits and vegetables, are also lower in calories.

While the sugars, starches, and vitamins in fruits and vegetables are broken down into nutrients and absorbed by our intestines, the cell walls of plants are not digested, and go on to form an important component of the stool: the bulk or roughage. The real benefit of fiber lies in its ability to expedite waste material transit time through the large intestines. Regular and complete elimination of toxic fecal matter is a prerequisite for optimal health. The longer that fecal matter remains in the colon, the more toxins are reabsorbed back into the bloodstream. Toxins reintroduced back into the body create the unhealthy internal biological environment that becomes a fertile breeding ground for harmful bacteria, funguses, parasites, molds, and other disease-causing pathogens.

Constipation is the most common and obvious sign of an insufficient amount of fiber and water in the diet. Dry, hard fecal matter slows down transit time through the colon. Straining for any reason during evacuation of the bowels produces pressure on all of the abdominal wall, causing the development of hernias, varicose veins (due to pressure on the long veins of the legs), hiatal hernias (upward pressure forcing the stomach into the chest), diverticulitis and diverticulosis (weakening and infection of the colon wall), hemorrhoids, and anal fissures and fistulae. Colorectal cancers are also more common in patients with lifelong habit constipation. This may be due to the extended and concentrated exposure of carcinogens to the internal surface of the colon, as a result of the hard dry stool and its slow movement or evacuation.

There are two types of fiber: soluble and insoluble. Fiber that partially dissolves in water is called *soluble* or water-soluble, while fiber that does not dissolve in water is called *insoluble* or water-insoluble. Both promote health, although in different ways

Water-soluble fibers, such as gum, mucilage, and pectin, dissolve in water, absorb water, and help soften the stool as it moves through the colon (the last 4 to 5 feet of intestines). These *soluble* fibers help remove cholesterol, bile acids, and heavy metals from the digestive tract. By coating the gut's lining and delaying stomach emptying, water-soluble fiber may regulate blood sugar by slowing sugar absorption after a meal, and therefore may reduce the amount of insulin needed. Water-soluble fiber is found in fruits such as apples, oranges, pears, peaches, and grapes, as well as vegetables, seeds, oat bran, dried beans, oatmeal, barley, and rye.

Water-insoluble fibers, such as cellulose, hemi-cellulose, and lignin, do not dissolve in water. These fibers act to scrub the lining of the gut. These *insoluble* fibers are found in certain fruits and vegetables, dried beans, wheat bran, seeds, popcorn, brown rice, and whole grain products such as breads, cereals, and pasta. Please refer to Table 12-5: Top Twenty Fiber Foods for a list of common fiber-rich foods.

Table 12-5

Top Twenty Fiber Foods

The following list of foods is high in dietary fiber and should be consumed daily for optimal colon health.

1. Dried beans, peas, and other legumes. This includes baked beans, kidney beans, split peas, dried limas, garbanzos, pinto beans, and black beans.

2. Bran cereals

3. Fresh/frozen lima beans, both Fordhook and baby limas

4. Fresh or frozen green peas

5. Dried fruit, especially figs, apricots, and dates

6. Raspberries, blackberries, and strawberries

7. Sweet corn, whether on the cob or cut off in kernels

8. Whole wheat and other whole-grain cereal products. Rye, oats, buckwheat, and stone-ground cornmeal are all high in fiber. Breads, pastas, pizzas, pancakes, and muffins made with whole-grain flours.

9. Broccoli

10. Baked potato with the skin

11. Green snap beans, pole beans, and broad beans (these are packaged frozen as Italian beans; in Europe they are known as haricot or French beans.)

12. Plums, pears, apples. The skin is edible, & high in pectin.

13. Raisins and prunes

14. Greens, including spinach, beet greens, kale, collards, swiss chard, and turnip greens

15. Raw nuts, almonds, Brazil nuts, peanuts, and walnuts

16. Cherries

17. Bananas

18. Carrots

19. Coconut

20. Brussels sprouts

WHOLE FOOD SUPPLEMENTS VS. INDIVIDUAL SUPPLEMENTS?

What is the best way to supplement the body with valuable nutrients? Whole foods. The whole is greater than the sum of the parts, even when it comes to nutrition. The different nutrients that are available and provided in whole foods work synergistically to provide health benefits superior to those derived when consuming individual nutrients that have been extracted from the whole food or created synthetically in a lab.

Also, supplements are called "supplements" for a reason. They were intended to support your body's health as merely an addition to your primary eating habits. Vitamins, or any other individually-isolated supplement, are not a panacea for creating optimal health.

GLYCEMIC INDEX & GLYCEMIC LOAD

Glycemic index (GI) and glycemic load (GL) are more recent ways of classifying foods based on the rate at which foods increase blood glucose levels. Up until a few years ago it was believed that if a food was composed of complex carbohydrates (starches) it would break down into sugar more slowly in your body than food composed of simple carbohydrates (sugars). Through research we have learned more about how foods affect blood glucose levels.

The glycemic index of foods is a calculation based on the glycemic response of foods, drinks, or nutraceuticals ingested by humans. Glycemic response is a numerical system that identifies the speed at which a food increases a person's blood glucose levels; the higher the glycemic index, the faster the rise in blood sugar. The glycemic response is influenced by many factors, including the amount of food you eat, how the food is processed, and the way the food is prepared. For example, pasta cooked "al dente" (firm) is absorbed more slowly than pasta that is overcooked. The glycemic index is an average of the glycemic responses measured from many individuals. When you eat a slice of bread, the flour from the bread is eventually broken down through the digestive process into glucose for energy. The same thing happens when you eat a piece of fruit, drink a glass of milk, or eat a chocolate bar. Each of these foods contains a different kind of sugar. Fructose is a sugar in fruit, lactose is found in milk, and sucrose is found in the chocolate bar. All of these different sugars are eventually broken down during digestion into glucose to provide energy.

The ranking of different foods based on their glycemic response was first studied by Dr. David Jenkins and colleagues at St. Michael's Hospital in Toronto, Canada. The research team conducted several experiments looking at the speed at which different foods affect blood glucose levels, and compared the numbers to those of a slice of white bread. White bread is given the glycemic index value of 100. Foods that have a value less than 100 are converted into sugar more slowly than white bread. Foods that have a glycemic index value greater than 100 turn into sugar more quickly than white bread. Foods with a low glycemic index break down more slowly in the body than foods with a high glycemic index.

Glycemic load is the glycemic index numerical value divided by 100 and then multiplied by its available carbohydrate content (in grams). GL takes the glycemic index into account, but is based on how much carbohydrate is in the food or drink tested. The glycemic load of a food or drink is numerically lower than its glycemic index. When considered together, the glycemic index and glycemic load can provide information beneficial in designing eating plans to help regulate blood sugar metabolism in conditions like diabetes and hyperglycemia, a pre-diabetic state.

However, one of the limitations of these rating systems is that they do not take into consideration the quality of the carbohydrate being consumed. GI and GL do not differentiate between high-quality and low-quality sources of carbohydrate. As a general rule of thumb, fresh, live, raw, organic fruits and vegetable are the best choice for low glycemic index and low glycemic load carbohydrate foods. As a general rule, fresh, live, raw, organic fruits and non-starchy vegetables raise blood sugar more slowly than most processed or refined carbohydrate sources.

Live Food, Live Body; Dead Food, Dead Body!

Whenever we violate Laws of Nature by eating foods that are not in alignment with (1) what humans were intended to eat based upon nature's design, (2) how our digestive system works and what foods it was designed by nature to digest, and (3) the true nutritional needs of our bodies, we will experience the consequence of that violation. Remember the Parkay margarine commercial? "It's not nice to fool Mother Nature!" Well, you can't fool Mother Nature and you can't fool the body. The quality of your health is a direct reflection of the truth about your eating and lifestyle habits.

When we look at humans in a natural environment we get an idea of what nature must have intended for the human body. In understanding how the body works as nature intended we know what foods work in the body and what foods will not work. In a natural setting, all living creatures (carnivore, herbivore, and omnivore) thrive on eating fresh, live, raw, foods.

All fresh, live, raw, foods, vegetable and animal, possess a life force energy that is present in all living things. Enzymes, destroyed during cooking and processing, have been identified as this life force energy. In order to be healthy, energetic, and disease-free, live creatures, like humans, need to consume live foods that possess this life force energy.

Every action has its consequence. Every consequence is an expression of some *truth* about the universe. Optimal health and wellness, like illness and disease, is merely an expression of the *truth* about our eating and lifestyle habits. There is no magic. All the rationalization, intellectualization, or slick marketing to the contrary will not change *truth*. Thus, it is true that *you are what you eat!*

WELLNESS MASTERY™ SUMMARY

Must Know!

1. It would appear that humans, as designed and created within the natural setting, are better equipped for "gathering" and eating fruits, vegetables, nuts, seeds, roots, and other wild plant life than for "hunting" and eating animal flesh.

2. Metabolic enzymes are produced by the body and facilitate or mediate every chemical reaction and cellular function in the body. The strength and quality of our immune response is attributed to metabolic enzyme activity.

3. Digestive enzymes are produced by the body and facilitate proper digestion.

4. Food enzymes are NOT produced by the body and are only present in live, raw (uncooked and unprocessed) foods (plant and animal). They are required during pre-digestion and are necessary for efficient and complete digestion and absorption of nutrients in the small intestines.

5. All food enzymes are destroyed when a live, raw food or beverage is heated above 115 to 118 degrees Fahrenheit.

6. Humans are the only animals on the planet (excluding domesticated companion animals or animals raised for human consumption) that stray from nature's menu by eating cooked,processed, and artificial foods.

7. Optimal health and wellness, like illness and disease, is merely a consequence and expression of the *truth* of our eating and lifestyle habits.

8. The different nutrients that are available and provided in whole foods work synergistically to provide health benefits that are far superior to those derived when consuming individual nutrients that have been extracted from the whole food or created synthetically in a lab.

9. "Live" foods (uncooked and unprocessed) contain life-force energy that does not exist in cooked and processed "dead" food. The more fresh, live, raw, organic food you eat, the healthier you become!

10. Whole food supplementation is superior to individual ingredient supplementation.

WELLNESS MASTERY™ ACTION

Must Do!

1. Eat fresh, live, raw (uncooked and unprocessed) organic fruits and non-starchy vegetables whenever possible.

2. Buy a juice extractor and begin juicing daily.

3. Drink at least one fresh, live, raw organic fruit juice in the early morning. Drink one fresh, live, raw, organic non-starchy vegetable juice in the late morning or mid afternoon. See Table 8-1: Basic Juicing Regimen and Recipes for a simple juicing routine.

4. Whenever eating cooked or processed food, supplement with digestive enzymes, as instructed on the enzyme package's label.

5. Shop for fresh certified-organic fruits and vegetables at your local natural food store, local outdoor farmer's market, or one of the organic produce sections now appearing in most of the larger grocery store chains.

6. Keep fresh, live, raw, organic fruits and vegetable available in the house for snacks.

7. Plan ahead. Keep fresh, live, raw, organic fruits or other natural, raw snacks at work.

8. Eat healthy foods before food shopping. It is easier to avoid the temptation of junk food when you are feeling nourished and well fed.

9. Eat more plant life and less animal products. Eat more raw foods and less cooked and processed foods. Eat more naturally occurring foods and eliminate artificial foods from your life.

10. Daily mantra: *"Live Food, Live Body; Dead Food, Dead Body!"*

CHAPTER THIRTEEN

PRINCIPLE #10

Physical Activity

MOVE THE BODY

> *All parts of the body which have a function, if used in moderation and exercised in labors in which each is accustomed, becomes thereby healthy, well developed and age more slowly, but if unused they become liable to disease, defective in growth, and age quickly.*
>
> —**Hippocrates,** Father of Medicine

NATURE'S DESIGN

Humans were designed as motion machines. Anatomically and biologically, the human animal was designed for movement throughout life. Movement stimulates numerous physiological processes that keep the body healthy, including increased oxygenation, detoxification, and elimination. Exercise—at least as we commonly think of it—is not really the key to health; movement is. Physical activity is one of your best stress management tools. The health of the body depends on the body's ability to keep physically active. The musculo-skeletal system—muscles, bones, ligaments, and tendons—is the primary system. Muscle constitutes the largest portion of body mass, between 30 and 50%. After metabolism, your muscles and physical activity demand the greatest energy requirement.

Every other anatomical and biological system in the human body is dedicated in some way to serving the function of our ability to move: the skin is the outer protection for the muscles; the pulmonary system (lungs) provides oxygen for energy; the circulatory system (heart and blood vessels) carries nutrients (oxygen and fuel); the digestive tract (mouth, stomach, small intestines, and large intestines) breaks down and absorbs nutrients for energy production and tissue repair and reproduction; the lymphatic system (white blood cells) breaks down and carries away waste products from cell metabolism; and the brain regulates all movement through the dedicated network of the skeletal nervous system (the autonomic nervous system—sympathetic and parasympathetic—is dedicated to all other functions of the body).

We possess conscious control over the skeletal muscles of the body as well as some conscious but limited control over other bodily functions that are primarily under autonomic control, such as heart rate, blood pressure, and body temperature.

THE PRINCIPLE OF RESISTANCE & ADAPTATION

The natural physical world operates and revolves around the principle of resistance and adaptation. Adaptation is a primary survival mechanism in all living organisms. Resistance is the force of opposition that stimulates this adaptation response within the body to accommodate the requirement of the situation in the environment. When confronted with opposition, an organism is stimulated to adapt in some way in order to accommodate the opposition.

Spiritually we grow stronger by overcoming spiritual resistance. Psychologically we grow stronger by overcoming mental resistance. Emotionally we grow stronger by overcoming emotional resistance. Physically we get stronger by overcoming physical resistance. Muscles grow bigger and get stronger based on the principle of resistance and adaptation. Resistance provides traction for forward motion in our life. Our body's immune response stays healthy and grows stronger based upon this same principle. Without resistance to stimulate an adaptation response, all body systems weaken.

PHYSICAL ACTIVITY & OXYGEN

If oxygen (see Chapter 7, Oxygen) is the most important nutrient of the body, what is the most important exercise? *Deep breathing!* Physical activity increases the depth and rate of your breathing. Increased breathing increases oxygen delivery to cells through increased circulation. Increased oxygen helps raise the pH (see Chapter 10, Acid/Alkaline pH Balance) and makes the internal biological environment of the body more alkaline.

PHYSICAL ACTIVITY FOR BONE & BLOOD ENHANCEMENT

Weight-bearing exercise increases bone density and bone volume. When you increase bone density and volume, you also increased bone marrow, found inside the long bones of the body. Bone marrow is important because this is where the body manufactures your red and white blood cells. White blood cells are the foot soldiers of your immune response. They attack, neutralize, deactivate, and destroy harmful and toxic substances in the body. Red blood cells carry oxygen from the lungs to tissues throughout the body, and carry carbon dioxide, a waste product of normal cellular metabolism, away from the tissue and back to the lungs for expulsion from the body. Regular physical activity therefore increases the body's white blood cell count as well as red blood cell count and oxygen-carrying potential.

PHYSICAL ACTIVITY TO STRENGTHEN
IMMUNE RESPONSE

White blood cells produced in bone marrow are an important part of your lymphatic system. Your lymphatic system, which consists of lymph fluid, vessels, ducts, and glands, functions as your body's sewage waste treatment facility. The health of your lymphatic system determines the quality of your immune response.

The body's ability to detoxify and neutralize harmful toxins is a critical function that we don't think much about until we consider that the body contains a three times greater volume of lymph fluid than blood. Lymph fluid contains various types of white blood cells, a primary defense against harmful foreign microorganisms and bacterial invaders of the body.

The lymphatic system, unlike the circulatory system, with its heart pump and blood vessels, has no single pump. Lymph flow relies upon body movement and breathing to facilitate circulation. Thus, physical activity strengthens immune response by stimulating lymphatic circulation, thereby increasing the rate of detoxification as well as increasing white blood cell production.

PHYSICAL ACTIVITY, DETOXIFICATION &
HEALTHY AGING

Physical activity "de-gunks" the body by speeding up the rate at which toxins are neutralized and eliminated from the body. Exercise increases circulation (blood flow), respiration (breathing), digestion (solid waste elimination), kidney function (fluid waste elimination) and the rate of metabolism (the combined process of cellular breakdown and rebuilding).

The more physically active you are, the faster your body deactivates and eliminates toxins. Stored toxins in the body are the culprits that speed up the aging process. A toxic internal biological environment not only accelerates the aging process but, more significantly, creates the ideal breeding ground for opportunistic harmful and destructive bacteria, viruses, funguses, and all manner and form of pathogens that lead to illnesses and chronic degenerative diseases.

PHYSICAL ACTIVITY FOR STRESS RELIEF

Physical activity, by dissipating the daily build up of negative energy in the body, is one of the best natural methods for releasing both psychological and emotional stress. It also speeds up the neutralization and elimination of toxic chemical substances from the body. Think about it. Eating, and specifically overeating, is one way that people express their frustration from mental and emotional stress. Those who exercise regularly report that it is not possible to engage in vigorous physical activity and hold emotional, mental, and physical stress energy in the body.

PHYSICAL ACTIVITY FOR WEIGHT MANAGEMENT

Consistent daily physical activity is the best natural method for losing fat, managing weight, and maintaining low body fat. Physical activity burns more calories than inactivity. Metabolic rate increases during physical activity. An unacknowledged residual benefit from regular exercise is an increase in metabolic rate for an extended period, thereby making your body more efficient at burning calories for hours after exercise.

Regular physical activity also regulates hunger through the appetite center in the brain. Research studies reveal that mice performing regular daily physical activity on a wheel treadmill stop eating at a certain point, no matter how much food is placed into their cages. The same study showed that inactive "coach potato" mice continue to eat long after the active mice had stopped eating. Food for thought!

INCREASE YOUR BODY'S FAT BURNING ABILITY

Obesity, the #2 risk factor associated with a higher incidence of all chronic degenerative disease, is primarily due to minimal physical activity along with unhealthy eating: poor quality and excess quantity. Statistically, America is a country that is overfed and undernourished. We eat too much of the unhealthy foods, not enough of the healthy foods, and sit on our butts way too much!

Glucose is the preferred source of energy fuel for the body, then fat, then protein. In the absence of available glucose the body will turn to breaking down fat and protein stores for energy. The body's ability to utilize fat for energy depends on the amount of fat-burning enzymes available. The more fat-burning enzymes available, the better your body burns fat. Extended moderate exercise stimulates the growth of these fat-burning enzymes. Although we burn fat for energy during aerobic activity, the real fat-loss benefit is derived from the increase in the number of fat-burning enzymes stimulated by increased physical activity.

Exercise also changes muscle chemistry in a way that helps your body be more efficient at burning fat for energy. Inactivity, on the other hand, changes muscle chemistry over time to require fewer calories. Extended inactivity causes a reduction in fat-burning enzymes, and the muscle then becomes less efficient at burning fat for fuel.

So what type of exercise stimulates the greatest fat-burning enzyme growth? The exercises that recruit the largest muscle groups in the body, the muscles of the buttocks, thighs, and legs.

The more muscle mass that is incorporated into an exercise, the less time is needed to stimulate the growth of additional enzymes that burn fat. This is why jogging is more effective at fat-burning and fat-loss than stationary bicycling, swimming, walking, or weight-lifting performed for the same period of time.

KEEP BONES STRONG & PREVENT OSTEOPOROSIS

Weight bearing activity keeps your bones strong. As long as there is appropriate mechanical stress on the skeletal system, your bones have a reason to maintain their structural integrity. A sedentary lifestyle weakens your bones. In the absence of weight-bearing activity, your bones have no reason to maintain their structural strength and begin to lose density.

Your body possesses adaptation mechanisms, by intelligent design, for the conservation of energy through efficiency. This intelligence dictates that the body will not maintain any surplus of muscle or bone not needed for current activity levels. The body maintains only that which it needs to function efficiently at this moment. When bones aren't being stressed, they begin to lose their calcium stores because they have no reason to maintain their structural integrity or the excess calcium.

Inactivity therefore causes the skeletal system to lose bone density by giving up calcium, the main mineral of bone composition. Research shows that healthy men who are restricted to bed rest lose calcium over time—as measured by the rate of calcium excreted in the urine—and lose bone mass in the weight-bearing bones at an even greater rate over the same period. When weight-bearing activity is resumed, the process reverses itself and the bones will reabsorb calcium, if available in the diet, in direct relation to the amount of the additional stress load. Bone density is regained at about the same rate at which it is lost. Astronauts who experience long periods of weightlessness while in space lose massive amounts of calcium from the weight-bearing bones of the legs, in spite of the fact that they are involved in regular vigorous non-weight-bearing exercise.

TAI CHI & HEALTH

Tai chi (pronounced "tie chee"), a 2000 year old Chinese fitness regimen, evolved from *tai chi chuan* which was originally developed to train the Chinese emperor's troops for battlefield warfare. Today, there are numerous styles of *tai chi* with the most common feature being slow, gentle, fluid, dance-like movements. Similar to both yoga and meditation, it helps relieve stress, increase flexibility, and build strength while being gentle on the joints.

The Chinese view illness and the physical manifestation of stress as a stagnation or blockage of the internal energy, what we call *qi* (pronounced "chee"). *Tai chi* is one method to release these blockages and promote the free flow of *qi*.

The slow twisting and untwisting movements while performing *tai chi* massage the practitioner's internal organs, increase blood circulation, optimize spinal nerve transmission, and reduce stress chemicals in the body.

YOGA & HEALTH

What is the best exercise for overall health and wellness? The best exercise is the one you will do consistently. Although conventional exercise—such as walking, jogging, swimming, and weight training—has tremendous physiological and physical benefits, yoga goes a step further. The mind-body connection that yoga can create serves to heal the mind (thoughts and emotions) and spirit as well as the body.

There are numerous forms of yoga. Therapeutic yoga incorporates breathing, poses, and meditation techniques to improve quality of life, reduce stress, and manage symptoms of various diseases, chronic conditions, and illnesses. Regular therapeutic yoga has been shown to improve the symptoms of asthma, back pain, fibromyalgia, multiple sclerosis (MS), depression, heart disease, and cancer.

The greater value of yoga lies in how it integrates and balances the spiritual, mental, emotional, and physical energies in your body. In India, the roots of therapeutic yoga go back thousands of years. Although used primarily as a physical exercise with a focus on physiology in the Western world, in India yoga was originally developed to open the flow of healing energy in the body.

A study reported in the June 2004 issue of the journal *Neurology* showed that patients with multiple sclerosis (MS) who practiced yoga for six months had significantly less fatigue than those who did not practice yoga. A 1998 study showed that yoga, more than conventional medical and physical therapy treatment, helped reduce pain and improve hand strength for people with carpal tunnel syndrome (symptoms of hand pain and weakness due to irritation and inflammation of the median nerve running through the wrist/hand), a typical repetitive motion injury.

Regular yoga participants report experiencing the benefits of decreased stress, increased energy and stamina, increased flexibility, stronger muscles, improved digestion, more restful sleep, and a greater sense of general well being. Yoga helps quiet the mind and teaches greater awareness of the physical body, which facilitates a greater awareness of self. A greater awareness of self is one of the pre-requisites for enlightenment and creating a more fulfilling life and peaceful existence.

There are numerous yoga systems that have developed over time. One basic yoga system called the "Sun Salutation" (surya namaskar) is a series of twelve basic postures performed in a single graceful flow—a simple balanced series of movements designed to enhance flexibility, strength, and aerobic capacity. See Exercise 13-1: Yoga "Sun Salutation." Doing the "Sun Salutation" first thing in the morning is a great way to start your day. Each movement is coordinated with the breath. Inhale as you extend or stretch, and exhale as you fold or contract. Different styles of yoga perform the "Sun Salutation" with their own variations. Practice these poses mindfully and you will experience improved flexibility and enhanced mind-body connection. This series of twelve positions is also an excellent warm-up exercise for any other physical activity or athletic sport.

EXERCISE GUIDELINES FOR AMERICANS

The United States Departments of Agriculture (USDA) and Health and Human Services (HHS) released the 2005 update to their Dietary Guidelines for Americans. Published every 5 years, the guidelines (www.healthierus.gov/dietaryguidelines) are the result of the most current scientific and medical research on how proper dietary habits can improve health and reduce the risk for major chronic disease.

These guidelines raised the bar on consumption of fruits and vegetables and put even greater emphasis on exercise than ever before, the strongest yet in encouraging regular physical activity, weight control, and dietary balance. These new guidelines stress personal responsibility, lifestyle balance, and significantly raise the minimum suggested activity levels. The message is clear: regular physical activity is essential to creating optimal health and well-being.

EXERCISE 13-1

YOGA "SUN SALUTATION" (SURYA NAMASKAR)

Source: www.yogasite.com (Reprinted with permission)

1. Mountain
Begin by standing in Mountain pose, feet about hip width apart, hands either by your sides or in prayer position. Take several deep breaths.

2. Hands up
On your next inhale, in one sweeping movement, raise your arms up overhead and gently arch back as far as feels comfortable and safe.

3. Head to knees
As you exhale, bend forward, bending the knees if necessary, and bring your hands to rest beside your feet.

4. Lunge
Inhale and step the right leg back

5. Plank
Exhale and step the left leg back into plank position.
Hold the position and inhale

6. Stick
Exhale and lower yourself as if coming down from a pushup. Only your hands and feet should touch the floor.

7. Upward Dog

Inhale and stretch forward and up, bending at the waist. Use your arms to lift your torso, but only bend back as far as feels comfortable and safe. Lift your legs up so that only the tops of your feet and your hands touch the floor. It's okay to keep your arms bent at the elbow.

8. Downward dog

Exhale, lift from the hips and push back and up.

9. Lunge

Inhale and step the right foot forward.

10. Head to knees

Exhale, bring the left foot forward and step into head-to-knee position.

11. Hands up

Inhale and rise slowly while keeping arms extended

12. Mountain

Exhale, and in a slow, sweeping motion, lower your arms to the sides. End by bringing your hands up into prayer position. Repeat the sequence, stepping with the left leg.

WELLNESS MASTERY™ SUMMARY

Must Know!

1. Anatomically and biologically, humans were designed and created as motion machines and require daily movement throughout life to stay healthy.

2. Muscle constitutes the largest portion of body mass, between 30 and 50%.

3. Weight-bearing exercise increases bone density and bone volume and keeps bones strong.

4. Regular physical activity increases the body's red blood cell and oxygen-carrying potential.

5. Physical activity strengthens immune response by stimulating lymphatic circulation and increasing white blood cell production.

6. Physical activity "de-gunks" the body by speeding up the rate at which toxins are broken down and eliminated from the body.

7. Physical activity is one of the best natural methods for dissipating negative energy created from mental and emotional stress.

8. Regular physical activity is the best natural method for losing fat, managing weight, and maintaining low body fat.

9. The body's ability to utilize fat for energy depends on the amount of fat-burning enzymes available. The more fat-burning enzymes available the better your body burns fat. Extended moderate exercise stimulates the growth of these fat-burning enzymes.

10. The consistent practice of yoga is spiritually as well as physically healing because it integrates and balances the relationship between spiritual, psychological, emotional, and physical energy in the body.

WELLNESS MASTERY™ ACTION

1. Practice Exercise 13-1: Yoga "Sun Salutation" at the end of the chapter. Perform five rotations of the twelve yoga positions of "Sun Salutation" every morning to start your day.

2. Identify several physical activities you enjoy and find ways to incorporate each of them into your daily routine.

3. Exercise with a friend, an exercise buddy. The buddy system is a great way to create support, consistency, and accountability.

4. Get in the habit of doing some form of physical activity for 30 minutes every day.

5. Keep a pair of comfortable walking shoes at work or in your car, and walk for 30 minutes during your lunch break.

6. If you are new to the exercise world, hire a personal fitness trainer to coach you. Your fitness coach should be able to customize a personal physical activity program that fits your lifestyle and fitness goals.

7. Change or rotate your physical activity routine and
    environment every 30 days. Variety helps keep activity
    fresh and interesting and stimulates the body in ways that
    continue to promote positive change.

8. Always buy the highest quality athletic shoes, clothing, and
    equipment. You deserve the best!

9. Sign up for a beginning yoga classes at your local gym
    or yoga studio and experiment with different classes and
    different instructors to find out what is the most fun and
    what works the best for you. Invest in a yoga video tape and
    yoga at home!

10. Do deep breathing exercises daily (see Deep Breathing
    Exercises presented in Chapter 7, Oxygen). Post deep
    breathing reminders on your nightstand next to your bed,
    on the mirror in your bathroom, above the kitchen sink or on
    the refrigerator, on your computer monitor screens in your
    office at work and at home, in the middle of your steering
    wheel or hanging from the rear-view mirror in your car,
    and carry it around written on the back of your business or
    calling card.

Wellness Mastery™
EmPOWERment Programs

Mission Statement

EmPOWER
**the human spirit to achieve highest potential,
contribute to the healing of the human condition
and improve quality of life.**

Workshops

All programs are designed and delivered based upon the
combined principles of (1) adult learning, (2) accelerated learning
and (3) experiential learning to maximize the learning experience,
behavior modification and skill mastery for each participant.
Participants will be provided with all class materials covered
during the programs.

FOR HEALTH PROFESSIONALS

(Medical, Chiropractors, Naturopaths, Acupuncturists, Therapists, Nurses)

WELLNESS & HEALTHY-AGING
(FULL-DAY / INTERACTIVE / CASE STUDIES)

Provocative, informative and always entertaining...learn how to make the paradigm shift to move beyond treating symptoms to become a "Healthy-Life Doctor." EmPOWER your patients to greater wellness utilizing proven natural therapies! Achieve greater personal fulfillment and success in treating chronic degenerative diseases based upon a greater understanding of the wholistic nature of humanity (the mind-body-spirit-emotion connection) and the Universal Principles (Spiritual Laws and Laws of Nature) that govern health outcomes.

For Individuals

Personal EmPOWERment Series
(30-50 minute modules / Interactive / Q&A)

Entertaining and provocative educational series that explores the wholistic nature of humanity (the mind-body-spirit-emotion connection) and the Universal Principles (Spiritual Laws and Laws of Nature) that govern health outcomes.

- **Empower the Doctor Within!** (Introductory 1-hr Keynote)
- **The Power of Mind**
- **The Power of Emotions**
- **10 Principles of Healing**
- **Emotional Intelligence (EI)**

Health & Healing Series
(30-50 minute modules / Interactive / Q&A)

This enlightening educational series explores the latest medical scientific research findings and the proven natural therapies for reversing and preventing the top chronic degenerative "lifestyle" diseases.

- **Reverse & Prevent Cancer**
- **Reverse & Prevent Heart Disease**
- **Stop Obesity—Now!**
- **Sugar Blues—Reverse & Prevent Adult Onset Diabetes**
- **Reduce Stress—The #1 Risk Factor for Disease**
- **Reverse & Prevent Alzheimer's & Parkinson's**
- **Reverse & Prevent Attention Deficit Disorder**
- **Natural Alternatives to Hormone Replacement Therapy**
- **Secrets of Healthy-Aging & Longevity**

For Corporations

A Blueprint for Corporate Wellness
(50-minute Keynote)

Maximize corporate performance. This program explores the new paradigm strategy for designing corporate wellness programs (employee wellness education and employee preventive health programs) that improve employee morale, enhance employee performance and reduce health care costs.

Leader EmPOWERment Series
Introduction to Emotional Intelligence
(50-minute Keynote)

"Emotional Intelligence" has been identified by human performance and organizational development psychologists as the essential measurable leadership skill, and the primary differentiator between good and great leaders. This presentation gives a cursory overview of the four basic emotional competencies that comprise Emotional Intelligence.

Spirituality in the Workplace Series
(50-minute modules / Interactive / Q&A)

Create a "sustainable organization." Learn how to make the paradigm shift in your organization from the exploitation of people to the empowerment of the human spirit as the ultimate corporate strategy for success. Maximize performance, productivity and profits through developing the existing human potential within the organization based upon the "whole-person" approach (the mind-body-spirit-emotion connection) and the Universal Principles (Spiritual Laws and Laws of Nature) that govern employee performance.

- Corporate Healing—
  The Ultimate Corporate Strategy for Success

- Leadership with L.O.V.E—
  The Ultimate Leadership Strategy

- Emotional Intelligence—
  The Heart & Essence of Leadership Potential

- Maximize Employee ROI—
  Optimal Human Performance in the Workplace

- Create Healthy Relationships—
  Master the Art of Effective Communication

- Resolve Conflicts in the Workplace—
  The Art of Dissipating Negative Energy

Sales EmPOWERment Series

The Art & Science of New Paradigm Selling

(50-minute / Interactive / Q&A)

Master the Art & Science of high-probability selling that flows effortlessly as a natural consequence of creating integrity relationships. Participants learn the 6 fundamental principles and skill-sets of successful selling, based upon a deeper understanding of the wholistic nature of the prospect (the mind-body-spirit-emotional connection) and the Universal Principles (Spiritual Laws and Laws of Nature) that govern successful outcomes during the sales process.

- **Take Charge of the Call—Are You in the Drivers Seat Throughout the Entire Process?**

- **Talk only to the Decision Maker—Stop Wasting Your Most Valuable Commodity, Your Time!**

- **Find Out About THEM...Are You Asking the Critical Questions?**

- **Create Value Before Discussing Price$$—Stop Shooting Yourself in the Foot!**

- **Flush Out All the Reasons Why & Why Not—Are You Missing the Real Issues That Are Killing Your Sales?**

- **Ask, Ask, Ask for the Order—Have You Mastered the Art & Science of the Close?**

Dr. Bizal will customize his talks and educational venues for you and your organizational needs. Visit The Bizal Group, Inc. at www.TheBizalGroup.com or call 949-222-6681 to speak directly with Dr. Bizal to discuss the possibilities.

Future Publications by Wellness Communications

Scheduled for Release in 2008

The Optimal Life Workbook

The Optimal Life—Booklet Series (#10)

The Optimal Life Cookbook, Empowering Healthy Eating

10 Principles of Healing—Booklet

Spirituality in the Workplace—Booklet Series (#7)

Scheduled for Release in 2009

Corporate Healing, The Ultimate Corporate Strategy for Success

Please contact us at:
www.WellnessCommunications.org
and register to be notified of release dates
of future publications

or email us at:
info@WellnessCommunications.org
to inform us of your interest in future publications

Dr. Stephen Bizal, D.C.
Wellness Practitioner &Wholistic Health Educator

Dr. Stephen Bizal is a wellness practitioner, wholistic health educator, certified corporate trainer, professional presenter, and executive and corporate wellness consultant based in Newport Beach, California. His passion for helping others achieve their highest human potential is the culmination of twenty-five years of experience in human performance enhancement in both the healthcare and corporate arenas. Dr. Bizal was the founder of Personalized Health & Fitness, Inc., one of the early pioneers in one-on-one executive health and fitness programs. His "Wellness & Healthy-Aging" workshop was the first wellness program approved for continuing education for chiropractors in California.

The Wellness Mastery™ EmPOWERment Programs enhance the quality of life, help achieve the highest human potential and empower health and healing. All programs are based upon the wholistic nature of humanity (the mind-body-spirit-emotion connection) and the Universal Principles (Spiritual Laws and Laws of Nature) that govern health. Dr. Bizal has been advising, teaching, and speaking on human potential, human performance and wellness for over 25 years.

His education includes a B.S. in Accounting from Pennsylvania State University; B.S. in Biology and Doctor of Chiropractic from Southern California University of Health Sciences; postdoctoral certifications in Disability Evaluation and Industrial Consulting. He was appointed Qualified Medical Evaluator (QME) by the Department of Industrial Relations, California.

Contact Information

DR. STEPHEN BIZAL, PRESIDENT
THE BIZAL GROUP, INC.

4533 MacArthur Blvd. Ste A#166

Newport Beach, CA 92660

Tel & Fax: 949-222-6681

sbizal@drbizal.com

Web Sites

www.DrBizal.com

www.SteveBizal.com

www.TheOptimalLife.net

www.TheBizalGroup.com

www.WellnessMastery.org

www.WellnessCommunications.org